Starting Treatment With Children and Adolescents

Starting Treatment With Children and Adolescents

A Process-Oriented Guide for Therapists

STEVEN TUBER AND JANE CAFLISCH

Routledge
Taylor & Francis Group
New York   London

Routledge
Taylor & Francis Group
711 Third Avenue
New York, NY 10017

Routledge
Taylor & Francis Group
27 Church Road
Hove, East Sussex BN3 2FA

International Standard Book Number: 978-0-415-88557-7 (Hardback) 978-0-415-88558-4 (Paperback)

Library of Congress Cataloging-in-Publication Data

Tuber, Steven, 1954-
  Starting treatment with children and adolescents : a process-oriented guide for therapists / Steven Tuber and Jane Caflisch.
      p. ; cm.
  Includes bibliographical references and index.
  ISBN 978-0-415-88557-7 (hardcover : alk. paper) -- ISBN 978-0-415-88558-4 (pbk. : alk. paper)
  1. Child psychotherapy--Case studies. 2. Adolescent psychotherapy--Case studies. I. Caflisch, Jane M. II. Title.
  [DNLM: 1. Psychotherapy--Case Reports. 2. Adolescent. 3. Child. 4. Psychotherapeutic Processes--Case Reports. WS 350.2]

RJ504.T83 2011
618.92'8914--dc22   2010038394

Visit the Taylor & Francis Web site at
http://www.taylorandfrancis.com

and the Routledge Web site at
http://www.routledgementalhealth.com

To the students, past, present, and future, of the doctoral subprogram in clinical psychology of the City University of New York at City College, with the deepest gratitude and respect.

—S.T.

To my parents and grandparents, generous and tireless play-partners who first invited me to be curious about the inner life in all its richness, messiness, and mystery.

—J.C.

Contents

The Process of Writing This Book

As this book is, above all, a book about heightening awareness of process as well as content in child clinical work, we would like to briefly describe the process of how this book came to be. Fundamentally, this book is a direct outgrowth of a doctoral-level practicum course that has been taught at the City College of New York for the past 25 years by Steven Tuber, the senior author, about the process of child psychotherapy. It is also the product of collaboration with a former student in this course, Jane Caflisch, who brought the perspective of a beginning therapist to the creation of the book from beginning to end.

This collaborative effort began with the process of choosing the 12 session transcripts that form the basis of the following chapters from over 200 transcripts presented in this course over the years, each drawn from a beginning therapist's first 10 sessions with a child patient. Over the course of many months, we read through each of these transcripts and met regularly to discuss emerging themes, to craft what would become the structure of the book, and to select those transcripts that felt most evocative from both a teacher's and a student's perspective.

Once the 12 transcripts were chosen, our collaboration took the form of supervision, with Steven Tuber as the supervisor and Jane Caflisch as the supervisee. Each week, we met to discuss a transcript, reading it aloud together to make the voices of patient and therapist come alive, with Steven Tuber providing commentary and Jane Caflisch engaging with this commentary from the perspective of a beginning therapist. In this way, our meetings mirrored the structure of the course, which is organized around listening to audiotaped sessions and "stopping the tape" to engage with the clinical processes at play.

These supervisory conversations became the substance of this book. Each chapter was sent back and forth between the two authors, with an eye toward both the overarching themes and the small details and toward maintaining the relevance and clarity of the commentaries for a therapist at the beginning of his or her career. Thus, while we use the pronoun "I" throughout the rest of the book to refer to the perspective of the senior author, Steven Tuber, as the commentaries follow from his experience as teacher and clinician, the voice of the second author was also integral to the unfolding of the process and content of the book.

Finally, this book equally owes its existence to the student therapists, child patients, and these patients' parents, who gave permission for their session transcripts to be used in this way. The sessions were originally audiotaped for the practicum class taught by the senior author to provide the basis for in-depth classroom discussions of clinical process. It is worth noting that when a tape recorder is introduced into a session it may shift the dynamic for both the child and the therapist. While in most of the sessions presented here the tape recorder is ignored and recedes into the background, it creates difficulty in some sessions. In other sessions, the child uses the tape recorder in remarkably creative ways, for example, addressing the recorder directly as an imagined third party or as an audience who would bear witness to the process unfolding in the room. We are grateful to each of these patient-therapist dyads for allowing us to serve as this audience and to learn from and with the beginning of their work together.

THE PURPOSE OF THIS BOOK

This book has two, somewhat overlapping, purposes. Its primary purpose is to be used as a process-oriented clinical guide for beginning child therapists. In this regard, it provides the beginner a "hands-on" experience of reading actual sessions between a second-year doctoral student in clinical psychology as the therapist and his or her first child patient in one of their first 10 sessions at work together. Our sense is that few student therapists have access to these types of clinical data; thus, the book can provide a welcome window into the how and what of a beginning clinical experience. This overriding purpose behind the book also provides a supervisory "eye and ear" to the clinical process between patient and therapist, presenting opportunities to stop and think along with a more experienced clinician at various points in a treatment hour. Making meanings out of particular play content will be intertwined with discussions of the process of the given session, with alternative pathways in play provided throughout. These pathways are not provided in a "manualized treatment" spirit but rather as a means of stimulating your thinking, encouraging your flexibility, and hence expanding your awareness of the multiple levels of experience of both participants at any moment in the clinical enterprise.

The book has a secondary purpose, one that is presented to readers at all levels of clinical experience. This purpose is a direct outgrowth of the variety of conceptual frames the senior author now has "in his bones" after nearly 35 years of practice, teaching, and supervising child psychotherapy. These frames are an amalgam of (a) certain core psychodynamic constructs, such as id, ego, and superego structures, integrated with theorizing about the quality of affect and the nature of the defenses used to tolerate and express affect; (b) theories of play and the development of the self, especially Winnicottian theory regarding the origins of self, other, and the capacity to play; and (c) of special interest, the concept of mentalization as it applies to child treatment—that is, seeing psychotherapy primarily as a means of fostering the child's development of a sense of psychological mindedness about the behaviors, feelings, and thoughts of themselves and others in dynamic interaction. The comments throughout each of the transcripts presented reveal the often-simultaneous use of many or all of these frames in understanding the child as a whole, complex person. While it is well beyond the scope of this book to provide even a concise introduction to all three of these frames, we strongly encourage the readers not well versed in these domains to immerse themselves in some of their classic readings to make their journey through the book more meaningful. We provide, at the end of this preface, a short list of suggested readings within each domain to enhance your appreciation of the clinical transcripts.

It is also important to note what this book is and what it is not. In its focus on creating an initial frame for the therapist and child to begin their work together, we hope to illustrate how this process-oriented approach can have broad utility to you as a therapist. This orientation also implies a deep respect for the patient as someone who can come to know him- or herself better with you as catalyst rather than creator of this new sense of self. But, there are many aspects of the therapeutic work that we do not comment on that are of equal or greater value and need to be part of your thinking and work as a child clinician. There is no reference, for example, to the broader social context of the treatment. Every one of these child patients is from an inner-city setting, and there is much to be said to better understand the meaning of that context in your work. There is no mention, moreover, of work with parents or of the impact of neuropsychological deficits or learning styles and difficulties in our work with children.

In our focus on psychological mindedness, we do not in any way mean to imply that this is the only way to provide help to your patients even within the session. For example, in addition to nurturing psychological mindedness, another essential role that the therapist may serve involves helping the child evoke better life strategies to cope with his or her environment. While such strategies are not addressed in these commentaries, we invite the reader to engage with the transcripts that follow with an eye toward integrating the process-oriented approach presented here with an awareness of the realities of each child's unique life circumstances. In addition, while the focus of this book is on the beginning phases of treatment, we invite the reader to think critically about the ways in which clinical process may unfold differently during the middle and termination phases of treatment, which are organized around markedly different goals and expectations. Each of these topics has been addressed masterfully by other writers in other venues, and we encourage the reader to seek out such perspectives as essential counterparts to the process-oriented point of view presented here. We do hope, however, that the focus on presenting real-to-life initial sessions and providing a heuristic for making sense of them will be of value in your further development within this deeply process-oriented profession of ours.

SUGGESTED READINGS

STRUCTURAL CONSIDERATIONS: ID, EGO, AND SUPEREGO PROCESSES

Brenner, C. (1973). *An elementary textbook of psychoanalysis*. New York: International Universities Press. The most concise yet comprehensive summary of psychoanalytic principles.

Freud, S. (1923). *The ego and the id*. London: Hogarth. Standard Edition 19: 12–59. It is always vital to read Freud's own writings in this area, and this short work provides a most useful depiction of the basic structures of the mind.

AFFECT AND DEFENSE ORGANIZATIONS

Fast, I., Erard, R., Thompson, A., & Young, L. (1985). *Event theory: A Piaget-Freud integration.* London: Taylor and Francis. This is a remarkable cross-fertilization of cognitive and psychodynamic contributions to how emotions and defenses are intertwined, a small gem of a book.

Freud, A. (1967). *The ego and the mechanisms of defense.* New York: International Universities Press. This is perhaps *the* classic text on the nature and structure of defenses.

WINNICOTT

Winnicott, D. W. (1971). *Playing and reality.* London: Tavistock. This is a lovely collection of a number of his most seminal works.

Tuber, S. (2008). *Attachment, play and authenticity: A Winnicott primer.* Lanhan, MD: Rowman and Littlefield. Twenty-five of Winnicott's most important papers are woven into a coherent narrative of his enormous contributions to theoretical and clinical work with children.

MENTALIZATION

Fonagy, P., Gergely, G., Jurist, J. L., & Target, M. (2002). *Affect regulation, mentalization and the development of the self.* New York: Other Press. This is yet another original condensation and explication of the concepts of mentalization and reflective functioning.

Slade, A. (2005). Parental reflective functioning: An introduction. *Attachment and Human Development, 7,* 269–282. This provides a beautiful translation of mentalization theory to work with parents.

Acknowledgments

There are many people to thank who have supplied their loving thoughtfulness to this work, and I am delighted to acknowledge them. First and foremost are the therapists and patients whose treatment sessions are reported here. Sharone Bergner was a most thoughtful reader of an early draft, as were Peter Fraenkel and Arietta Slade. Jeremy Safran, Eugene D'Angelo, David Crenshaw, and Sebastian Santostefano were also most useful in their advice and comments about the book. Jodie Meyer was absolutely essential in providing the last review of the manuscript, while Anna Moore, the associate editor at Routledge, has been a staunch supporter of the work through to its publication. Last, my thanks go to my coauthor, Jane Caflisch, for providing a process of writing that was as rich as could be.

—S.T.

Thank you to Steve Tuber for the opportunity to collaborate on this project in its moments of little d's and big D's, perseverance and inspiration, work and play; to my supervisors Laura Gold and Denise Hien, the best examples I could have hoped to have; to my classmates and colleagues at City University, whom I admire deeply and whose company I am truly grateful to have along this rocky, rewarding path we're following; to my family and friends for your support, wisdom, and humor, for floating around together in the world of feelings and for keeping me rooted in the solid world; and to Han Yu for building a shared home vast enough for both playing and reality.

—J.C.

About the Authors

Steven Tuber is professor of psychology and past director of the doctoral program in clinical psychology at City University of New York/City College. He has written over 100 papers on the interplay of child assessment and treatment and is the author of the critically acclaimed book, *Attachment, Play and Authenticity: A Winnicott Primer*, a 2009 finalist for the Gradiva Prize, awarded by the National Association for the Advancement of Psychoanalysis for the outstanding theoretical work of 2008.

Jane Caflisch is a doctoral student in clinical psychology at the City University of New York. She works clinically with children, adolescents, and adults and is involved in research examining attachment and mentalization in the early stages of child psychotherapy.

1 Setting the Frame for Psychologically Minded Treatment

INTRODUCTION

A Chinese proverb inspired the basic premise for this book: "Give someone a fish, they eat for a day. Teach someone to fish, they eat for a lifetime." At the risk of sounding facetious, for the purposes of this work the proverb can be rephrased as "Give a child* an interpretation, he feels good for a day. Teach a child to feel comfortable with the mindset that allows him to make his own interpretations, he can feel good for a lifetime."

SETTING THE FRAME

Upholding the idea of being psychologically minded (a perhaps less-unwieldy term than *mentalization*, which is employed interchangeably) as a goal of therapy has a powerful and obvious implication that somehow being psychologically minded is better than not being psychologically minded. That is a remarkably 21st century thing to say as the notion of a young child even having a mind, much less a mind that could be very much affected by its psychological milieu, has only had a history of roughly 100 years. It has only been in the last 15 or 20 years, moreover, that there has been heuristically vital thinking about when and how this capacity for reflective functioning (RF) and "mentalizing" evolves (Fonagy, 1991; Fonagy, Gergely, Jurist, & Target, 2002). Linking recent advances in attachment theory with the advent of RF has placed the ability to put yourself in the role of the other as an essential state of being, one that allows for enhancements in the capacity to be a better parent, friend, spouse, and colleague. If these enhancements are real, which I believe they are, then enacting a process by which you serve as a catalyst toward your child patient's growing capacity to look reflectively at his or her own mind and the minds of others becomes a most worthwhile therapeutic endeavor.

The potential value of this mind-set for the child is enormous. If a child can be helped to think about experience as a process and not simply as content, the child remarkably enhances his or her problem-solving capabilities. It allows the child

---

* For the sake of simplicity, unless explicitly stated, we use the word *child* to refer to a child or adolescent patient.

not to be drowned in the bath of immediate affective experience, in the tension and the awfulness of an abrupt dysregulation. It puts affective intensity into perspective and creates a way to regulate and balance affective life. As Bucci (1997) put it in a different context, the process of verbalization, while retaining a connection to bodily and affective experience, allows for the potential transformation of that experience. At the least, this enhanced affective balance increases the likelihood that the child is going to behave better in the world, and this behaving better in the world in most circumstances winds up causing other people to behave better toward the child. Even at a basic behavioral level, therefore, enhanced reflectivity often creates a bidirectional, cyclical pattern between child and parent or child and teacher that can make a child's life so much easier and more benign.

From a teaching perspective, there is a most useful corollary to psychologically minded child clinical work: It puts less pressure on you, the beginning child therapist. One of the most difficult burdens about being a child therapist is a feeling, "This poor child is in pain; the family is disrupted. How am I going to make this better?" This state of mind is particularly challenging because, unlike most adults, young children are not able to come in and say, "I'm really having trouble with X," or "I don't quite understand why I do Y." Yet, young children will symbolically enact a broad range of difficulties right in front of you. Since you often have little idea what to make of this symbolizing, what to make of this re-creation of deeply personal events, if you do get caught up in, "I have to make sense of this content, I have to interpret this particular content," you will find yourself feeling remarkably inadequate most of the time. Even if you "figure out" the content and can make some interpretation that sounds reasonably correct, most of the time the child will not know what to do with your response or will not have any useful way to place it in his or her cognitive framework in a manner that would allow the child a true accommodation (in the Piagetian sense of a discernible shift in the structure of the child's thinking). The child may indeed assimilate your remarks because he or she feels that you are trying to be kind and the child has come to trust you as a benevolent person, but the child is not going to be able to apply it to the rest of his or her life outside the therapy room. By contrast, this notion of creating a child clinician, of nourishing a state of psychological mindedness that allows the child to make his or her own interpretations, takes you "off the hook" of having to come up with an exact interpretation that not only fits the moment but also is useful long afterward.

Of equal importance, this reflectively minded stance is inherently respectful of the child's inner life and of his or her potential for broadening and deepening this inner life. This framework is about helping the child to make sense of personal experience rather than you making sense of this experience for the child. It stresses children's humanity, it views them as capable of problem solving, and it accentuates your role as a catalyst. In Winnicottian terms, it turns the therapeutic endeavor largely into the creation of a holding environment, a potential space for the child to explore. That exploratory process and your honoring of that exploratory process are exactly the means by which the child becomes psychologically minded. You say to the child, "This space, this child therapy room, is really a place where you can let your mind go—to sort out, to make sense out of, to get rid of, to interpret, to externalize, to come to grips with a whole variety of inner experiences." Your role as a therapist is now to help contain that experience by pointing out in a variety of ways what it means to be thinking about thinking and helping the child to articulate what it feels like to be thinking and feeling. So, the notion that the child can expand his or her way of feeling about him- or herself, can become more aware of him- or herself as a feeling person, and can begin to put words to what that experience is like is actually the "royal road" toward helping the child develop a richer and more differentiated internal life. To say this in another way, these are the two fundamental jobs of a child clinician: psychological tool creation and tool enhancement.

This tool creation/enhancement process occurs in several ways. One way is through simple modeling. Say, for example, a 7-year-old begins treatment by asking you, "Is this your job? Do you see a lot of kids? Do you just play with kids all the time?" You can answer that in a way that is self-reflective: "I wonder what it'd be like to have a job where you played with kids all the time, where you talked with kids about their worries all the time. What do you think that'd be like?" You formulate it as a question that asks the child to comment on the process, and you do it in a self-reflective mode, reflecting out loud, that shows that you are comfortable thinking about questions and questioning. You do not have to rush to an answer, you do not even have to answer the question, but you are comfortable articulating that this is a worthwhile, valid question. The process that you model ideally allows the child to say, "When I think of a question, when I'm curious about something, it's okay to be curious, and I can actually think about that, and I can imagine that process." If you ask that question and the child says, "I think it'd be so weird, 'cause kids can do crazy things," then you can say, "Crazy? What would crazy feel like?" "Well, crazy feels like when I get mad at my sister, and I have all these punching, biting feelings, I just so want to do something terrible to her." What might in other contexts be seen as the child being "bad" is now placed in a context of "crazy." In other words, the feeling is still being disowned but is less dominated by superego-fueled prohibitions, making it more open to exploration. This allows you to respond: "A lot of brothers have those kicking and biting feelings about their little sisters. It's very hard to have a little sister." You have now validated the child's statement, you are validating the child's experience, and again, depending on where the child goes with that, you can further expand on it. But, it comes from your initiation of the process by asking a question out loud and serving as a model of what it is like to reflect on an inner experience.

In the vernacular of this chapter, you are trying to set a frame, and the frame is that this room and this time in many ways are a unique time and a sanctuary of space. You and your patient can talk about things and feel things and wonder about things in a way that we often do not have the time to do anyplace else. So, wondering about where feelings come from, wondering about what a feeling feels like, wondering about what to do with ideas, and keeping that sense of wonder and curiosity at the forefront of the process can come to be experienced by the child as an antidote to feelings of shame and guilt. Indeed, these can come to serve as an antidote to the entire family of superego prohibitions that so often dominate the reasons children believe they are entering treatment in the first place. In this sense, a reflectively minded model is very much an ego psychology model in that it is all about enhancing and vitalizing one's ego strength. Creating or elaborating on a child's dance of curiosity and competence is at the heart of what it means to enhance ego resources and therefore at the heart of what it means to have an ego-oriented approach to experience. Creating a child clinician thus by definition creates a more emotionally resourceful child. It is in this context that the first conceptual frame I described, that of the heuristic value of core psychoanalytic concepts, meets with the third conceptual frame I described, mentalization, so that "tool enhancements" (i.e., ego resources) are placed in the context of greater psychological mindedness (i.e., mentalization).

Crucially, the fact that you are going to take this "ego" approach does not mean that the child's clinical picture is not dominated by vindictive, rigid, superego-based feelings that can be horrifyingly cruel and malevolent. It does not negate that there are powerfully aggressive, sexual, and amorous feelings in a young child. But, part of what you are doing by focusing on curiosity, by focusing on wonder, by modeling a self-reflective process is essentially saying that every affective experience is worthy of being wonder producing. Indeed, the way that you use your psychological ego strength is in no way to deny these sorts of experiences but in fact to accommodate those superego-generated and id-generated experiences within this ego-based, curiosity-driven, resourceful context. The more we can bring terrifying feelings within the domain of one's flexible ego resources, the less terrifying they become. In turn, the less primitive one's id experiences become, the more those aspects of life can be integrated into the self. As we set the frame for self-reflection, we are saying to the child that these affects are not forbidden to talk about. They are not so overpowering and terrifying to both of us that they can never be mentioned. Rather, they are things that we can wonder about and try to make sense of because they have *meaning*. The very process by which we go about trying to make meaning out of these incredibly scary feelings and ideas makes them less scary. All of that is built into this notion of setting up the frame of therapy as a self-reflective process.

If by the end of such a treatment approach you have set a frame within which, when your patient experiences an intense feeling, the patient can (a) be unafraid of it, (b) find words to articulate it, and (c) if necessary, try to find someone who can help the patient try to make sense of it, you have helped that patient to build the bedrock of how every one of us copes every day. That process is what grounds us. That process is what takes a harsh, awful feeling of disappointment, shame, or incompetence or an incredibly infuriating aggressive or sexual experience and tames it somewhat, links it, binds it to something you can make sense of and for which you can feel some degree of mastery. Isn't that what we would want to enhance in our patients of any age? But, particularly in treatment with young children who are just beginning the process of learning how to do that, working to enhance that capability seems to be a valid and timely approach to psychotherapy.

THE ROLE OF CONFLICT AND THE ROLE OF ANXIETY IN THE THERAPIST

Now, part of why this approach is particularly useful is because a child does not come into therapy just by chance. The child comes into therapy because there are a series of conflictual experiences that are making it hard for the child at this moment in time to do three things: to articulate a problem, to bind that affective experience to ideas, or to go to other people and derive clear reassurance of support and help in problem solving. The child is overwhelmed by a particular series of events, whether these events are internally derived or externally created by people around her. Thus, the child is particularly hungry for, is particularly in need of, this kind of reflectively minded resource enhancement. Therefore, the more you make therapy about creating an environment in which you can enhance those capabilities, the more useful you will be to your child patient.

Having said all that, there is a great difficulty. The great difficulty is that you are anxious. As beginning therapists, it is hard to sit in the room and just be there, to do what Winnicott called "going on being," by which you are able to listen in a way that allows you both to go with the child and be very present and at the same time to be reflective enough so that you are able to ask: "What is this child communicating to me? To what extent is the child clear about what he or she is communicating to me? How can I get the child to be clearer about what he or she is communicating and how he or she is communicating it? How can I get the child to be more sophisticated about this communication process, in particular about this communication process as related to the conflicts and the struggles and the symptoms that the child came in with in the first place?"

Attempting to overcome this anxiety begins with the first things you say to the child. When I first meet a patient, I will say: "Do you know why you're here today?" Most of the time children will say no to your question, even if they "know" exactly why they are there. Or, they will make up something like, "My mommy says that I have to stop biting my nails," or "My mommy says that I have to stop being mean to my sister." We are all on routine ground here. I then ask the question, "Well, do you know what I am, and what I do?" Usually, they say no, and I describe myself as "a feelings doctor or a worry doctor." I explain, "Kids have lots of different feelings inside, and lots of worries, and I'm really good at being able to listen to and play with kids and help them figure out where these feelings come from. If we can figure out where these feelings come from, we can sometimes make those feelings a lot easier and a lot safer." That is my introduction to therapy. I do it that way because I want to let the child know that, whatever the reason that he or she is coming, for me the child's behavior is not that important. It is much more the child's inner state of mind that is important, and I am interested in the child making sense of this state of mind.

So, as early in the treatment as I can, I want to put out there that this is my approach; this is how I am viewing the patient. I am hoping that in time what is called the treatment alliance will be built on an agreement to make sense of feelings. This is not about the child liking me or me liking the child, although that is going to be important. It is about exploring and honoring the fact that the child has a mind, a mind that is full of feelings and ideas that can become jumbled and at war with one another. My job is to help the child figure out the source of this jumble and what the child can do to feel less jumbled and less at war.

That leads to the next problem, which is that if the child was already reasonably capable of figuring out this jumble, the child would not be in therapy. So, we are setting as a goal something that is difficult. There may be in the first session or two a kind of willingness to take a look at him- or herself in this new way because it is different and sort of tantalizing. But, relatively soon after that, once therapy loses its novelty and habitual or transferential paradigms come to the fore, a whole slew of states of mind and feeling states will conspire to prevent you from helping the child become more mindful. In other words, the child will develop resistance, and a variety of defenses will be mobilized not to *let* you help the child think as a clinician because thinking like a clinician at this point is terrifying.

RESPONDING TO CHALLENGES TO THE FRAME

If the first part of your job is articulating a frame, articulating a method, articulating a hypothesis about the notion of where feelings come from and about this notion of being psychologically minded, the nitty-gritty becomes how you respond to challenges to that frame. For example, you may find yourself saying something like, "I see that dragon looks very strong. I wonder what it would feel like to be that little boy when that dragon is towering over him?" "Let's go play with Legos" may be a common reply, with a rupture in the play indicating that your attempt at creating a reflective stance completely backfired. You make an attempt to help your patient reflect, and the child shows you by literally going someplace else that he or she cannot reflect at that moment. Perhaps what you can do then is to say, "Hmm, sounds like it's time to have some Legos feelings instead of dragon feelings. I don't know what happened to make those dragon feelings go to Legos, ... but we can go play with Legos." You allow the shift to happen, but you acknowledge the shift by creating a process that says, "Something happened here." Maybe the child cannot think about that for even a second and will make a Legos model for another 30 minutes. It is even probable that this is what will happen at first. But, little by little, you are suggesting that there is a reason why the child has shifted to Legos instead of just sitting with a feeling or an idea. Over time, what you are hoping is that the percentage of time during which the child can reflect develops from near zero at the beginning of treatment to a significant percentage of the time as the treatment progresses. Indeed, a measure of treatment progress can be the degree to which such reflective capacity increases.

THE ROLE OF CHRONOLOGICAL AND DEVELOPMENTAL AGE IN FRAME SETTING

Now, you need to keep in mind that this shift is very much affected by the age and the developmental capacity and level of the child. If I were to have one thing to say to you, one incredibly concrete thing you can do as you start out as a child therapist, it would be to read developmental psychology textbooks, and then reread them, so that you have developmental milestones in your bones, as Winnicott put it. It is essential when you are sitting with a patient to know, "This is what typical 7-year-old patients are like. This is what their cognitive capabilities are, this is what they tend to think and not be capable of thinking." When your goal is to want this child to be more psychologically minded, that is relative to what is capable for a 7-year-old. We cannot expect the child to have the abstract thinking of a 15-year-old because if the child is 7, no matter how sophisticated and wonderful the child is, the child cannot do it. So, if you set up the frame *that* way, the 15-year-old model, by definition you are setting up a treatment that is going to fail because you are expecting your patient to do something the child is not capable of doing, and the child is going to hear your sense of disappointment that he or she is not being sufficiently sophisticated. So, everything I have been saying about creating psychological mindedness is bounded by age and development. If your patient is under 6 years old and thereby still dominated by preoperational thinking, there will be limitations to how much the patient can "get" the concept of thinking about him- or herself as having feelings because a preoperational child is almost by definition without a sustainable capacity to maintain a reflective stance. So, sometimes you are going to have development as your worst enemy because it is going to be really hard, cognitively speaking, to sustain mindfulness. By contrast, concrete and certainly formal operational thinkers can have the capacity to take a step back and look at themselves reflectively for far longer periods of time.

At this point in these introductory statements, I am reminded of a student's comment:

> A young child who I work with is often all over the place, and my supervisor kept saying that I should say, "Whoa, everything just changed all of a sudden!" For some reason it was hard for me to get myself to do that, but the one time I actually did it is the one time he visibly calmed down. It was really powerful.

That is such an important point because, at any age, children are capable of feeling that they are understood, even if their capacity for articulating why is not there. You can pick up a 1-year-old who is feeling fidgety, and if you can warmly hold the child, he or she suddenly becomes relaxed and less squirmy. Haven't you just made an interpretation, in a way? The child literally could not say anything yet nonetheless felt understood. Perhaps your 5-year-old patient, who really cannot articulate his or her haphazard process, was similarly calmed simply by giving the patient structure. Simply commenting, "We were doing A, and now we're doing B," and communicating in your tone that you are not afraid of the fact that your patient has spiked in affect, can be effective in getting the affect to feel more under control. Much of what you do as a therapist is through your tone of voice and through your courage because for you to be able to finally say, "Whoa, something just changed!" when it feels new and unnatural takes a lot of courage on your part. When you can courageously say that, and say it in a tone of voice that is caring at the same time that it expresses that you do not know what is going on, that models precisely the idea that this child's behavior, this child's inner state, cannot be so toxic and terrible that you are blown away. It is the fact that you can articulate something outside the immediate moment that detoxifies the child's experience of self at that moment and causes the shift in behavior.

Thus, a large part of this process of being psychologically minded and reflective is also another way of saying, "I'm not afraid of your inner world. I'm commenting on a shift in your inner world because I'm not afraid of it. If I'm not afraid of it, over time you're going to be less afraid of it." That is enormously healing and useful for a child to hear. That is what Bion (1962) meant by containment, and what Winnicott (1958/1965) meant by a holding environment. The 15-month-old boy is having a tantrum, and he's picked up by the mother and held; for a while he is squirming and squirming and fighting and fighting, and then after about 30 seconds he calms down and puts his head on her shoulder. That is literal containment. But, you do that for your patient by being able to say, "Whoa, what's going on here? We were talking about this, and then suddenly whoa! Look at all these feelings that came up." That is putting your arms around the child's experience. That is saying that there is a limit to it, that it is not just going to blow up. The child has no idea at that moment what is happening, but the child does know that he or she is suddenly feeling completely undone and is suddenly getting viscerally overwrought. You put a boundary to it by making that statement, and that is in some way containing.

The same student may respond: "I've found it's much more containing than saying, 'It's very hard to say goodbye.' That was what I was used to saying at the end, but it was much more effective to say, 'Whoa, everything changed!'"

That is a wonderful distinction to make because when you say, "It's hard to say goodbye," that is a statement of content. And when you make an interpretation to anybody of any age, it is only useful when the person is 1 millimeter from it him- or herself. But when you are 6 years old and you suddenly feel like you have to leave prematurely, because your inner world is that chaotic you are not sure if you are ever going to come back, and someone says to you, "It's hard to say goodbye," you are nowhere near that statement. The child has no idea how to contain what is felt as an exacerbation of feeling, so the child has to be concrete and say, "No, it's not!"

By contrast, when you comment on the process of the shift, "One minute you were here, and the next minute you're there," that feels right because the child was playing and now suddenly is disrupted and does not know why. The child feels better understood by your commenting on the process rather than by your making a specific content interpretation. That, to me, is really the bedrock of good child therapy. When you comment on the process, you give the child a feeling of being so much more profoundly understood, and then, wonderfully, the more understood the child feels, the calmer he or she gets; then in fact, the child might even hear an interpretation. If you try to address the child's emotional arousal head on by commenting on content and the child does not have the ability at that moment to take a step back from the arousal, your interpretation almost always backfires. The child grabs hold of the content with a need to deny or dismiss it, and this pulls you toward the temptation to further address this content, creating a vicious circle. When this happens, you are going to want to slowly but surely get back to talking about the process, talking about shifts in affective state, shifts in ideas, without necessarily saying, "This means so-and-so," but instead, "This feeling seemed to shift to that feeling, did you notice?" That allows the child to compose him- or herself, and then eventually content interpretations may be made.

BROADENING THE FRAME

It is hoped that what happens over time is that you will find moments when a child can label an affect and reflect on his or her internal process and other moments when the child cannot. As you get to know your child patient, you get to see when the child can be more psychologically sophisticated and other times when it is much more foreign. Over time, your job then becomes one of broadening the frame (hence Section 3 of this book). For example, you and your young boy patient may both become adept at saying: "Whoa, one minute there were all kinds of angry feelings that the dragon was having, and the next minute those angry feelings just disappeared! I wonder where they went?" But, the child might not be able to do that at all about fearful experiences because although the child is comfortable being the angry dragon, he is still terrified of being the little boy who can get dominated by the dragon. So over time, when you try to make that same statement about anxiety, he may not be able to hear it at all, and the play may get even more disrupted and more chaotic. You begin to learn what the affects are for the child to reflect on without becoming disorganized and what the affects and the states of mind are for which the child is nowhere close to being able to reflect. Over the course of treatment, you are going to broaden that frame, broaden that capacity to touch more and more of the child's affective experience, so he can be increasingly articulate within that domain. Thus, if the first task we are proposing is setting the frame and the next is responding to its challenges, the third, the middle phase of treatment, is broadening that frame, making the challenges increasingly accessible to reflection.

Although beyond the scope of this volume, it is important to note that as you are reaching the end of treatment, you may be able to deepen as well as broaden the frame. In that last phase of treatment, if you get there, the work begins to look much more like the summary of treatments described by master therapists, a treatment in which interpreting content is the prime aspect of the work. Once you have been working with a child for that long a time, there are going to be certain affective states that the child is not only curious about but is also capable of exploring on a deeper level. You are no longer content asking the general question: "I wonder why that feeling went from A to B?" You start to say things like, "It sounds like every time that dragon is angry, there are very scary feelings that also come up, and that the more scared the dragon becomes, the angrier he becomes!" Now, you are not only labeling simple affects but also putting multiple affects together. That is obviously a more sophisticated process, and it is something that typically happens much later in the treatment, speaking to experiences like ambivalence and multiple states of mind. This then leads to "genetic" interpretations, such as, "There's part of that dragon that *hated* his mommy dragon for doing that, and yet he felt so scared because he needed his mommy dragon. And when he was little, he *really* needed his mommy dragon, and he was afraid that if he got mad at his mommy dragon, that mommy dragon would just get rid of him, and he'd have nobody." As clever as this interpretation might be, it can only begin to make sense to your patient if the work has been done to allow him to talk about and articulate what it means to have a feeling in the first place and to be able to reflect on the process of where feelings go and what happens to them.

THE ROLE OF DEFENSES

Importantly, this notion of framing as a means of affect regulation enhancement has until now neglected the vital role of the defensive processes. When you make the comment, "Boy, one minute that person was feeling something and the next minute was feeling something else," what that implies is that a defensive operation occurred and shifted the child away from one experience to another. This process of improving psychological mindedness is by definition linked to the fact that affects can be scary, that we create structures to make them less scary, and that sometimes these very structures can make it hard for us to understand what we are feeling. It therefore becomes crucial as the treatment deepens not simply to label affect but to label defenses that are being used by the child as a means of escaping affect. For example: "Now I get it why you don't want to talk about that stuff and why you changed the subject because it seems that every time we talk about your mom, there are so many strong feelings that come up—angry, and sad, and happy, all at the same time. And it gets to be so strong that you don't want to talk about it at all. I get it. And that's when you change the subject." As a more elaborate interpretation of defenses can be heard by the child, the child's psychological mindedness not only broadens the frame of his or her experiences but also deepens the level of affect that can be experienced. It is hoped that by the end of a long-term treatment you have actually been able to look at affects in relationship to one another and affects in relationship to their defenses. If you have done that, then the child is really quite a sophisticated clinician. The hope is that if the child now is that sophisticated she does not need you anymore. She can use what you have done to help her do much more on her own.

I am reminded of Freud's comment near the end of his life when, during an interview by the BBC, he was asked to define the purpose of psychotherapy. He purportedly replied, "The purpose of psychotherapy is to replace the misery of neurotic life with the misery of everyday life." This is an especially hard truth to face in treatment with children and adolescents. You can have done tremendous work with your patients, and they can be so much more reflective about all kinds of feelings, but they may still have to cope with an alcoholic father, an abusive mom, parents in the middle of a divorce, or the realities of poverty. There are miseries in their everyday lives that they still have to deal with, and you cannot make those disappear. But, what you can do is to give them the most sophisticated toolbox they can have to try to take on those everyday life miseries. That is a lot to give somebody, even when the challenging realities of a child's life outside the treatment room can be deeply difficult to witness.

Students have responded to these oversimplified introductory statements with the following types of questions and comments:

> It's definitely a challenge. When I've tried to make comments like, "It's hard to have a brother," and things like that, I've gotten a number of times, "You talk too much, stop talking," or physically in the room sort of hiding, climbing up on the radiator. So the challenges are really resonating, and I haven't yet gotten past that point. My supervisor and I are working on making more statements, because I ask a lot of questions.

One way to reframe it is that you're not teaching them a lesson, you're commenting on what's going on in the world around them, to show them how you do it. So it's not as much about whether you ask a question or make a statement.

I appreciate students' candid responses to these opening generalities because they help to clarify what I mean by responding to the content of a child's actions or words. I think a common mistake that beginning therapists make is that their questions are too often a function of content. Questions like "Why did the man do that?" or "Why are you feeling so-and-so?" rarely lead to further elaborations by the patient early in their treatment. When supervisors do not want you to ask a question about content, they may ask you to make a statement. Often, such a statement as "Boy, that dragon looks unhappy" can be quite useful. But, to take either the question or the statement and have it be about the process within which a particular content is subsumed tells the child something quite different. It tells the child that wondering about the process is really useful. That is what I am trying to push you to do, to frame your responses such that they enhance the child's curiosity about their mind.

PROCESS VERSUS CONTENT

This distinction between process and content is elusive at times. This book attempts to tame that elusiveness by using actual transcripts of students' psychotherapy sessions as its primary text. I review specific moments in these sessions during which the distinctions between content-based and reflectively-based interventions can therefore be made more explicit. It is hoped that will be of use to you as you begin your clinical career.

One of the reasons I think a reflective-based approach is a useful way to go about engaging child patients early in their treatment is that when you are just learning, the "inquisitive" position can be far more limiting to both you and your patient than the reflective position. A content-focused approach can often make the child experience therapy as: "I have to answer this question or else I'm failing therapy. He wants to know why I'm angry, but I don't know why I'm angry. … What do I do?" This is in opposition to "So this whole process of coming to therapy is about thinking out loud. Hmm, I can do that, I think that's okay. He's not really telling me what to do or making me give him an answer, he's just sort of wondering along with me, and we're sort of wondering aloud about where these feelings come from."

I realize I am painting this distinction in a black-and-white way to make a point when it is far subtler at times. I stress this distinction here for two reasons. First, the initial sessions of a treatment are crucial in setting up a framework for what future sessions will be. Second, as a beginning therapist, the pressure to understand your patient is relentless and deservedly so, making questions about content especially tantalizing. "How else am I going to find out what's wrong with the child and provide help if I don't know the 'what' of the child's thinking?" It takes a great deal of tolerance for ambiguity and frustration on the therapist's part to aim at creating an atmosphere of mindfulness, a search for the "how" in a child's affective and cognitive life, when you may have almost no clue regarding the "what" of their behavior. But, the pressure in the search for the "what" and later the "why" behind the child's symptomatology can be too relentless, and then it is easy for the child to feel like you are probing intrusively. That in turn makes the child more defensive and makes more of the session a battle, which is not useful to anybody. Coming in and saying, "Let's see where this goes, and I'm going to follow along, and in places where I don't understand the transition, I'm going to wonder aloud what made that transition," is a softer, more flexible opening stance. Depending on the child's level of mindfulness entering the treatment, the child may sometimes be able to help you and sometimes not, but even when the child is not, even when you are really lost, you can still model the message that, "It's not so terrifying to be lost; we can handle this being lost together. I'm still curious, and our curiosity can still be here regardless of how much we don't know.'"

On the other hand, students often have the experience, especially in the first sessions, that when they begin to ask questions it really opens up the therapy. Their child patient may be very verbal, and asking questions may allow him or her to play and talk.

That raises another important distinction: the difference between intake and therapy. In an intake, especially if you are not going to be the child's ongoing therapist, you have to ask a host of basic questions simply to ascertain a working diagnosis. When you do an intake, there are data that you need to get, period. That is why it can be bumpy if you have done the intake to switch suddenly to being a therapist, and why ideally I do not think you should do both. I think at first you should learn how to do intakes from a more diagnostic perspective.

This distinction between consultation and ongoing treatment implies an important switch that must be explained to the child if you are assigned a therapy case because now the child is expecting you to continue to ask them all these questions. But, you can say, "When you first met Ms. Smith, she asked you a lot of questions because she was just getting to know you and trying to figure out why you were here, but we don't need to do that so much. We're really here for a different reason. It's not so much about asking you a million questions; it's really about us figuring out together where and how your worries and feelings can be scary to you." Although you are always a diagnostician in every phase of work with your patients, this distinction between initial and ongoing work with the child bears emphasis in an explicit way with the child to make explicit your manner of approach.

A BRIEF COMMENT ABOUT LANGUAGE

The aim of this book is to attain as strong an "experience-near" (Mayman, 1967) approach to child work as possible inasmuch as this phenomenological method aims to link affective experience with reflective capabilities. One method repeatedly employed is the use of language that does at least one of these three things: (1) uses the child's language whenever possible as a starting point; (2) is precise and sparse, fitting with the child's level of linguistic comprehension and attention; and (3) uses an action-dominated type of language, heavily imbued with verbs or stark adjectives.

Derived from both a Piagetian and a Winnicottian perspective, action-oriented language is how language is first experienced. In Piagetian terms, the child is first and foremost a sensorimotor being, experiencing the world as a series of actions and reactions from which cognition evolves. In Winnicottian terms, the baby turns the mother into a series of verb-nouns: She is a nipple-giver, warmth-maker, smiling face-maker, and so on well before she ever becomes the concept "mother." Even after a child masters language, his or her strongest emotions are still expressed via tears, shrieks, gasps, and sighs, suggesting that we never fully give up the visceral, nonverbal link to our affective life. Technically, we can use this visceral affect life fruitfully in our child work if we use language to describe feelings in an action-dominated manner. Thus, the child's smashing of a toy figure by a giant can be called "smashing feelings" rather than angry feelings, especially if the child has described this behavior in the play by a word like smashing. This can be an extremely useful way to connect with a child's affective life on an immediate, visceral level rather than on an intellectualized level. Because the whole purpose of language in early life is as an accompaniment to action, I often find that children are able to hear and respond much more fully to this level of description than the more "experience distant" language of words like angry, sad, or worried. There will be repeated examples of this use of action language throughout the text of the transcripts.

THE ROLE OF PLAY IN THE REFLECTIVE PROCESS

Before I turn to actual transcripts of patients and therapists in the beginning phase of treatment, we need to take a few minutes to talk about play. Here, the second pillar of my conceptual frame, the role of play and the development of a sense of self and other, becomes fully integrated with the prior frames of psycho-analytic constructs and mentalization. Why should you work so hard in a therapy with a child to get the child to play, and what does play mean to a child? For Winnicott, perhaps the greatest of play theorists, the capacity to play is not at all a given but arises out of a particularly "good enough" relationship between mother and baby. By mother, I mean not necessarily literally or solely mother, but the environment into which the baby is born. A child who cannot play is an impaired child psychologically, and if the child is this impaired, then the overwhelming bulk of your therapeutic work will involve getting the child to the point at which he or she first can play. The ability to play is a remarkable achievement; hence, often in child therapy that capacity will become precarious and will become the barometer of a child's capacity to tolerate difficult affects at difficult intensities. When the child cannot sustain the capacity to play, you will notice that what happens in the room between the two of you changes qualitatively and meaningfully. If play is itself therapeutic (Tuber, 2008; Winnicott, 1962/1965), then helping the child regain the capacity to play in the wake of intense affect becomes a guiding principle of your work. This guiding principle in turn leads us right back to the premise of this book: creating clinicians in your patients. Playfulness provides the laboratory for the child to master almost an infinite variety of experiences of the self in relation to other people and in relationship to different affects. The more the play can be maintained and not break apart, the greater the child's affective range becomes, the greater the child's affective tolerance becomes, and the more differentiated his or her sense of self and others becomes.

In large measure, this is because the very nature of play is all about the child taking different positions. One minute the child is the mother, the next minute the child, the next minute the robber, the next minute the person robbed. The fluid shifting of roles also provides a host of precursors to the capacity to have empa-thy, the capacity to see the world from other people's positions. A reflectively minded treatment therefore consists largely of making comments about, wonder-ing about, and enhancing the child's curiosity about what all the protagonists in the play might be thinking or feeling at a given moment without (and herein lies the art of being a skilled play therapist) ending the play itself. For example, if the child has identified viscerally with a mighty dragon that is scaring all the people in the household, you can take on the voice of the people who are frightened by this dragon. You can also switch back and take on the voice of the fright-ened part of the angry dragon. Or, you can take on the voice of the fully angry dragon. But, by helping the child engage with what the different protagonists are thinking or feeling at any particular moment in the play, you are enhancing the child's psychological mindedness and creating the mindset that therapy is above all else an experience of developing reflective capacities in a safe space. This goal of creating a child clinician is achieved by enhancing a child's capacity to play despite stressful affective conditions. Play is, at its core, a reciprocal process in which mind, self, other, and affect are interwoven. Accordingly, it is through the process of play that the child develops the capacity to comprehend the content of another person's mind and the content of his or her own mind. So, having said that, where does play begin? There is significant agreement among many, if not most, developmental theorists that in the first weeks and months of life, the vast majority of a baby's life is much more "merged" with the mother in that the baby does not have a clear sense of the boundaries between his or her internal experience and the external world. Winnicott said it like this: "It's possible to describe a sequence of relationships related to the developmental process and to look and see where playing belongs. So first, baby and object are merged in with one another; baby's view of the object is subjective, and the mother is oriented toward the making actual of what the baby is ready to find" (Winnicott as cited in Tuber, 2008, p. 120). This means that baby wants breast, mother provides breast; baby wants to look out, mother props the baby up to look out. The mother's "good enough" sense of attunement and sensitivity is what allows the baby to start to have positive experiences about the world.

Now, what happens over time, and this is where Winnicott provided a crucial and heuristically vital part of his theory, is that the mother is not perfect in her attunement. Because the mother is not perfect, the baby is going to have multiple states, it is hoped for small periods of time, during which the baby's wishes do not come true. Baby is hungry, and it takes mother 12 seconds more than the baby would like to get upstairs, unbutton her blouse, and put the baby on her breast, for example. In those 12 seconds, the baby is not falling apart, but the baby has a sense that what he or she wants does not come instantaneously. There is a period of disruption, and for Winnicott, the period of disruption is crucial because it allows the baby to realize over time that, in fact, mother is separate from the baby. This time lag creates, we adults surmise, an experience within the baby that "there must be something outside of me that I have to wait for in order to get what I need." So, the first inklings of the world being outside the baby's subjective experience start to emerge.

In Winnicott's view, if this time lag is not too severe (and the measure of its severity is solely a function of the baby's tolerance for the delay without becoming overwhelmed), there develops a degree of repudiation of this mother: "How dare you not be there immediately?" But, if the mother is there in a short enough period of time, then the baby accepts the "lagging" mother: "Okay, you weren't here immediately, but it's good enough because you came along, so I'm grateful anyway." This sense of things still being all right in spite of the disruption of care allows the baby to begin to perceive the mother as separate from him- or herself. In Winnicott's poetic phraseology:

> The object is repudiated, reaccepted, and therefore perceived objectively. This complex process is highly dependent on there being a mother or mother figure prepared to participate and to give back what is handed out. This means that the mother is

in a to-and-fro between being that which the baby has the capacity to find and, alternatively, being herself waiting to be found. (Winnicott as cited in Tuber, 2008, p. 120)

This mother-infant paradigm, by which the mother provides sufficient but not omnipotent care and can allow for repudiation, reacceptance, and gratitude on the part of the separating yet interactive baby, provides key parallels to the experiences between you and your child patient in the therapy office because when the child can play and forget about you for a while, your job is to not jump in and say, "Oh, hello, remember me? I'm your therapist!" When you wait, the child will then, at some point, readapt to you *if the child needs to do so.* The art of child therapy is recognizing a moment in the child's play when your comments can amplify, clarify, or call into benign question some aspect of the play without disrupting it. The transcripts presented in the rest of this book are an attempt to make this "art" less magical and to provide you with a more vivid, "in-the-trenches" sense of when and how to enhance the child's mindfulness through the medium of her play. There is one other piece of the mother-infant dyad that provides for an enhanced understanding of play origination. Consider the baby playing "peek-a-boo" with his or her mom. From the baby's point of view, each time the baby makes eye contact, he or she has an experience of "magical" power because of the mother's always being consistent and reliable enough to be there to be seen. Yet at the same time, when the baby turns away from the mother, she experiences existence without the mother for that moment. There is a dance between baby and mother with being and not being. The baby can then start to develop an in-between space in which she can begin to take the mother for granted. This allows the baby the enormous advantage of being comfortable being alone, at least for brief periods of time.

The capacity to play is also tremendously affected by the capacity to be alone. Often, children can play if they have you hovering and paying attention every moment, but as soon as you lose attention, they can easily dysregulate. They are constantly asking you, in one form or another, to get involved in the minutiae of their play—serving as a prop, holding an action figure, and so on—keeping you constantly involved for fear of losing your connection. As a matter of fact, they are spending so much time directing your play that they may never really play in a spontaneous way, and that is because there has been a disruption in their basic capacity to be alone, which trumps the autonomous nature of their symbolic capacities. In the midrange of the capacity to be alone are children who play readily and easily and can indeed lose themselves in play without fear across a wide range of affective content. Their loss of the capacity to be alone or even to play in general is episodic and often provides a vital clue regarding the nature of their deepest fears and inhibitions. Look at all of the transcripts in this volume with an ear toward when and how the capacity to play or to be alone is mitigated and what can be done to help the child recover this capacity. At the other end of this spectrum are children who desperately create an alone world because they constantly fear intrusion. These are children with whom you have to be amazingly delicate in not intruding on their play or even making a comment on their play because the slightest comment or gesture can leave them and their precarious capacity for play feeling violated. Thinking about this spectrum of continuity of play in this manner is another way of saying that the nature of the child's attachment status can be derived through the assessment of their capacity to be alone and at play. One can make, I feel, an easy parallel among the intrusive, preoccupied parent with the child who is constantly afraid you are going to intrude on his or her play; the largely dismissive parent with the child who wants you to constantly be involved in his or her play; and the secure parent with the child who can play by him- or herself for long periods of time and tolerate your making comments on this play without it becoming disrupted.

One last link needs to be made from the capacity to be alone. This capacity allows the child the space to explore his or her environment, creating the literal and figurative milieu for play. This space is an intermediate zone, a place at first dominated by the same alternating omnipotent and helpless feelings the infant may experience with the mothering person but now focused on a world of objects, of *toys*. Precisely because one's comfort with this world of objects depends on having a good enough, secure base to return to when the manipulation of these toys goes awry affectively, the baby alternates between attachment behavior and play. Play is precisely so special a developmental achievement because it implies both a modicum of security and the need to work on and expand experiences of both omnipotence and need for closeness. The to-and-fro between self and others is first expanded to objects and then to the symbolic representations of others and objects. The arena in which this to-and-fro occurs was called by Winnicott a *transitional space*, and all the actions, real and symbolic, performed in that space in between are called *transitional phenomena*. The baby's ability to co-create this in-between world is the world of play.

THE ROLE OF HATE AND AGGRESSION IN PLAY

I stress that repudiation is an integral part of both the separation experience and the capacity to play because one of the greatest things about play is that it allows for the largely safe expression of all kinds of aggressive, hateful feelings. If I go to my mom and she yells at me and says, "No, you can't wear that dress, go up to your room," and I go into my room and take my doll figures and have a dragon come along and swipe the mommy figure and throw her to the moon yet nothing terrible happens, then I am mastering my aggression toward that mommy figure at the moment. I am expanding internally on what it is like to hate my mother, while in reality both my mother and I are surviving. Ideally, when I come out of the room after I have had my time-out, my mommy would be able to say, "I was really mad at you because you shouldn't have dirtied your dress like that. Do you understand why I was mad?" "Yes, Mommy," I reply. "Okay, let's go play." Because this mommy now shows that she can go back to being the loving person she was even though she was mad, the child has the experience that her mommy can tolerate her aggressive play without undue retaliation, allowing the child to feel more capable across a wider array of affective experience.

For so many of the children with whom you will work as a therapist, this negotiation will have had limited success. If the mother cannot articulate why she was angry or reach some affective resolution with the child, then the child's experience becomes a more precarious mixture of affects that are too readily felt as toxic, either in the child's experience of self, of his or her mother, or both. If the child cannot detoxify the experience through subsequent play or direct resolution, the now-toxic self-experience is likely to be defended against in a manner that is prone to symptom formation. It may interfere with attention in school, it may interfere with friendships—indeed, many of the symptoms of childhood that bring children to your office have much to do with the capacity to manage and work through loving and hating feelings in the early years.

THE CAPACITY TO PLAY

The ability to manage loving and hating feelings, of course, is linked to the bidirectionality of the parent-child interaction. On the one hand, if the child does not have the capacity to play well, then you realize how limited the child's resources are to cope with whatever symptoms arise as the child does not have a viable arena in which to work symbolically through the variables that create the symptoms. On the other hand, part of what makes the work so difficult with a child patient who has a limited capacity to play is how likely it is that his or her mother, father, or both may also have diminished playfulness and hence a limited capacity to understand the importance of play. These parents will make little sense of your explaining the nature of play therapy, which in their eyes is at best frivolous or, at worst, dangerous.

Work with parents is a topic beyond the scope of this volume, but the assessment of a parent's playfulness is crucial as you decide whether your child patient is best suited for a play therapy of any kind, especially one in which the capacity for mindfulness will be of particular interest. Part of what you are doing in the intake process, then, is an assessment of both parent's and child's capacities for playfulness and hence for reflection and empathy. By assessing who is more impaired across these dimensions, the intake begs the question of who needs the work more, the parent or the child. The answer to that question in many ways is going to help determine your approach. If you feel that a parent is play impaired but the child has the capacity to play, then you are going to be much more oriented toward helping the parent become more capable of handling and receiving the child's play. If in fact the parent has a sufficient capacity for reflection and thoughtfulness but the child's impairment in play is at issue, much more work has to be done for the child. Students often ask how much they should let the child "just" play and how much they need to narrate the play. I am reminded in this context of Winnicott's comment: "I think I interpret mainly to let the patient know the limits of my understanding" (Winnicott, 1971). I am strongly biased in favor of the implications of this comment. I would say that the most creative processes occur when the child is comfortably playing alone. That is when the child can most likely get to unconscious conflict, or even conscious conflict, and your role is to gently point out where the play is going, keeping the child working on the play. The optimal child therapist experience is one in which he or she does not have to say anything the great majority of the time. The ideal experience is also one in which the therapist bears witness while the child plays and masters the conflict. The therapist intervenes only if the child is getting overwhelmed or bored by the play, and at that point the therapist's job is to make some type of comment or connection that gets the child back into the transitional space of playing. In the best of all worlds, the child creates his or her own therapy, and you are waiting to be called on as a vital catalyst. The catalytic work may be as simple as providing the space for the child to play or as profound as making active interventions on the behalf of re-creating the lost capacity to play. The remainder of this volume speaks directly to this spectrum of intervention.

Section I

Setting the Frame

Twelve case transcripts are presented in this book. We divided the cases into three sections. The first section is composed of four cases for which the work is largely conceptualized around the creation of a framework for self-reflection. The second section highlights sessions in which there were repeated open challenges to the creation of such a frame and explores ways to respond to these challenges. The final section taps sessions in which a self-reflective stance by the patient was available so that the work was focused on broadening this frame. These classifications are of course arbitrary; there are aspects of each category in all of the sessions, but it is hoped that the grouping of transcripts in this manner is more salutary than off-putting. We provide the transcripts of entire sessions rather than vignettes to give a greater sense of the rhythm and pace of a session because, too often for our taste, only the most evocative highlights of a session are provided in the literature, making it hard for beginning therapists to get a feel for what a "typical" session looks like from beginning to end. All the sessions were conducted by therapists seeing their very first child patient, and all were within the first several months of treatment.

Importantly, other than the age and gender of the child, we provide only the child's presenting symptoms and no other historical information. Part of the reason for this is to preserve confidentiality (although all patients, their parents, and their therapists gave permission for using these transcripts). But more fundamentally, we chose this approach because we are far more concerned in the first few months of work with a child with establishing a process of how to consider the child's verbalizations, as opposed to how to best link the particular content of these verbalizations to the child's psychological history. As described in the

Preface, the beginning therapist may often feel drawn to focus on content, yet the child will not be able to engage meaningfully with this content until a frame is set for reflection on process. The content of a child's history will naturally become far more salient as treatment progresses and a treatment alliance is fully established. We believe, moreover, that if the alliance is established largely through the child's acceptance of a self-reflective stance as a useful tool in the child's ongoing psychological life, then that alliance will more readily allow the child to supply more of the work toward self-understanding. The child will have been "taught" how to fish rather than primarily waiting for the "fish" (interpretation) from the therapist.

Section I provides four case transcripts. In each case, the child was largely unaware of, but not hostile toward, the notion that his or her feelings and thoughts can have a meaningful link to his or her behavior and the behaviors of others. In Chapter 2, a 13-year-old boy uses the board game Trouble to struggle with highly conflict-laden themes of aggression and submission. In Chapter 3, a 7-year-old boy uses dinosaur figurines to enact powerful experiences of aggression and loss. In Chapter 4, a 9-year-old girl wrestles with the loss of her previous therapist as she begins work with a new clinician. Last, in Chapter 5, a 14-year-old boy uses the treatment hour to forestall an experience of "having to explode" after years of suppressing a deeply felt experience.

2 A 13-Year-Old Boy

This child was referred due to a history of school failure and recent deaths in his family. I call him A and refer to each subsequent case with the next letter of the alphabet.

A enters the room, sits down, and stares out of the window.

T: I know you like this view.
A: —
T: So how are things?

Although innocuous, the question begins with a focus on content, asking, "Tell me about things in your life," as opposed to, "What's been on your mind?" or, "So how will we start our work today?" Sometimes, it is exactly these innocuous moments when you really have an opportunity to communicate something meaningful about process. When I say, "How are things?" by definition I am asking you to tell me about your day, but as a therapist, I am not really interested in the events of your day so much as what is on your mind and what you feel.

A: Good.

The question, "How are things?" sets the child up for this one-word response, which moves away from process and toward "good versus bad." Most of the time, unless a child is engaged in the treatment in a very verbal way (which is unusual for a teenage boy), almost every content question you ask will inspire a one-word good-versus-bad response. If you asked a process question, you might still get such a response, but the answer would at least be moving toward an engagement with process.

T: They're good?
A: —
T: What's new? Seems like something's on your mind.

Better, as it attempts to engage his mind.

A. I'm looking at that blimp.
T: Oh, I didn't even see that blimp. I wonder how it floats up there. Do you have any idea?

An interesting, open-ended process question, but still too intellectualized. While it may give him a chance to show his competence, it turns the session toward extraneous ideas at best and exposes the child to feeling ignorant. If the therapist asks, "Do you have any idea?" and the child says no, he may automatically begin to feel vulnerable about not knowing something. As we will see, much of this session becomes completely preoccupied with this child's grandiosity and need to demonstrate his competence and domination. Especially in working with children with these particular preoccupations and vulnerabilities, asking a question that could leave the child feeling ignorant is risky.

A: It's real light.
T: It's real light?
A: Mm-hmm, anybody could pick it up.
T: Oh yeah?
A: Except for real little people.
T: Little people. It looks small from here, but it's probably bigger if you go closer to it, right?
A: —
T: You think you could pick it up?
A: Yeah, it's full of air.
T: It's full of air. So it's sort of like a big balloon?
A: —
T: Do you ever wish you could fly one of those?

Again, this is a content question that is likely to gain a one-word yes or no answer. Instead, I might say, "I wonder what it would feel like to fly one of those?" inviting the child to speculate about a feeling. Noticing the child's lack of responsiveness to my questions so far, I might also simply stay quiet, leaving space for him to direct the session at his own pace.

A: —
T: No? Why not?
A: Too slow.
T: They're too slow; you like speed? What would you rather fly?
A: A warrior plane.
T: A warrior plane? So, that means that you would be in some sort of combat or war?
A: (Shrugs shoulders.)
T: Probably? What kind of war?
A: —
T: Overseas or here?
A: —
T: Would it be your own plane or would you have a co-pilot?

Asking so many questions leads to briefer answers and makes the session all too content based, especially when these questions probably would not lead to either metaphoric or direct depiction of his inner life. After he says "warrior plane," I would ask, "I wonder what it would feel like to be in that kind of plane?"

This question could open the door for the child to express all sorts of feelings, including aggressive ones.

A: (*Unintelligible.*). He would be doing the driving, and I would do the shooting.
T: Ok, so you wanna do the shooting, and he's gonna do the driving? Or the flying I guess.
A: —
T: And what are your targets you think?
A: Enemy airplanes.
T: What did you say?
A: Enemy airplanes.
T: Enemy airplanes, so you're getting other airplanes down. Hmm, I wonder what that would feel like, to shoot things up in the sky like that. What do you think?

Wondering about the feeling is useful here but could get muddled by the shift to a question about thinking. Ideally, a person should be able to distinguish thinking from feeling, but one can easily overwhelm the other. For example, when asked to describe how a character is thinking and feeling on the Thematic Apperception Test (TAT) (Murray, 1938), a popular projective story-telling measure, many people cannot discriminate between the two. Either they become too intellectualized and block the question about feeling or they are so dominated by feeling that they cannot tell you what their character is thinking without giving all kinds of affect. To help avoid this confusion, if you are asking a question about feeling, you should avoid using the language of "thinking." Asking, "What do you think?" can elicit a purely cognitive response instead of a response that could have had more vitality or affective resonance. Clearly differentiating thinking from feeling in your questions may also provide a model to help patients become more aware of the ways in which thoughts and emotions may overlap yet remain distinct.

A: —
T: What do you think it would feel like?
A: —
T: I am sure things would go by pretty quickly up in the sky. Pretty fast.
A: —
T: You have to make sure you're not shooting at any of like any of your own planes. Be careful about that.
A: —
T: What else, what else are you thinking about?

So hard to get him going, like pulling teeth. Since children will often respond concretely to questions about what they are thinking about, "What else is on your mind?" could gain more of a response and could tap more closely into the child's affective life. If we think of the mind like a landscape that includes feelings as well as ideas, expressing curiosity about a child's mind creates a space to explore both these inner experiences.

A: —
T: Does it still feel funny to come here and talk about stuff?
A: It never felt funny.

An important shift to try to talk about process in the room, but he quickly denies difficulty. One way the therapist might encourage a reflective stance, especially with an adolescent, could be by revealing something about the contents of his or her *own* mind. Being transparent in this way could both model the reflective process and help ease the child's anxiety, making it easier for him to speak. For example, the therapist might acknowledge that he or she realizes that he or she is pushing the child in a way he may not like and wonder about this: "Well, I want to agree with you about it not feeling funny, but I also can't help but notice how many questions I'm asking of you, almost like I'm being a reporter. And yet the more questions I ask, the less you say. I wonder what to do with that?"

T: It never felt funny? It feels comfortable?
A: (*Nods head.*)
T: Seems like it could be a little bit funny to come here and talk about things sometimes. Sometimes you may not feel like talking at all.
A: —
T: What do you feel like doing now?

The therapist feels the need to shift the tone and action of the session, as if they have reached a roadblock, but a shift to doing should ideally be accompanied by a further comment about process: "Seems like we're a bit stuck now. I'm not sure if we should speak, be quiet for a while, or do something. What's it feel like in your head?"

A: You can pick a game.
T: I'm sorry?
A: You can pick a game.
T: You want me to pick it?
A: Mm-hmm.
T: Which game do you want me to pick?
A: Your choice.
T: My choice? What an honor. (*I go to the games and pick Trouble.*)
A: —
T: Now this will be new—uh oh! I spilled all the pieces on the floor. What color do you want to be?
A: Blue.
T: Which one?
A: Blue.

T: Blue? OK. Which one should I be?
A: Green.
T: Green? All right. Let me put this to the side so it won't get in the way.
A: (*We set up the game. A sets two extra pieces to the side.*)
T: You don't need those two?
A: —
T: Who should go first?
A: (*Unintelligible.*) I don't know how to play.

A potentially powerful admission on his part, speaking to his honesty and trust in the therapist. Do you comment on this, or treat it nonchalantly? I would be reluctant to comment at this point since this is the first time the child is showing his vulnerability, but I would keep this moment in my mind as the session progressed.

T: You don't know how to play? Do you want me to read the instructions?
A: Mm-hmm.

This might have been a moment to address the sensation of not knowing how to do something: "Not knowing how to play something can be a very confusing feeling. What's it like?" This creates a frame for being curious about what ignorance or inadequacy feel like.

T: All right. Maybe it's on the back. Keep poppin' and hoppin' to get all four of your pegs to the finish line first and you win. So I think what happens is you press that, right (the bubble thing with dice in it) and then the die in there tells you how many spaces to go.
A: And you know I don't think you have to pick a certain number to come out of home.

This statement implies that he may indeed know something about the rules of the game after all, but may not be willing to admit this. Such a "white lie" is hard to address at the moment without seeming accusatory, but it is something to keep in mind for a later session if it comes up again.

T: You have to what?
A: I don't think you have to get a certain number to come out of home.
T: I don't think so either. I don't think it's like Sorry. This is a little different.
A: You can go first.
T: Oh—.
A: (*Unintelligible.*) And you can go again when you get a two.
T: What did you say?
A: Two, you go again next time.
T: You think so? Let's see, no. All right. POP! Four. So here's start, wait that's the start. One, two, three, four.
A: POP!

T: Ah, same one. (*A brings his piece around the board.*) POP! Two. One, two.

A: Go again.

T: Oh yeah, I like that rule! POP! Three. Um ... one, two, three.

A: POP! (*Gets a two.*) POP!

T: Nice. POP! Three, one, two, three.

A: POP!

T: POP! Six, one, two, three, four, five, six.

A: POP! (*Gets a two.*) POP!

T: Oh the double one. Oh, you're catching up! POP! What is that? Four. One, two, three four.

A: POP!

T: Oh! Six, almost home! POP! Three. One, two, three.

A: POP!

T: Double, double again.

A: POP!

T: Wow! You've got one home, another one out. POP! One, two, three, four, I'm home.

A: POP!

T: POP! Let me see, I think I'll make this one go up one.

A: POP!

T: POP! Ok, one more.

A: POP!

T: Five, two, three, four, five. Wow, you have one home, one blue guy out already.

     This seemingly innocuous statement opens up a critical theme in play therapy, namely, how competitive can the therapist be in a game? Or, more broadly, what is the role of expressing "healthy" aggression in child therapy? As always, this is a diagnostic question that should be based on your diagnostic impression of how vulnerable to aggression your patient is, the patient's resources to stay within the frame of play in the face of aggression, and so on. Your tone of voice here is critical. Can you convey a competitive feel and a sense of pleasure in the rivalry of the game in such a manner that the child can respond well? Gauging the child's reaction to shifts in your tone of voice will often allow you to gather a preliminary impression of how fragile the child is in this regard.

T: Gotta catch up here. POP! Let's see. One, two, three, four.

A: POP!

T: POP! Two. One, two. See this is different from—oh yeah, double double! POP! Five, one, two, three, four, five.

A: POP!

T: This is different from Sorry. Because in Sorry you know you have those other rules where you can switch people out and all that stuff. Let me see. POP! Four. One, two, three, four.

A: POP!

T: I do wanna know what happens when you land on top of another player though.

A: You go back.

T: They go back home? POP! Let me see. … I'll take one more out. One, two, three.

A: POP!

T: One, two, three, four, five, six. You keep getting a lot of sixes. High numbers. I keep getting ones.

Here again, the issue of competition is clear. The therapist is lamenting her bad luck and the good luck of her opponent. It might be useful to add an affect to this lament: "Even though I know it's luck, it's a frustrating feeling when things seem to be going so well for you and so poorly for me. Will I ever get good luck?"

T: POP!

A: POP!

T: POP! One, two, three, four.

A: POP!

T: Three. POP! Four, I'm gonna bring out my last guy. One, two, three, four.

A: POP!

T: Your turn at three. POP! Six.

A: (*Unintelligible.*)

T: Hmm? Oops, I forgot. (*I start to move his piece instead of mine.*) One, two, three, four, five, six.

A: POP!

T: Oh, it's getting close here. POP! Anyone can win! One, two three, four.

A: (*Unintelligible.*)

T: What did you say?

A: (*Unintelligible.*)

T: (*I am using his piece again.*) I did it again! What do you think I keep doing that? I can't tell the difference between blue and green. Ok, let me get focused, oh oh. One, two, three, four.

A: POP!

T: POP! Um, let's see. Now I could, according to you go one spot and send this guy back home. (*I can move ahead to where one of A's pieces is and send his piece home.*) What do you think I should do?

Now the plot thickens! The therapist has usefully made overt her choice of how aggressive to be in the game, but she puts the burden of this choice on the patient and asks him what he thinks as opposed to feels about the choice. I'd be more inclined to say something like: "A tough choice here. A part of me feels like it would be mean to capture your piece, and so I should just move my other piece, but another part of me knows it's just a game, and I should play to win."

A: I don't know.

T: You don't know? What do you want me to do?

A: Anything.

T: Anything? 'Cause the last time we played Sorry and I had the same choice you said that I could do that, but if I did that you would remember it.

Here, the therapist viably brings back a past session to use as a scaffold for linking feelings with behaviors. This has the doubly positive impact of linking his behaviors with feelings over time and of showing him that she is not afraid of his desire for revenge (his statement that he will remember if she plays to win).

A: Not this time.

T: Not this time? Oh! Well what's different this time?

A: —

T: Hmm?

A: (*Motions for me to make my move.*)

T: All right, this is what I'm gonna do. (*I make a passive move—move another piece that does not interfere with his piece.*)

A: POP! (*He moves his piece on top of one of my pieces.*)

T: OH! You sent me back home! Even after I, I didn't send you back home that time? What's that about? You sent me back home even though I showed your piece mercy, and I didn't send you back home?

Even though she is explicit about her decision not to be aggressive, she is frustrated by his choice not to be so kind. Voicing this frustration is tricky as it may evoke excessive guilt in the patient for his desire to win. It would be better to acknowledge his aggression rather than focusing on guilt: "So I was playing with too much worry about how you'd feel rather than feeling comfortable playing to beat you, but you felt comfortable playing to beat me. That's important for me to understand."

A: I told you.

T: You told me what?

A: That you could do anything you wanted.

T: Oh, so that was my choice. And I just, I should have been more aggressive, all right? POP! Four. I'm gonna get this guy back out—one, two, three, four.

A: POP!

T: OH! Again A! You're sending me back home! OH! OH! This is competition isn't it?

A: It's a competition to get all of your people back home.

T: You're trying to get all my people back home? You don't want me to win, huh?

Here, both patient and therapist are openly confronting the aggressive aspects of the game head on, so the content is honest and real. It would perhaps be a useful moment to add: "Man, winning feelings can be so strong, they really make our minds work with such focus and desire!" This models a process of mentalizing about what the other person feels and thinks about when competitive.

A: —

T: Ok, POP! Five, okay. One, two, three, four, five.

A: POP!

T: POP! This is a pretty good game so far, pretty exciting. One, two, three, four, five, six.

A: POP!

T: Again! (*He sends one of my pieces back home.*) How am I supposed to win if you keep sending my pieces back home?

A: You're not supposed to win.

T: I'm not supposed to win? So why are we even playing?

A: (*Unintelligible.*)

T: So, so what?

A: 'Cause I know you're not gonna win.

T: 'Cause you know I'm not gonna win, that's why we're playing? Hmm … I don't know if I like that. So, no matter what I'm never gonna win, is that what you're saying?

A: Yeah.

T: So, I should just be prepared to lose every time?

A: Uh huh.

T: All right. It doesn't feel good to lose over and over again.

An interesting moment. He is speaking as if *he knows* he will win, a kind of grandiosity that would likely be too easily punctured if addressed head on this early in treatment. Yet, it does provide a moment to reflect: "I wonder what it would feel like to be so positive that I can't lose? That's such a powerful feeling. And here I am, feeling the opposite, like I'll lose over and over again. That's a feeling that makes me feel so small and weak."

A: (*Unintelligible.*)

T: See, I know I could have, but…You think I should next time? Get back at you?

Asking him this question places him in an impossible position.

A: Yeah.

T: Yeah, you think I should?

A: Yeah

T: All right.

A: There's always gonna be something waiting for you.

T: What did you say?

A: There's always gonna be something waiting for you.

T: There's always gonna be something waiting for me. Ooo wow. That sounds like somebody wants to get back at me if I do something to him.

A useful comment. The therapist might also say: "It feels like I should be worried inside about what you'll do next, like there's no escape from your revenge. That's another weak-making feeling." As we have discussed, turning nouns and adjectives into verbs to describe feeling states, like "a weak-making feeling," can be an extremely useful way to connect with a child's affective life on an immediate, visceral level.

T: To his piece that is. OK, one, two, three, four.
A: POP!
T: POP! I'm not sure how I feel about, you know, getting back at you as they say. What do you think about it, do you think it's always the right thing to do?

Here, the therapist is addressing the issue from a superego-driven point of view, focusing on whether revenge is right or not as opposed to acknowledging the naturalness of its origins. While this approach is completely understandable, it is contraindicated clinically because you do not want a child to give you a rote response describing what a "good-boy behavior" or a "bad-boy behavior" would be. Instead, you want to do the opposite: to show that the acknowledgment of aggressive feelings is not a toxic thing to acknowledge or communicate, and that in fact the more you can communicate it and the other person can tolerate it and not fall apart, the less toxic you feel inside about your aggression, which allows this aggression to be tamed. This experience, in turn, strengthens ego resources, which can be used to battle id feelings and to mediate superego demands.

A: (*Unintelligible.*)
T: You do? What is important to you about it?
A: (*Unintelligible.*)
T: Yeah, getting people back.
A: I'm gonna get you for no reason.
T: I'm sorry?
A: I'm still gonna get you for no reason.

Very important to recognize the patient's authenticity here. This is a powerful admission on his part, and his comfort with telling this to his therapist speaks to the degree of trust that has formed between them.

T: You're still gonna get me for no reason, so you're just gonna get me back no matter what, that's what you're saying? OK. POP! One, two, three, four, five, six.
A: POP!

T: OOOH, I did not realize the situation. This is not good. You have three home already, and I only have one. POP! This, somehow, and I keep getting ones.

A: POP!

T: This is not looking good for me. OOOH! Game over. Your prediction came true.

A: I won.

T: You won. Now what happens? (*A starts arranging his blue pieces around the board, sort of marking his territory.*) You are doing a different version of the game?

A: No. I beat the red, beat the yellow, and I beat the green.

T: I can't hear you.

A: I beat the red, the yellow, and then I just beat green.

T: You beat the red, you beat the yellow, and then you just beat the green. When did you beat the red and the yellow?

A: I don't know. I'll pick the next one.

T: What did you think of this one? Not exciting enough?

A: No, too easy.

T: Too easy. Too easy to beat me?

A: No. That's way below—(*unintelligible*).

T: What's way better?

A: That's way below—(*unintelligible*)—to beat you.

T: It's way what?

A: Below.

T: What do you mean below?

A: Like—

T: So it's below easy beating me, is that what you're saying?

A: Yep.

T: Oh gosh! That is just ugh!

A: So I don't have to be scared that I'm gonna lose cause I always know I'm gonna win.

Another intense and authentic statement by the patient that both announces his confidence and acknowledges anxieties that he may have, just not with the therapist in this game. I might have added: "Yes, I know what you mean by it being scary to have to think about losing—what a relief it must be to not have to do that!"

T: Oh, I see, ok, all right. Well, what would happen if I started to win some of the games, what would happen then?

A: That would never happen.

T: That will never happen. OK, so. What do I do about this, A? What do I do about losing and losing and losing? What can I do? I don't like this feeling.

A frank and authentic comment by the therapist. It might also be useful to speak directly to feeling hopeless and helpless as these are likely to be the underlying experiences the patient is denying by his insistence that he has nothing to fear from his therapist, even though this game is largely a game of chance.

A: Try winning.

T: Try winning? Ok. Try winning? What else can I do? Tell me your secrets.

A: Try winning.

T: Alright, here we go, Connect 4. You know I tried to do the motivational speaking last time, I think that helped a little bit.

A: When?

T: When I was talking to my chips and stuff.

A: Um, you didn't lose that game?

T: Um, I think I won one of them.

A: Nah.

T: I think I talked to my chips and I said—

A: No you lost.

T: I lost? This is a terrible, terrible feeling right here, A. I hate losing!

Here, the therapist is beautifully evoking her sense of how badly she feels, but she could take it further. First, she could acknowledge again the helpless, hopeless feelings and then contrast them with his omnipotent feelings. Ideally, over time the goal should be to help the patient see how these feelings alternate and then to see the ways in which these feelings can mutually influence one another, that is, attain true ambivalence.

T: (*The chips fall out from the bottom of the Connect 4 game.*) Oh! What happened?

A: You planned that all out.

T: No, I did not, I did not plan that all out.

T: (*Playing the game.*) Another good game on our hands.

A: Where?

T: Hmm?

A: Where?

T: Right here.

A: No it's not.

T: It's not? Why?

A: 'Cause you're not gonna win.

T: It can still be a good game though, can't it?

A: Not if you keep losing.

T: Not if I keep losing? Well. I think I can still have fun. I can try. I can try to win, as you say.

A: Not gonna happen.

T: Not gonna happen? I need motivational speaking, and you keep telling me I'm gonna lose, I'm gonna lose, I'm gonna lose.

A: Alright, you're gonna try to win.

T: Yeah, exactly.

A: You're gonna lose.

T: I'm still gonna lose even if I try to win?

A: Mm-hmm.

T: Oh boy, what am I gonna do? Why do I even play if I'm gonna lose every time?

A: (*Unintelligible.*)

T: Why do I even play? Maybe we should just retire the Connect 4 game. I'm always gonna lose, I'm never gonna win.

A: 'Cause maybe you could try to win sometimes.

T: I could try to win sometimes? But you told me I'm never gonna win.

A: I know that.

T: So.

A: So, try winning sometimes.

T: But I can't win, according to you!

A: Try harder! You gotta try harder.

A fascinating exchange, with the patient taking on the role of the omnipotent self and projecting the impossible dilemma of trying harder even though it is hopeless onto the therapist. I would add: "Where do I get the strength to try harder if the hopeless, small feelings are so strong?" This invites reflection and curiosity about the active process of feeling hopeless, which may come to be a useful frame for the patient.

T: So, if I try harder, then I might be able to win?

A: No.

T: No?

A: No.

T: So what can I do and why should I even play if I'm never gonna win.

A: It's fun beating you.

T: It's fun beating you—fun for you.

Here, both patient and therapist can openly acknowledge the sadistic pleasure the patient feels in beating her. The fact that the therapist can acknowledge the patient's aggression without retaliating too vehemently and her ability to stay so engaged with him despite the losing are enormous strengths she brings to the session and will be of great potential benefit to the patient going forward.

A: Yeah.

T: So that's why I should play?

A: Mm-hmm.

T: To keep you entertained?

A: Yeah.

T: Yeah, even though you keep telling me that I'm never gonna win, that's fun? What do you think it is for me, though? You think I have fun losing every time?

Here she is trying directly to get him to think of what losing feels like, and he responds …

A: (*Unintelligible.*). But if you practice you'll get more better.

… with some hope for her.

T: Oh, that's a good point. Yeah, I think so. So you think if people practice enough they can get better at what they're doing?
A: —
T: No matter what. So if I practice for 100,000 years?
A: Nope, still not gonna win.

Now, he sadistically dashes all her hopes.

T: Still not gonna win. What if I went and I met the man who created Connect 4, and he told me—
A: Still not gonna win.
T: Still not gonna win? How would I ever possibly win?

Again, speaking directly to her hopeless state, and the clash between hope and hopelessness, would be a more useful way to help him become more mindful of her (and eventually his) experience of helplessness.

A: Think of your own strategies before the game starts.
T: Alright, let me try, let me try to do that. Okay? Try to make up my own strategy. Whose turn is it?
A: Yours.
T: My turn? Let me pay attention. You have this game at home right?
A: Nope.
T: No you don't? I thought you did. I was gonna ask you who else you were able to play with Connect 4 if you had it.
T: (*Keep playing game—I see a winning move to make.*) You know what A? You're right, if you keep trying, if you keep, if you try …
A: You won 'cause I let you win.
T: You let me win this time? You let me win? Thank you A.
A: You're welcome.
T: You're trying to help me with my self-esteem?
A: Nope.
T: No? What were you trying to do?
A: To help you see that if you try to practice with the different strategies.

T: Mm-hmm.

A: But now next time I won't have to hold back on you.

T: Oh, ok, so you were being easy on me this time.

A: Mm-hmm.

T: It seems like every time I win, you say you let me win.

This is a most difficult situation interpersonally for most therapists. The patient is ego-syntonically and steadfastly displaying a grandiosity that is difficult to manage gracefully without one's own aggressive/competitive feelings coming to the fore. It may have been a prime moment to try to reflect: "It's a very weak feeling inside to believe that it's hopeless for me, that I'm at your mercy."

A: That was the first time I let you win, and you get to go first.

T: And I get to go first, woo—I feel like the last time—

A: You're still gonna lose.

T: Excuse me?

A: You're still gonna lose.

T: Hmm. Hmm. Well we'll have to see won't we?

A: No, I already know!

T: You already know, oh, you can predict the future?

A moment when further reflection on hopelessness, or perhaps anger, could be useful: "It's hard not to want to fight these hopeless feelings and to get back at you because I feel so small."

A: Yes, you lost Connect 4.

T: What is that, 5 minutes from now?

A: Yeah, probably.

T: What's gonna happen after 10 minutes?

A: You're gonna lose some more again.

T: And what's gonna happen in 15 minutes?

A: That's too far for my predictions to go. There's no more.

T: That's too far out in time?

A: No, I used too much.

T: What do you mean you used too much?

A: Like when I'm using all my powers. They're down for today.

A fascinating moment. He's able to find a way to limit his grandiosity without "losing face." The therapist could encourage reflection with a comment such as: "I wonder what it feels like to shift from power to feeling that's it's down?"

T: Your powers are down for today? So you only have one prediction for today?

A: No, that was three, two.

T: That was two?

A: I used some at school, too.

T: You what?

A: I was doing some at school.

T: You went through some at school? What were your predictions at school?

A: That there was gonna be some nasty lunch.

T: That there was gonna be a nasty lunch? OK, and did that come true?

A: Yup.

T: Okay. And what else did you predict at school?

A: I had to come up and beat you again.

T: At school you were predicting that?

A: Yeah.

T: So, when did you think that today?

A: When I sat down to lunch looking at my lunch.

T: You're sitting at your school, looking at your disgusting lunch, and you're
      thinking that you're gonna beat me later?

Wonderful how she uses his word *disgusting* here to mirror and amplify his
affect related to the food instead of keeping it as an intellectual idea. This patient's
ability to be so real with his therapist throughout this session likely owes much to the
fact that she is so comfortable labeling and validating his experiences with affect.

A: Yeah. Well that's not really, that was like a plan.

T: That was a plan, okay. So you didn't even have to predict that, that was more
      like you just knew. All right, let's see about this prediction. Let's test it
      out. (*I drop a chip.*)

A: I predicted you would go there.

T: You have a lot of predictions today, huh? Maybe you should save some of your
      energy, and I could get another prediction from you later.

A: All right. You've gotta lose.

T: I've gotta lose? If I win, I wonder if I'm gonna be able to get another prediction
      or not. 'Cause that might change your last prediction, you know?

A: No.

T: I wonder why they made these chips red and black anyway.

A: 'Cause, you're go!

T: I'm just trying to stall A, come on, give me a break. I'm just trying to stall. You
      told me I'm gonna lose, you think I'm looking forward to that?

A deft move by the therapist. Acknowledging her stalling leads to a direct
question to him regarding her state of mind while not challenging him head on.

A: Yeah.

T: You think I am? What benefit am I getting out of losing every single time?
      What good is it for me?

An interesting dilemma presents itself here. She is trying to depict her hopelessness but asking him to explain it. This places him in a tough spot as it encourages

his power yet tugs at his guilt at the same time. It might be more useful to turn that dilemma into a statement: "On the one hand, a part of me just feels like the losing will never end, so I am almost hoping you'll cut me some slack. Yet, if you do, I'll feel like you're just letting me win. So, either way it feels like I'm trapped being a loser."

A: I don't know.
T: But yet I look forward to it?

She touches on the theme of masochism in light of his sadistic dominance, but he cannot pick up on it at this point. It might be worth a "throwaway" comment like: "So why would I want to keep playing if I know I'll always lose? Is there a part of me that wants to be a loser?" By "throwaway" I'm implying that it is most unlikely that the patient could respond usefully to this statement at this point in the treatment, but it may serve as something for the therapist to refer to in later work.

A: Mm-hmm. I knew you was gonna go there. (*I blocked him from winning.*)
T: You knew I was going to go there? This is a tough, tough game, anybody's game! Right?
A: (*Shakes head.*)
T: No? It's not anybody's game?
A: It's just my game.
T: It's just your game.
A: And as I predicted you lost.
T: Oooh! I lost already? I don't see how? How did I lose already?
A: I know you lost, it's coming up.
T: Oh my goodness. We haven't even finished, and you're already telling me that I lost. I think I still have a chance. What do you think?
A: No.
T: No? No chance?
A: No chance? (*He drops some chips.*)
T: You're trying to distract me over there by dropping the chips?
A: No.
T: Your turn. What about now, you think I have a chance now? Maybe?
A: No.
T: No, no. Let me see. So, is your school lunch bad everyday, or?
A: Nope, just that was the worst.
T: Was that today or yesterday?
A: Yesterday, yesterday we had some soggy nuggets.
T: Soggy nuggets? So what's it like, the school?

The therapist shifts from the intense aspects of the play to discussing school. While it provokes the interesting banter that follows, he wants to stay in the moment. It might have been fruitful to stick with the "disgusting" quality of the nuggets to see if that type of affect would engage him.

A: It's fun sometimes.

T: It's fun sometimes?

A: Yeah.

T: What's it like meeting all the new people and everything?

A: —

T: Yeah. What's fun about the school so far?

A: I don't know. It's just fun.

T: It's just fun? It's just fun?

A: Yeah, they don't give a lot of homework.

T: Uh-huh.

A: That's all though. I think you're just trying to stall me.

T: Ahh! Actually, I haven't heard you mention your school so much, so I kind of wanted to hear about your school. Is that so wrong?

A: No, you're just trying to stall me, trying to make me forget the game. It's not working this time.

He turns her talk about school right back to their intense power struggle over play. This is his way of saying that the metaphor of the play theme is far more important and alive than shifting to a school discussion. There is too much transference, too much intensity in the playing out of this power paradigm for him to want to shift gears, and there is not any anxiety generated in him so far. He has stacked the deck too heavily in his favor around the play for him to want to give up the dominant position.

T: It's not gonna work?

A: It never did.

T: You don't believe me, you don't believe that I just wanted to hear about your new school?

A useful challenge to the paranoid flavor of his response.

A: No, I don't believe it.

T: You don't believe it? Even if I tell you it's the truth you don't believe it. I wouldn't lie. Have I lied to you before?

This might have been a most useful time to articulate a reflective stance: "So I wonder what would make me so desperate to win that I'd pretend to ask you about your life only to try and distract you. I'd have to be so hungry to beat you that nothing else would matter. Where would that hunger come from?"

A: Probably.

T: Probably?

A: Yeah.

T: Hmmm. I wonder why you think that.

A: 'Cause you're just trying to stall again.

T: You think that I'm just being competitive and that—

A: No, you're not competitive. You're not the competitive type.

T: I'm not the competitive type?

A: No.

T: What kind of type am I?

A: The wack type.

T: The wack type! Oh again! But last time you called me wack it was just because you said I was not good at Connect 4.

A: See that's the same thing I'm talking about!

T: The same thing I'm talking about. So I'm not wack generally or wack at Connect 4—like please clarify.

A: All the games you lose.

T: All the games I lose, okay.

A: Yeah, you lost like Trouble, Battleship, Sorry.

T: Mm-hmm.

A: Battleship again.

T: Oh boy!

A: Sorry.

T: You are going through this painful history of my losing!

The therapist could amplify this affect with a comment like: "It just makes me wish I could be deaf and not have to hear all the ways I'm small and weak."

A: Connect 4 like 80 times.

T: Oh! Why are you bringing this up?

A: 'Cause you keep on trying to stall me, so I'm trying to stall you.

T: I am not trying to stall you! I just went.

A: (*A puts in chip.*) I just went also.

T: Let's see. I still think it's a pretty good game here, I do. I still think there's a slight possibility that I could possibly win the game. (*I run out of chips.*) More chips, more chips.

A: Are you stalling again?

T: I'm stalling? I'm just trying to work this out in my mind why I am even playing this game.

A: What situation are you talking about?

T: What situation am I talking about? This one right here! The one we're looking at right here, this Connect 4 game. I'm in a situation you're telling me no matter—(*he starts to put a piece in, skipping my turn to go*) uh oh, I'm not gonna lose my chance! I am not gonna lose my chance. Didn't I? OK here we go (*I drop a chip*). I want to, you know, I want to express how you know a little bit here about what, I'm thinking and you're telling me what's your prediction (*A sings something*). This looks like a really tough game (*A sings something*). I don't have any other choice I have to go right here.

A: And I have to go right here.

T: (*We complete a game in which all pieces are in the board and no one has won.*) In the history of our Connect 4 games …

A: No no (*unintelligible*).

T: … let me just, in the history of our Connect 4 games, I don't even think that we've even been able to—

A: (*Unintelligible.*)

T: You think that I'm getting better?

It is probably not useful to ask him for soothing words as he is so ego-syntonically enjoying his power at the moment.

A: No.

T: What do you think happened?

A: I think I went too easy on you.

T: You went too easy on me again?

A: Yeah, let's start over.

T: All right.

A: You won last time, but.

T: You won last time?

A: Yeah.

T: Nah, I think you would probably say you won last time.

A: No, I think it was you, you won right?

T: Oh, the time before this. (*We start a new game.*)

Her easy willingness to keep on playing despite losing is having a salutary effect on him. It speaks to her tolerance, and to her containment, in Bion's sense, of his grandiosity and his hunger for dominance in that her wish to continue shows that she can survive. In Winnicott's language, she has been repudiated, so perhaps she can be reaccepted on the patient's terms. In the context of the play, his acknowledging her victory is a major reparation on his part. It raises the interesting question of whether the therapist should comment on this reparation. She might say: "It makes my feeling small less painful to know that I won a game."

T: So, so far school has been fun?

A: —

T: Yeah? And what about, what else beside the little homework is fun about school?

A: My friends.

T: Oh yeah? You didn't tell me about who they are.

A: Just about that big-headed Malaysia girl.

T: Big-headed Malaysia?

A: Yeah.

T: Are you still friends with her?

A: Sometimes.

T: Sometimes? Are you friends right now?

A: I don't know.
T: You don't know? What's going on?

I would have pushed the process here over the content, so instead of asking for more details, I would have stressed: "Not knowing how you feel or where you stand with a friend, that's not an easy feeling at all. I wonder what that feels like for you?"

A: —
T: Hmm?
A: Nothing.
T: Nothing? Nothing's going on but you don't know if you're friends with her? I
        don't understand.
A: I'm setting my plan.
T: You're what?
A: Setting up my plan.
T: You're setting up your plan.

Our child patients tell us, far more dramatically than our adult patients, when we've hit a dead end. What's fascinating is how he is doing the obverse of what happens in most child play: Instead of retreating from the play at a moment of anxiety or conflict, he returns to the play. It is easy to see how the comfort of his dominance in these board games is vastly safer than his not knowing where he stands with friends in the real world, especially with women. The fact that he is beating a woman so consistently here must be an important part of the transferential paradigm.

T: Okay. Oh. I still don't understand why I'm playing if I'm always gonna lose.
        That's one thing I'd like to know.
A: —
T: Hmm?
A: Nothing.
T: I'd really like to know that. Why do you think I'm still playing?

She is trying so hard to get him to process the "why" of her playing, when a focus on *how* she feels playing, especially her ambivalence about playing in the face of certain defeat, might be more evocative. He literally does not know yet how to even address her question, so he has to say "I don't know." I would argue that one of the ways to assess the usefulness of the treatment might be to measure over time his development of the capacity to see her point of view affectively around themes of competence and inadequacy.

A: I don't know.
T: You don't know? Oh (*I block him from winning*)—you have no idea?
A: I knew you were gonna block right there.

T: If I didn't, then what would happen?

A: It was a prediction.

T: I thought you were all out of predictions. Wow, you see how you did that both sides? (*Sets up his chips so he can win vertically or horizontally.*)

She shifts to an admiration of his skills for the first time.

A: I know.

T: So tell me more about your friends at school.

A: All right. I was just trying to stall it as long as I can so it won't be as painful as I thought it would be.

T: (*Laughs.*)

A: 'Cause you lost, so I was just going to stall.

T: Are you being me right now?

A: No.

T: You're stalling right now.

A: Today was good at my school—

T: I'm sorry?

A: Today was good at my school.

T: Oh?

A: We had gym ...

T: Mm-hmm.

A: ... and then, we came out ...

T: Mm-hmm.

A: ... went upstairs, had lunch (*unintelligible*)—packed up for home ...

T: Mm-hmm.

A: ... , lost (?), came here.

Another moment of "reparation." He tells her about school (something he knows she wants to talk about) as a response to her admiration?

T: What do you mean lost, what? What did you say, packed up for home and then what?

A: Oh no. I packed up for home and went home.

T: Oh you did?

A: Yeah. Then I came here.

T: Mm-hmm.

A: And then the first two games nobody won and then you won. And I wanted you to hold every like—(*unintelligible*)—now this one, you lost. (*He drops in winning chip.*)

T: OH! That was painful. Oh boy!

She is admirably able once again to tolerate his victory and acknowledge her "pain."

A: I was trying to stall it.

T: You were stalling it. That last little chip.

A: —

T: Now here I am, here I am, listening to your wonderful story about your wonderful day and here I am, I didn't even know you were about to put that last chip in.

She is able to tolerate his "sadistic" pleasure at savoring his victory yet can voice her affect meaningfully.

T: (*We start new game.*) Boy oh boy. Hmm. So did you really do that to make it less painful for me?

Here, however, she asks a question that would involve too great a loss of "face" on his part to answer positively. He is not at all at a place yet where he could voice concern for her as it would make him feel too small. We are thus getting a window into the origins of his dominant play: He must disavow self-doubt and vulnerability to maintain a sense of vitality.

A: No.

T: What did you do that for?

A: For all of the stalling you did.

T: What? You already had your chips in place already, you didn't need to stall, did you?

A: Yeah.

T: Why did you need to stall?

A: 'Cause, for fun.

T: For fun?

A: —

T: What kind of fun is that?

A: Pretending.

T: Hmm?

A: Pretending.

T: What did you say?

A: Pretending.

T: Ahh. So you were pretending so that I wouldn't notice that I was about to lose, is that why?

A: I think you already knew.

T: You know, I gotta tell you I didn't.

A: You're go (*I drop chip*). But you stalled again. I won. I told you about my day— (*unintelligible*)—was fun.

T: Unfortunately, unfortunately (*I have a winning move*), unfortunately.

A: —Took it off.

T: I took what thing off?

A: This.

T: No I didn't.

A: Keep stalling—(*unintelligible*)—and you took it off.

His invincibility is getting punctured, and he resorts to accusing her of stalling or even cheating (the tape is unclear) to maintain his self-esteem.

T: That would be the only way I could win?

A: One win to one win.

T: One to one? So this is the final game? Of—

A: No two more. Whoever gets three wins.

T: Whoever gets three wins?

A: You can go first.

T: Okay.

A: Don't lose.

T: Don't lose? I'm still gonna lose?

A: Mm-hmm.

T: Oh boy. One day you gonna have to predict to tell me if I'm always gonna lose.

A: Yeah. 'Cause I made up the whole game today.

T: What do you think it feels like to always lose?

A: Don't ask me, I never lose that much, you lose over and over!

T: Well, you know, I'm just trying to get your opinion on it because I'm trying to figure out still why I'm playing, you know what I'm saying?

A: My opinion is I never lost so I don't know how it feels.

Again, he is telling us the limits of his capacity for empathy or reflection. He does not want to even begin to imagine what the therapist feels because it would be too dangerous. It's likely that he has too severe an either-or dichotomy regarding competence. His defenses then must be employed to externalize the "always-a-loser" experience and to project it onto the therapist so he can maintain his "always-a-winner" experience. The therapeutic question then turns on whether he can be helped to develop a continuum of competence with less-severe all-or-nothing defenses. The argument here is that modeling and depicting a curiosity regarding this all-or-none experience will attenuate it over time.

T: So you never lost?

A: Well I lost but only like two times.

T: What about like besides Connect 4, have you lost anything else before?

A: No.

T: You never lost before?

A: Like what?

T: You know.

A: Some other things but that was only like one time. I don't know how it feels to lose over and over again. If you say to somebody you should ask an expert like Ms. X.

T: Oh! I'm an expert on losing?

A: Yeah, you lose all the time!

T: Well, at least I'm an expert on something, right?

A: Losing—that's not good.

T: It's not good to lose?

A: No.

T: Why not?

A: It's wack.

T: It's wack? What's wack about it?

A: Losing.

T: Right, but what's wack about losing?

A: I don't know, you know!

T: Expert, expert winner, tell me.

His aggression has taken a toll here, as she pushes him to speak about her state of mind, something he cannot and will not attempt.

A: Expert winner? Oh, I don't really know how it feels to lose cause I'm a winner.

T: Right, right.

A: You should usually ask a loser.

T: But I wanna know—

A: How it feels to win? It feels great!

T: I mean—

A: You should try it sometime.

His sarcasm is so intense, yet she recovers beautifully …

T: Maybe I should try it sometime? What about things that you don't win? You
	 know what I mean?

A: Like what?

T: I don't know, things that maybe happen at school, things that happen at home.

… and she is able to far more diplomatically and delicately poke holes in his invincibility by shifting to home and school. While she is not "staying with" the play here, it seems worthwhile to see if he can sit with the question of not feeling as "waterproof" in other parts of his life.

A: Oh we don't be having nothing at school and I don't wanna go to no spelling
	 bee, so if I do have to go I'm gonna get wrong on purpose so that's not
	 really losing.

T: So if you do have to go to the spelling bee, you'd lose it on purpose?

A: Uh huh.

T: So you wouldn't have to go? But the feeling of losing, it's kind of like a sad—
	 it's kind of like—what does it feel like to you? I know you've rarely,
	 rarely felt it, maybe only one or twice in your life.

He maintains his defenses regarding losing by discounting the relevance of a school "loss," so she tries to see if he can acknowledge sadness—a worthwhile effort to get "underneath" his preference for aggression as an antidote to depressive experience.

A: When I first felt that I had to get payback so I got payback.

Strikingly, he denies sadness and maintains aggression as the way to keep his self-esteem intact. "Payback" becomes the focus rather than sadness.

T: So when you first lost you had to get payback?
A: Yep, when I lost (?).
T: So how did you get payback?
A: By beating—
T: Mmh.
A: See, if you want payback you can try beating me. But we know that ain't never gonna happen.

Yet again, we see him bring the discussion back to their play, as this is an arena where he feels such dominance that his defenses remain impermeable. He can always project onto the therapist his hopelessness and helplessness.

T: So what about when something happens that makes you feel like you lost, like, not even a game, like I don't know, something going on in school or like at home or something like that. Would you feel the same way, like you'd have to get payback?
A: No.
T: No? How do you feel in those situations?
A: I don't even know.
T: Do you know what I'm talking about?
A: No.
T: (*Laughs.*) What do you think I'm talking about?
A: (*Inaudible.*)
T: Right.
A: And that's all.
T: What did you say?
A: And that's all.

He's completely in denial over the acknowledgment of a loss of any kind. I might have stuck with his comment about how beating him is never "gonna happen." To model her experience as the victim, the therapist could try commenting: "It's an awful feeling to never be able to get payback. It feels so helpless." Or, to see if the patient could reflect on his defensive posture, she could try: "I wonder what it would feel like to never fear getting payback?"

T: And that's all?

A: Mm-hmm.

T: 'Cause there can be different kinds of losing, you know what I mean? Don't you think?

A: No.

A: Your go or my go?

T: I don't remember.

A: You're copying me!

T: Let's see—one, two, three, four, one, two, three, four. I don't remember. I went first so I think it's my turn.

A: You're still copying me.

T: I am? Well I am trying to learn from the expert. You told me that I could always try to try harder, so that's what I'm trying.

T: (*Playing Connect 4.*) Where should I go?

A: Right here

T: Is that gonna help me win?

A: Yeah. Well, it should.

T: It should. Should I trust you?

A complex moment. Given his need to dominate, asking for his help is likely to stir up his sadistic fantasies even further. Perhaps a different kind of statement, rather than a question, might be preferable: "A part of me wants to ask for help, a part of me wouldn't trust your help, and a third part of me feels weak for asking. It's so hard to know what part to put out there."

A: Yeah.

T: —

A: (*Drops winning chip.*) You lost.

T: Oh!

A: I won't do that. (*Begins to remove his winning chip.*)

T: Oh, are you taking it back?

A: Yeah, I was gonna have to block you anyway so, you lost. You lost, and I blocked you.

T: So you're taking it back? I wonder why. I wonder why.

A: It's too easy.

Once again, he sticks to his invulnerability as his reason for helping the therapist. It might have been useful to say: "I wonder if there's a part of you that feels sorry for my poor play, even though there's a stronger part of you that enjoys beating me all the time?"

T: It's too easy? You want a harder way to—a challenge?

A: No, well if you could bring it. But—

T: If I could bring it, but that's basically impossible, right?

A: Yeah.

T: According to you, I could never be as good at this Connect 4 game, huh?

A: No.

T: Let me try this. (*I drop a chip.*)

A: Let me try this. (*A drops a chip, mimicking my phrase.*)

T: I see something, I see something, somehow—

A: What, right here? (*Referring to a winning setup.*)

T: Yes.

A: No. (*A begins to move one of my chips that would create a winning move out from the board.*)

T: Hey what are you doing? I think that piece needs to stay in there—what, you saw that.

A: No—can I? 'Cause I figured out from you.

T: Oh! I don't know about that rule.

A: (*A puts two chips in at the same time.*)

T: So now I can put in two chips then if I want to? Is that what we're doing?

A: Oh wait, but it's still my go. (*Unintelligible.*)

T: Okay, so now we're both winning because now I can put in two chips. And now we both won!

A: No. I won twice.

T: You won twice? And I only won once?

A: Mm-hmm. (*A continues to put chips in the board after I have stopped playing.*)

T: And now how many times have you won?

A: (*Counts the number of ways he has Connect 4 on the current game after he puts all his chips in.*) One, two, three, four, I mean one, two, three, four, one, two, three, four, one, two, three, four.

T: How many times was that?

A: (*Unintelligible.*)

T: I don't know.

A: One, two, three, four, one, two, three, four, one, two, three, four, one, two, three, four.

T: How many times?

A: One, two, three, four. Four, four.

T: So you won four times, and I only won one time.

A: Well—a few more times. I won four.

T: So you won four, so you are the overall winner. Is that right?

A: Yeah, yeah—that didn't help.

T: My, what is helping me?

A: The black.

T: The black chips. I tried that last time, remember?

A: Yeah and that then you was kind of wack.

T: Well A, actually it's time up again. Gotta try that out next time. Gotta put these chips away.

A: It's too late, you lost again.

T: Oh, well you told me I was gonna lose anyway, right? So, should I not have my hopes up at anytime?

A: Well, if you think you could beat me. Practice.

T: Practice? And maybe just maybe one day.

A: No.

T: So, I'm confused.

A: Practice. Get your strategies up. I'm probably still gonna be better, and you're still gonna lose.

His adding the word *probably* is important here. It is the first tentative giving up of his need to be invulnerable. I do not think I would comment on it just yet, but it would be important to remember for a future session as the first chink in his defensive armoring.

T: Okay, so I'll practice, get my strategies up, you'll probably have a better strategy?

A: No.

T: And I'm still gonna lose. Is that what you said?

A: Yep.

T: Yep? Maybe next week you can tell me again why I always want to play in order to lose. 'Cause I'd like to know.

A: Don't it feel good?

T: What did you say?

A: Don't it feel good?

T: Doesn't it feel good? What do you think it feels like?

A: Don't ask me, I don't know.

T: You don't even know.

A: I think so, I think you feel happy.

T: You think I feel happy that I'm losing?

A: Mm-hmm.

T: Why do you think that?

A: 'Cause well, every time you lose, you never get mad about it.

This is a fascinating moment as he takes her "good sportsmanship" as masochism and her lack of anger as lack of disappointment. He reveals here his concrete experience of affect as something you show rather than something you experience. I would have said something like: "Well, it's sure true that on the outside I may be looking like I don't care, but inside I have many different feelings, especially feeling weak and dumb and frustrated."

T: How do you know?

A: Because.

T: Didn't I just say before I hate to lose?

A: No.

T: I don't like to lose! I don't think anybody likes to lose. Especially over and over and over and over again.

A: You said you're like the world champion of losing.

T: That's true, I have a special title so, maybe it's not so bad.

This reaction probably masks the therapist's frustration again, so I might have said: "Losing feelings really sting, so being the world champion of losing would feel like being stung all the time."

T: But, yeah, I don't think you believe that either. All right, ready?
A: I'll beat you next time.
T: You'll beat me next time? So just get ready for it?
A: I'm ready.
T: You're ready already. Okay.
A: So just get ready to lose.

The therapist could reflect on the complex feelings stirred up by being put in this position: "It is very hard to get your feelings ready to lose. You have to do a lot of protecting yourself to not feel that small all over again. But I'll try."

T: Oh boy.

The patient's strong attachment to the therapist is clear, although predicated on his assuming a dominant position. Work directed at slowly loosening this need to dominate will likely reveal a whole host of depressive, vulnerable, and inadequate feelings, the working through of which will be enormously helpful to him.

In this first transcript, we have touched on themes that will be repeated throughout: the benefits of a focus on process, on *how* the child processes the behavior in the room as opposed to the what of his behavior or the therapist's; the usefulness of placing one's thoughts or comments in the form of a question when possible, to build on the child's sense of wonder about his own mind and its processes; and, more subtly, an emphasis on which underlying feelings could be driving the content of the child's play, in this case his underlying hopeless and helpless feelings that mask his bravado and grandiosity vis-à-vis the therapist.

3 A 7-Year-Old Boy

B presented as an oppositional, easily frustrated child who was aggressive toward his peers and suffered from receptive and expressive speech delays as well as mild motor impairments. It should also be noted that when the child and therapist are described as "hitting, beating, or pushing one another" at various points in the play, they are referring to their figurines hitting each other.

B: They should put it back how I left it.
T: Someone messed up the dinosaurs.
B: Yes.
T: Oh, because other kids play in this room, too.
B: But they don't need to mess up my order of dinosaurs.

The child enters the room and is immediately filled with righteous indignation. How can we understand this well enough to help the child reflect on his experience? Certainly, it is well within the egocentric thinking of a 7-year-old to expect that the playroom would remain as it was the last time he came. It is also striking that the play of the last session was meaningful enough that he immediately wants to resume the play as if he never left. But, can we say something more specific to this child about his need for order? Is this the most affectively relevant experience for the child. If so, a comment such as "I wonder what it's like for things to feel out of order." might be useful. If what is most relevant is anger at others rather than the anxiety of disorder, it might make more sense to say, "It can be very angry-making if others don't leave your playing alone." In either event, it might have been more useful to comment on his affect rather than explaining that the room has to be shared.

T: Let's see.
B: Hey, who ruined my potato man? And who ruined my other potato man! (*Voice escalating into madness.*) Who ... have done this? Whoever did this ... are dead. They took, messed up my big daddy potato man? Arrrghmm!

How quickly the child is furious! Even expressing murderous rage does not calm him. He is livid to the point of grunting within seconds of entering the room. Unlike the child in our previous case, whose denial seemed impervious, this child's conflicts are right at the surface, presenting the therapist with the dilemma of how to modulate affect and enhance defenses. This dilemma raises questions for technique: How does one attempt to tamp down the child's rage—by acknowledging it directly, or by attempting to dilute it through distraction, minimization, or other regulatory strategies?

B: Oh. (*Tone reduces.*) What happened to the face? You see?
T: The face part went over there.

The therapist chooses the latter approach, simply noticing and reviewing what happened to the toys. While this validates the actual events that have upset the child, it does not touch the child's affective experience. The other approach might be typified by a statement such as, "The louder your voice, the more I know that some very strong feelings are going around in your mind. What does that feel like?" This links behavior (his escalating voice) to his inner life. Expressing curiosity about this connection between outer and inner states may lay the foundation for further work on modulating and mirroring his inner experience, which seems capable of all too intense explosiveness.

B: Where?
T: Some parts of the face that were on this guy, are on that guy, it looks like, right?
B: No. Not. (*Fumbling around in bins.*) Where are the rest of the dinosaurs? They're only a little bit. What do kids do with you when they here?

He speaks directly to a common theme with young children beginning play therapy, especially in a shared space, namely: Who physically "owns" the play space? How vulnerable is the child's play and creations to the violations of others? What are the child's fantasies about such a violation? This child's comments suggest that he imagines the other children seen by the therapist do "bad" things, stealing or disrupting toys, with the implication that the therapist does not stop them. A useful comment could be, "The toys that are important to you don't seem safe. I wonder what that feels like?"

T: They play with the toys, just like you.
B: Wanna play?

Importantly, despite his outrage, he can quickly reorganize and wants to play, a resilience that is noteworthy and an important resource for the child. The therapist could comment on this resilience by placing the two affects side by side: "The wanting-to-play feeling is even stronger at this minute than how strong it felt to have your toys messed with. Sure, let's play." Acknowledging these two feelings at once will serve as a key precursor to the child's eventual development of the capacity for ambivalence.

T: Sure, let's play with them.
B: Wait, let me put them in order, and you pick the … the guys. Oh, I have a better game. I'm gonna move the dollhouse up. I'm gonna be in the back with the good guys, I mean, with the bad guys. And you have to lock all of the place up.
T: I have to lock it up?
B: Yeah, and I've to try to go in and find you.

T: So this is the front of the house?

B: Yeah, you have to try to lock it really hard.

T: I have to lock the toys?

B: I'm Tromastome. This guy.

T: Tromastome.

B: Which one you want to be, from here?

T: Remember this guy? His arm kept falling off?

B: Yeah, you wanna be him?

T: Hmmm ... .

B: Why you don't pick him, too? Both of them?

T: I think, yeah, maybe I'll pick this guy. He's kind of funny looking, isn't he?

B: And I'll pick these two. You have to pick two, and all of you? A lot of good guys.

T: Pick two? Pick another one, then? (*I'm always following his rules, and have no idea what the game is.*)

Yes, indeed! So much of play therapy with young children is to be led into a personally symbolic land where you do not know the rules or even the landscape. It takes enormous patience and tolerance for ambiguity to allow the play to develop without rushing to have it make sense to you.

B: Yeah.

T: Ok then, I'm going to pick her! She looks strong.

B: Hey, where's the toy box? There's none there? I'm gonna look in there (*the big box in the corner*). I've never looked in here. What is this?

T: That looks like a hand puppet.

B: It's not here. Let's start playing. Lock up the house.

T: Lock up the house? What does that mean, lock up the house?

B: Oh, you don't have more pieces for the house?

T: There are blocks here, is that what you mean?

B: Yeah, lock the door. Lock the door and lock the windows.

T: Lock the door and lock the windows.

B: Yeah, here's the truck.

T: So, I want to protect these dinosaurs from the bad guys outside?

A worthwhile and understandable attempt by the therapist to get at the purpose of the play. With the same tone of voice, it might be preferable to ask: "I'm trying to follow what we'll be doing in this important play, but it's so hard to know why these doors and windows need to be locked. I wonder why?"

B: Yeah.

T: Okay. (*I start blockading the openings of the dollhouse with the furniture blocks.*) Like this?

B: Yes. No, not leave it out the window (*my piece was protruding out*). You have to lock it really hard. The part from downstairs. ... There are no more cars like that?

T: I guess not. Doesn't look like it.

B: What is this? Spelling? (*He points to a Scrabble game on the shelf.*)

T: Mm-hmm, spelling. You want to play it?

B: Yeah. Let's play. You locked up?

While he is a bit distracted for a moment, the power of the play reorganizes him, and he comes back to it.

T: Not yet.

B: You better lock up the downstairs. You have to lock up really hard or I come in. I'm gonna get a stronger guy, too. Hmm.

A vital question here is who he is most going to identify with, the aggressor trying to penetrate the house or the fortifiers seeking to protect it? How fluid will these identifications be? Will being the angry penetrator flow directly from his anger at (and identification with) the other children who penetrated his play, or will he focus on the anxiety generated by the aggressors? Following his lead in this regard will help the therapist decide which affects to consider.

T: How was your day at school today, B?

The therapist breaks the plane of the play by bringing in school content. Something about the unclear nature of the play may be pushing her to want to distract him, but he is undaunted. If at all possible, letting the play develop is key, even if you cannot yet understand its nature or purpose, because play is the language of the child's authenticity and the vehicle for his creative attempts to master his emotions.

B: Good (*he answers before I finish asking the question*). I didn't know there was a purple triceratop!

T: Okay.

B: You have to hide the dinosaurs.

T: Hide them, right?

B: Away from (*inaudible*). What's in here? Stuff that you can play with, build? (*He's waiting for me to finish hiding and blocking.*)

T: Legos. Do you know what Legos are? They're like blocks.

B: Yeah. But there are no humans. Why are there no human blocks?

T: Yeah, they're just shapes, that you can build together. Have you ever played Legos before?

B: Yeah, but it was humans.

T: Human Legos?

B: Yeah, it had people heads, you had to make them human.

This is now the second time he is distracted from developing the play, but once again pulls himself back to it.

B: You locked downstairs? You want me to go in there and help you?
T: Yeah, will you help me? I locked the upstairs. (*He comes over to my side.*) Why are we locking up the windows?

Again, a perfectly innocuous question, but shifting the gist of the question to include affect might be more amenable to his self-reflection: "These locking up feelings seem *very* important. I wonder why?"

B: Because I could come in through the windows.

The therapist's concrete, content-oriented question yields a concrete, content-oriented answer instead of a more reflective one.

T: Mm-hmmm.
B: Because maybe I could climb up through the back and I go in.
T: It's pretty blocked up, huh?
B: Yeah, but downstairs we need more pieces. Do we have no more?
T: Yeah, there are no more blocks, huh?
B: Yeah, but there are more blocks in that room. There's one of this. There's blocks in there.
T: Hmm, well, we can't go in that room right now because we're in this room, so. That's one way. (He puts the truck inside the house to block it up.) Okay!
B: We are ready.
T: We're ready to play?
B: But wait. Wait a minute. Wait, I'm gonna get a stronger guy in here. If I get one, that means you get one.
T: Okay.
B: I'm gonna get this guy. Wait, time out. This one, this one, this guy's head.
T: Oh, his head fell off. There you go, is that right? (*He tries to reattach the head to the body.*)
B: Oh, it needs to be fixed. Why it's not fixed? Why it's not going through?

Yet another distraction, this time with another broken toy. It appears that the toys being broken stir up an anxiety that interferes with the development of the play. Given that the play itself is linked to penetration and safety, it is as if the underlying theme is showing up everywhere he looks.

T: You want me to try and help you?
B: Like that?
T: Oops. Let's see.
B: Okay. I think I'm gonna pick this big guy.

T: Looks like this is the head piece, but …

B: Okay. Let's just start. Ok, you need to hide your dinosaurs.

T: I'm trying to get his head on. (*I'm persisting for some reason.*)

B: I'm starting.

T: You're starting? Okay, I'll play without a head. Okay, so. (*He takes one of his pieces and starts to barge in through the windows.*) Hey!

B: You have to hold it! Now I'm going through the front. Oh, I can't. Oh, I'll just go through this way.

T: No!!! Did you get in?

The play finally begins! Now, the therapist must really be alert to nuance and remain flexible. The child is likely to shift perspectives and characters at a moment's notice, wanting the therapist to follow his lead at times yet becoming quite frightened of his own impulses at other times. The play is paramount, so the therapist should keep her words to a minimum, trying to serve as a catalyst to the unfolding play without adding comments that could lead the play too far from where the child seems to want it to go. Intuiting how best to facilitate this unfolding can be difficult at this stage in the treatment as this is only the third session with the child. Because there is little play history between child and therapist, it will likely be a challenging task of attunement to discover which themes the child most needs and wishes to express in this session.

B: Yeah. One.

T: The truck's not stopping you? You got in through a hole?

B: Yeah. But the truck is stopping me from going all the way in.

T: Yeah?

B: Ouch. I said I'm going in. (*Pushes really hard this time.*) Arrgh! When I go in, that means I get to go on that side and you get to come on this side.

T: We switch sides? Ok. Do we switch pieces? Switch players?

B: Actually, no, I get to go on this side so I can know where you are.

T: And what do I do?

B: Oh, you get to stay there. Arrrggh. (*Keeps pushing through.*) Did you hide all of the dinosaurs? (*Tries to push his way in.*) Did I get in?

T: Um-hm. I think you made it in! You made it in!

The therapist is doing a fine job of both following the lead and rules of the play and expressing dramatic affect that appears to match where the child is going with his penetration. At this moment, she is identifying with his identification with the aggressor.

B: Now *WHERE* are the dinosaurs? Oh, they are not! Oh! You hid them in a really good place! Oh I bet they're right here!

He is so appreciative of her hiding prowess! She hid them just well enough to be a slight challenge but not so well that they are gone. This reminds me of the optimal game of hide-and-seek in which it would be a disaster not to be found but a bore to be found too quickly.

T: Ahh! There they are! You found them!
B: Are there more?
T: Yep, there's more!
B: You don't know I'm here.

This is a crucial moment in the play. He is invested enough in the experience that he is much less self-conscious and wants her to dive into their newly created and shared transitional space. This is true playing and must be protected if at all possible.

T: Be careful! The enemy is in the house. Hide dinosaurs, hide! Be very quiet!

The therapist adapts terrifically, voicing instructions to the dinosaurs as a true playmate.

B: But now, now you have to look in the other room. Oh, the dinosaurs are taken.

He shows his appreciation of the therapist's playfulness by immersing himself directly in the play.

T: Be very careful, dinosaurs!
B: Look!
T: Ha! Is there someone on the roof? Is there someone on the roof of my house? (*His character is coming from the roof, and I bring my player up to check. B hides his character as I approach.*) Okay. I don't see anyone. I'm heading back down. Guarding my dinosaurs.

With the play progressing so well, the therapist can simply continue the play or take advantage of this hiding moment by doing a bit of emotional foreshadowing: "At first it felt very scary inside to think of someone trying to break into my house through the roof, but I don't see anyone. I'm feeling a bit better, but it's still scary to have these about-to-get-hurt feelings!" If such a statement does not disrupt the play, it would be a worthwhile element to add. If the child gets distracted by the comment, the therapist learns the hard way to keep silent.

T: Oh! I hear something. Is there anyone up there? (*I bring my character back up, and B slams his character into mine, hitting it out of my hand. It goes flying down to the floor.*) Ah!
B: He's evil, he could do that.
T: Wow. I think he's hurt.
B: Is he broken? Oh. I thought he was broken.

T: No, you can't see it, but he's hurt inside. It hurt a lot.

The therapist begins the process of describing internal feelings.

B: I had to do it. Because I'm evil.

This is a fascinating statement by the child because it simultaneously implies that he knows he did something bad (with guilt attached) and that he is compelled enough by the character's evilness to do it anyway. A comment that touches on this ambivalence might be: "The evil part of the guy had to hurt him, but another part of him seems confused, almost like he shouldn't have done it. What does this back-and-forth feeling feel like?"

T: What do we do? Now we can't play anymore because he's hurt.
B: No, nothing hurts him because he's rock. He's made out of rock. Hey, I'll start hurting. Now you hurt my feelings, you made me angry. (*Taking on a character voice.*) Raaaaaugh! That's what you're supposed to do right now.

The child is directing now, wanting the therapist to help enact the play. Crucially, he makes a distinction between his physical invulnerability (he's a rock) and his feelings getting hurt. This may be amplified by the therapist: "So, even if his outside can't be hurt, his inner feelings can be."

T: Is that what he's supposed to do?
B: Yeah. Nothing hurts him. That makes him mad.
T: Hmmm, seems like they're just going to hit each other, aren't they?

The therapist gets a bit too caught up with the actual behavior of the charac-
ters as opposed to their feelings. To return to a more reflective stance, she might observe: "Nothing can hurt him on the outside, but the hurts sure make him feel strong angry feelings on the inside."

B: Yeah.
T: Then, what happens if they keep hitting each other?
B: Yeah, then the rest comes. They call for more bad guys. They have more
bad guys.
T: Then more people start hitting each other? Everybody hits each other?
B: No, more people will go in the house. Try to get me, but it's not gonna work!
T: Hmmm, now I'm afraid to go up there because then you'll hit me.

It might be more helpful to verbalize the fear in the form of an open dilemma: "A part of me wants to go up there and fight, but another part of me is afraid of getting hurt and feeling weak."

B: No, you're stronger than me. You're made out of rock. And you could go fly like this. Swish swish!

T: What are you made out of?

B: Oh, I'm made out of water.

T: Made out of water?

B: And fire. Actually no, water only.

T: So what's your special power?

B: Special power? When you hit me, your hand goes through my body.

T: Oh, because you're like water!

B: Yeah, and I could go like this … swooosh! Right here, when you try and hit me right there.

T: Hmm, let's see. (*I try to move toward him, and he moves away.*)

B: Try to get me. … (*Taunting a little in his voice.*) Swish!

T: Now I'm afraid. Now's he's afraid. I'm going to head back down inside where it's safe.

B: Fine. I'm sorry about hitting you. I'm going.

T: Ohh. That's okay.

B: But now he's not a bad guy. And this one, he's a good guy. He's the good guy, too. And that guy. I want to help you.

T: Hey. You came here to help us?

B: Can you please let me in? I'm a good guy, too!

T: All right! You turned into a good guy, let's see.

B: I've been a good guy. I just wanted to say hi. But hurry up, the bad guys! There's only one bad guy!

This is a striking sequence. It begins with his delight in his power and invulnerability, leading to a taunting voice that causes the therapist to slip a bit between staying in the voice of her play figure and being afraid herself. When her figure starts to retreat out of fear, he quickly identifies with the frightened figure and becomes an ally. His aggressiveness and "badness" must be denied. It could be extremely helpful to point out this rapid retreat by the child from his aggression: "I wonder what could make that guy want to drop his bad guy feelings as if they never happened and only want to be a good guy." This puts his defenses metaphorically in the limelight and provides a scaffold for future references to why defenses are useful.

T: Should I open up the windows?

B: No, close it!

T: Close it?

B: Yes! The bad guy's comin' in. I'm comin' in!

Importantly, we again see his alternating of good and evil feelings, so we might say: "Good guy feelings and bad guy feelings go back and forth, it's so hard to know which one to be!"

T: Where?

B: Downstairs!

T: Ah! Oh my gosh, no! Don't come in!

B: (*He's pushing his way in.*) Awooooooo, ahoooooo! He's calling for more bad
        guys. Ahoooo. Yes, I'm the strong guy. Can you open this door?

T: Oh no, no, don't come in! (*Continues to push his way in.*)

B: Alright, I'm coming through the window. I'm coming up.

T: No!

B: Oh … oww.

T: I must save the dinosaurs!

B: Ahooooo, ahoooo!

T: I'm being attacked by the bad guys.

B: Ouch. Now, forget about it. And the dinosaurs … evil? Ahhh … help us! We're
        turning evil! All of them are evil. It's me, open that door.

The therapist could comment on the feelings stirred up by this unpredictability: "Evil to good and good to evil. It's so confusing why the guys keep changing that nothing feels safe."

T: No!!!

B: It's me, Triceratop! Let me in! I'm not a bad guy. I'm a good guy.

T: Alright, good guys come in, I guess.

"But how can I ever be sure who will stay good and who will trick me? It's so scary when you're not sure." A comment like this may heighten his awareness of feeling unable to trust either his own aggression or that of others.

T: That's the rule? Where'd he go?

B: Why it's hot in here?

T: Where? Are you hot?

B: Yeah, the dinosaurs is hot.

T: Oh, the dinosaurs are hot. Because the house is warm and safe.

B: No, but can you please open the windows?

T: Nooo!!!

The therapist could express her uncertainty about whether to believe this character: "He's acting so politely, he must be a good guy, but I'm so not sure. I don't know who to trust!"

B: Please? It's hot! (*He's trying to get in, and I'm blocking him.*)

T: Are you a good guy, or bad guy?

B: Brother, brother! Good guy!

T: Oh, okay. Come on in.

Again, having the therapist voice her uncertainty through the play might allow the child greater improvement over the sequential way he experiences them in this play scene.

B: Where's my brother? And I tricked you! I'm a bad guy!
T: You tricked me? Oh no!

This could be a moment to comment on the inner experience of being tricked: "What an awful, scary feeling it is to be tricked! I don't know if I can feel safe anymore."

B: My brother is a bad guy, too.
T: Where's your brother?
B: You had … ? (*Struggling block sounds.*) Get me away from him! Hey, where is he?
T: Where are they?
B: The guy that was just here? (*I hid him from B's sight.*)
T: I don't know! Where'd they go?
B: Oh, you took him. Where's the guy that was just here?
T: I don't know! He disappeared, like magic!
B: For real, where is him?
T: Where'd he go?
B: The dinosaur, that was just there. In there. I mean it. Where is he?

Another striking moment. Although the therapist is not fully aware of this, the child has lost his capacity to play for the moment in light of his fear that the figure has actually disappeared. It is likely that the alternation between evil and goodness masks his underlying fear that being "bad" will result in his losing someone precious. A comment such as: "Losing feelings can be so scary that it's hard to keep playing, I wonder what could make such strong losing feelings come into our play?" might be a way to point out the loss of distance to the patient without unduly alarming him and may help him regain his balance and resume playing. By loss of distance, we mean that the child's easy balance between what is play and what is reality is blurred. The sequence is also a vivid reminder of the precariousness of the play space and how quickly play can overwhelm defenses, at least momentarily. Play is always at the balancing point of being real and not real and can easily tip into being far too real. When this happens, the child must retreat from the play, and the therapist must help him regain his balance.

T: They disappeared, like magic!
B: No. Who did it?
T: Do you see it down there?
B: No.

T: That's strange.

B: Right there.

T: Hey!!! They hid under the truck! How'd they get there?

B: Hey you put them there!

He reassures himself that it was not "magic" that hid the dinosaur but the therapist, as his loss of the ability to play at that moment makes the idea of magic far too terrifying. The child is still somewhat thrown by his blurring of play and reality, making the therapist's "magical" disappearance of the figures too direct a challenge to his reality testing.

T: They were hiding.

B: Now, give me my brother back. Or I tell the rest of the bad guy dinosaurs.

T: Okay, here you go. Hi brother.

B: Hi brother. Right. You are the bad guy? No. Now get out, you bad guy! Help me get away from that evil! Guys! We're getting in the house.

Another sign of his resiliency. He can go right back into the play and gear up for further aggression.

T: You're getting in the house?

B: Get into an army! It's time for a fight! Okay, but we have to split up. Two, two, and two. Okay. You, T-rex, you go downstairs.

T: I go downstairs?

B: No, me. (*We're hiding.*) No, you don't know where I went.

T: Where are you?

B: You don't know where am I.

T: I see you. Look, I see you through the hole!

The therapist is a bit too unaware of how frightened the patient was by his own aggression and the way in which this aggression stirred up his underlying fear of loss. In the play now, the patient identifies with a figure who hides in order to master his fear of loss. It is a form of peek-a-boo. The therapist, not knowing this, says that she can see him, which disrupts his play. I might have said: "It's scary to not know where you are. It makes me feel very unsafe inside."

B: Huh?

T: I see you!

B: Where?

T: Here.

B: No, you supposed to lock the door. The doors are supposed to be locked. You can't see me.

T: I can't?

B: Yeah, because the door is open. I'm right here. What are you talking about, you see me? Ahhh! Help me, brother!

T: Are you falling? Let me help you!
B: Help!

The dramatic shifts in his play, from wanting to be the therapist's enemy to wanting her friendship, speak to the child's fluctuating experience of alternately identifying with the aggressor and feeling the danger of his aggression. Offering to help in the play was an astute move by the therapist, but I would have also continued to voice the shifting of these states: "He's asking for help, and I'm so not sure. A part of me wants to help my brother, but another part is so not sure if I'll wind up in danger. Oh well, I'll help him and hope it's okay."

T: Here you go! Safe! Inside! Made it. Almost fell down. (*I help his figurine, which is falling from the roof, and grab him, bringing him into the house.*)
B: Thanks.
T: No problem, anytime!
B: And what happened to. ... You told me you didn't trust that guy, the large triceratop.
T: This guy?
B: Yes. That's the bad guy!
T: I'm not a bad guy anymore, remember? I got knocked off the roof! And your friend knocked me off the roof!
B: No, we are the good guys.
T: Okay. Come on in, then. Come into the house.
B: No, you are the bad guy.

The child is made too anxious for the moment by his aggression and so has to project it onto the therapist's figure ...

T: I'm not bad. I'm not bad, see? Come on in, I didn't block the windows.
B: No, not *you! That* guy!! Run!!!

... and then onto a third dinosaur, so that he can protect the therapist, symbolically, from the aggression.

T: Which guy?
B: That dinosaur, that yellow dinosaur, that lizard guy!
T: Here, you guys want a lift downstairs?
B: No! No, there's a guy downstairs.
T: Let's see. Are you a bad guy? You don't seem so bad to me.

Here again, it might be more profitable for the therapist explicitly to voice her ambivalence about trust rather than simply voicing one feeling: "It's so hard to be sure who's good and who's bad anymore."

B: Argggggh. (*He hits me again.*)

T: Oh. … I keep getting knocked down by the bad guys.

B: You can't get me.

T: That yellow dinosaur sure is angry, huh? Why is he so angry?

This is an important move by the therapist to note an affect and see if the child can respond. A bit more reflective language could model curiosity about these affects: "He's sure acting angry, I wonder what he's feeling inside." or "I wonder what being that angry would feel like inside."

B: Where is that guy?

T: He hit him over the edge?

B: Where's that rock guy?

T: This guy?

B: No, the rock.

T: This guy?

B: Yes. Oh, are you okay? I'm sorry what that guy did.

The patient expresses a remarkably blatant need to undo his aggression and make reparation.

T: I know, he sure was angry. Why was he so angry? Why did he hit me?

The therapist is adept at moving the discussion back to the figure's anger and avoiding the superego-dominated need to focus on the apology. Again, the language used by the therapist could be fine-tuned to create a more reflective stance: "What would it feel like to be that angry dinosaur, and what would make those angry feelings stronger than other feelings?"

B: Because he's evil! His boss told him to. I was faking being bad, a bad guy.

T: You were faking it? But you hit him over the roof!

B: Yeah, because he's a bad guy, and I'm protecting these two dinosaurs.

T: Are bad guys angry? Get angry? Do bad guys. …

The child's shifts from aggressor to protector are growing more rapid and frequent as the play "heats up." Rather than focusing on bad guys being angry, I would stay with the idea that both good and bad guys have feelings that shift from one to the other as this is what seems to be upsetting the child.

B: Nobody hit my brother! (*He hits me again.*)

T: Oh man, everybody's hitting each other.

B: Nobody hits my brother.

T: Is he angry, too?

B: Hey, how he could climb on top of the roof? (*He's discovered that the rubber dinosaurs can stay on the slanted rooftop.*)

T: He stays there, huh? He's rubber, so I think he sticks.

B: Look.

T: That's kind of cool, huh?

B: Look.

T: But not this guy.

B: And not this triceratop. Let's try here. Oh my God. How about here? No. This doesn't stick down there.

There is again a shift from being in the play to concretely focusing on the figures being able to balance on the roof. The child has a need for respite from the alarming aggressive impulses stirred up by the play. The fact that this respite involves content about being able to balance on a precarious place is quite "overdetermined."

T: It doesn't stick there?

B: Look. Soon we're going to switch sides. Switch players.

T: Yeah? Oh wow, he sticks over there. He also sticks over here. On this side.

A: Brother, right? Are you evil? You gotta talk for him. Are you evil?

T: I don't think I'm evil.

This might be one of those moments in the play when the therapist, speaking in a whisper as an aside, asks the child, "Should I be evil?" This gives the child mastery over the flow of the play, with the whisper making it clear that the therapist is temporarily putting the play space in abeyance to get clarity. This approach often works better than answering the child's question directly as it gives a clearer sense of where the child wants the play to be headed.

B: Then how you hit those guys down.

T: I guess I was pretty angry about something. I felt like they were going to attack me.

The therapist again is adept at linking anger to behavior, but it might also be useful to model curiosity about the source of these angry or "evil" feelings: "I don't know where my evil feelings came from or why they are stronger right now than my good feelings."

B: No, you evil. You work for them. Pshuu, Pshuu. (*Hitting noises; he hits me.*)

T: Oh, why is he hitting me?

B: 'Cause you're evil! He's evil!

T: I'm evil? I'm the bad guy? Then get off me! Get off me! Off! All of you! This is my roof!

She adjusts immediately to the child's needs to have her be the evil figure, so the play takes on a more alive, visceral quality.

B: Oh … now they are really angry. What did you do to our family??? Pshuu, pshuu!

T: Get off my roof!

B: Never.

T: Off my roof! This is my roof!

B: Come get us first.

T: Ahh! Whooo, hoooo. (*We are hitting each other.*) Oh! Got one down. (*One of the figurines fell.*)

Reflection on what it feels like to be the evil figure might be an important element to add to the play: "A part of me is so full of wanting to destroy this family. Why am I doing this? What is going on with my feelings?"

B: No. I got him.

T: You got him?

B: This guy, is not dead.

T: Oh, I'm off the roof.

B: You, don't hurt my friends. Thanks. Now I got, oh! Sorry. Hmmph. (*Hits me again.*)

T: Oh, you hit him. You hit the rock guy.

B: Oh, sorry, I didn't see that. I didn't see him. Now, that guy. Where's that dinosaur? Oh, this guy? He needs to go in here and get those guys. And. ...

T: Those?

B: Yeah. And he needs to push this. Actually, the rock, I mean not the rock guy. This guy is evil. So yeah, that guy. This guy, will push this. (*He's putting the dinosaurs into the truck.*) Here. Gotcha.

T: These guys push these guys away?

B: Yeah.

T: He's driving the truck?

B: No.

T: Oops. It's like a pickup truck, a dump truck. (*I spill over the guys in the truck.*)

B: But can you stop doing that? (*Soft voice.*) Now the good guys have to come and get 'em.

The fact that he can interrupt the "reality" of the play to tell her to stop and can then switch right back to the play is an enormous strength. This ease in moving between playing and reality suggests a better prognosis for this child as the therapist may use his capacity to play to engage him in an exploration of a great deal of his inner life.

T: They gotta chase? Are these the good guys?

B: Yeah.

T: I'm gonna try to. ... (*He bangs right into me.*) Ahhh!!! I can't fight against a truck! If you're gonna hit me.

B: Oh yeah? Well, fight against me! And, oh yeah? We're an army! Two against one.

T: Two against one. Hmmm. ...

B: Let's be fair.

Yet again, we find him fluctuating between the wish to dominate ("two against one") and the feeling of guilt ("let's be fair"). The fact that guilt arises as soon as he creates a triad adds a potentially useful piece of diagnostic information as his desire to be fair was previously more a function of an imbalance in power within a dyad. Will there be more instances of oedipal triumph or guilt?

T: I guess I should get my friend, here, to help me.
B: Seems I should get my friend, here, to help me. Get them! Get them! Arrgh-
　　　pow! Arrrgh-pow!
T: Hey!
B: I got you! (*Keeps hitting me.*) This one is stronger than you!
T: Yeah? How do we know?
B: Because this one has bigger muscles than him.

Can he be more "phallic"?

T: I don't think so!! (*He starts hitting me.*)
B: I keep hitting you!
T: I know! Why do you keep hitting me?

He seems almost surprised at his continued aggression, and she adeptly expresses curiosity about this. However, a focus on exploring "what" that state of mind is or "how" that state of mind feels will likely generate more self-reflection than a focus on "why" he is being aggressive. It might also be more useful to stay within the metaphor of the play figures: "A part of him feels so superstrong that he wants the other guy to know what it feels like to be the strongest."

B: Because I have powers. I could go fast. Wheeeish, whish.
T: I could go fast, too.

This attempt to match his power might stir up his need to prove himself in battle, which could interfere with his capacity to reflect on his state of mind.

B: No, you can't. You only can turn into water.
T: Oh, I'm the water guy? Then you can't hit me because …
B: I just got you. 'Cause this guy's fast. Hmmph. You cannot get me. Or you can-
　　　not attack me. Swisssh. Arrrgh. … Pooosh. Oh this one can't do this.
　　　Only this guy. He could hit rock and cracks and go see you. Pish pish.
　　　… Oh, goes everywhere.
T: Like that?
B: (*He moves the figurine back and forth really fast.*) No you, then I go under,
　　　and you don't know where am I. And then you go stand up. No, you go
　　　there. And you go like that.
T: All the way up.
B: No, like this. Phoosh. Like that.

T: Oh, okay.
B: Try. I didn't even hit you.
T: Oh. (*I laugh.*) Oooh!
B: Like that.
T: Like that?

He does indeed become immersed in a battle that stirs up enough anxiety for him to need to create a break in the play.

B: Oh, what time is it? It's time to switch.

He remains consistently mired in the either/or nature of his aggressive feelings. Now he must give up his "badness" and place it on her shoulders.

T: It's time to switch? Okay.
B: Now I'm the good guy, and I have to lock up the house.
T: Okay.
B: I'm Tromastome, and I have the dinosaurs. I have all of the dinosaurs. And I have to hide all of the dinosaurs. Can you help me?
T: You want me to help you? You need help locking it up?
B: Yeah.
T: I can help you. Should I do it from this side?
B: Yeah. (*I stay on my side. He is moving things around silently.*)
T: I think we need the truck again to block this guy.
B: I got it. Hmmm. Potato man, too. This guy can go there. And goes here. Where should potato man go? Oh yeah, here. Where the little potato man?
T: Oh, in there. I put him in there.
B: In there? I'm going to get him. No peeking where I'm going to put the dinosaurs.
T: Okay.
B: Is it almost time to go?
T: Nope.
B: Yes!
T: What's going on over there?
B: I'm looking for a place to hide the dinosaurs. And you don't know where I'm putting them.
T: You're hiding them from me?
B: Yup.
T: I gotta try to find them, right? I gotta try to get through the windows. Did you hide them well?
B: Not yet. Now I have to lock up the place good. (*Silence.*) There's nothing in the potato man. Nothing.
T: No? You didn't hide the dinosaurs in the potato man?
B: Nope.
T: You sure? Should I come and check?

B: Nope. There's nothing in there. For real. You can't go up, because it's. ... When I say start, then you start. (*I sense he's blocking me, getting anxious that I'm starting to head into the upper floor windows.*)

T: Okay, so where are my guys?

B: Your guys?

T: Yeah. Don't you have them on that side?

B: Oh, yeah. This guy, and one more, this guy.

T: So, are these bad guys? All of them? How many guys?

B: Okay, start.

This is a beautiful example of taking a break from the play and going back to the therapist to create a shared physical space, almost like an intermission between scenes with the actors now also serving as stagehands. Themes of hide-and-seek predominate in the setting of the scene. It makes me think of his need to retreat to developmentally earlier, separation-anxiety issues as a respite from the more intense phallic and even partly oedipal nature of his aggressive play.

T: Start? All right guys. It's our goal to look for the dinosaurs. All right, what's the plan? (*I'm verbalizing what we're doing. I feel the need to say it aloud so he knows what I'll do.*) I'm going to take the downstairs. I'm going to take the upstairs!

She is speaking out loud as an important means of communicating her wish to be involved in the play. She might again give an "offstage" whisper to him to get further instructions about how he wants the play to proceed.

B: No, don't go upstairs. First, you have to look downstairs.

T: First, I go downstairs? All right. If you say so. What's in here? Ah, I got in!

B: You didn't got in.

T: I got in!

B: Ahhh ... how'd you got in? Oh man! Wait, you could skate with this guy. (*Discovers wheels on the bottom of the figurine.*)

T: Oh yeah? That's cool. I didn't see that. It rolls? It doesn't really work, huh?

B: You try. Wait.

T: Kind of.

B: What is that? You try.

She is a bit too successful in penetrating his defenses (literally and figuratively), so he gets distracted by the wheels of the figurine as a way to modulate himself. She might say: "I think he got in so fast that the guys inside started to have all sorts of worries. I wonder what that was like for them?"

T: Does anything work with the button? Kind of, not really. All right, so what about the second floor? We got one guy down on the bottom floor.

B: Which guy, which guy? Let me see.

T: This guy, remember? I came in through here.

B: Wait, start over, start over.

T: What do you mean?

B: Start over, start over.

T: What do you mean start over? I'm inside already!

B: No start over. I made a mistake. I forgot to put this …

T: Oh jeez. I got all the way inside, and you made a mistake? (*Rumbling blocks.*)

She has gotten a bit too carried away with the penetration of her figure. He needs to undo the play to avoid the anxiety of becoming defenseless.

B: Now, start.

T: Ok, I'm going in here. I got in. I'm on the ground floor.

B: I got you. I got you.

He reverses the play to deny his anxiety.

T: What do you mean I got you? I got in!

B: No. I got you. You don't remember, I hit you in the head? And you got locked out.

Now, he is trying to rationalize his undoing of her penetration.

T: I sent in my other team member, right here (*laughing*). I got in! Why don't you let me in the house! I got in (*laughing*)! Fair and square, right?

When she focuses on her triumph, he feels even more vulnerable.

B: He starts to hit … hit, hit.

T: Ahhh ahhh! Oh my goodness. So angry! I thought we were the bad guys!

B: Huh?

T: I thought we were the bad guys.

B: Yeah, and I had to attack you. So you can't come and get the dinosaurs.

This causes his figure to turn into full-blown counterattack mode.

T: Oh my goodness (*laughing*)! Holy moly.

B: Now you can't get in.

T: I don't want to get in because someone's going to hit me if I come in.

B: Okay. Try.

T: I don't think I want to anymore, because I'll get hit. I was trying to get the dinosaurs but I keep on getting hit!

Although she is voicing the fear in her figure and its resulting avoidance of the aggression, she would do better by framing it in the context of a dilemma: "Those guys are so powerful that I'm filled with two opposite feelings. Part of me wants to run away and part wants to fight, but it feels very scary inside."

B: Okay. You could start now.

T: I don't want to go in now because I don't want to get hit.

B: No, I'm not going to hit. Nobody's in there. Down there. There's only one person on the left side, he's sleeping.

T: Should I come in now? No one's going to hit us?

B: But you have to be quiet.

T: I'll come in on that side now. (*I move over to the other side.*) Did you hurt yourself?

B: Yeah.

T: Let me see. Just now? Did you scratch yourself just now?

B: No, before. (*There is a tiny scrape on his finger.*)

T: Yeah, when did you hurt yourself?

B: I don't know.

T: At school?

B: No. Just right now.

T: Just right now? Is it okay?

B: Yes.

T: Do you need a Band-Aid?

B: No. It doesn't hurt. Not that much.

The force of his aggression and her fearful avoidance makes his experience of this aggression too toxic, so he shifts the play, putting the aggressors to sleep. He strikingly then notices an "injury" to himself, as if the boundary between play and reality was upended by the intensity of his fantasy. His fear of his own aggression results in his getting injured, suggesting a castration theme that fits with his triadic upset earlier, and putting us on the lookout diagnostically for future signs of castration fears. A useful comment on this process could be: "Sometimes it's very upsetting to play with guys getting into fights and then to have yourself really get hurt."

B: Now, you have to say "those animals are cute" first. (*He's taking more animal toys out of the bin beside him.*)

T: Those animals are really cute. Look at those cute piggies. Now I gotta look for the dinosaurs.

B: (*Making cute piggy noises.*)

T: Aww, what a cute little piggy.

B: (*Making horse sounds.*)

T: And a cute little horse.

B: Wanna ride it? Wheeee.

T: That's a really cute horse.

B: Wanna ride it? Wheeeee. You have to ride him.

T: Can I get on you and ride you? Oh, cool!

B: Wanna ride me?

T: (*I make horse trotting sounds.*) Dooh, dooh, dooh. Can you give me a ride up to the second floor please? Sure.

B: Let's pretend this is a horse.

Once again, he creates an interlude in his play. The intensity needs to be softened, and significantly, he can use his fantasy play to self-regulate. The degree to which he shifts into "cuteness" and "baby play" to retreat from his aggression is striking and hints at the anxiety stirred up in him by his previous play. One way to make this shift more conscious might be to say: "Boy, it feels much safer to ride on these horses. All those fighting guys were making for some very scary feelings."

T: Yeah, okay.

B: Wait, no. This guy.

T: Oh, there's a horse. Can you get on the horse?

B: No. This is my person.

T: It's too small.

B: Where you find this guy?

T: She was right here.

B: Oh, I meant to put her right there. (*Places her on the second floor of house.*)

T: Okay, let's get on the horses and try to find the dinosaurs.

B: Follow me!

T: Follow the piggies?

B: (*Making soft animal noises.*)

T: (*Making trotting noises.*) I'm going to follow the piggies. Hey, wait for me! I'll ride this horse right up to the top floor.

B: Hey wait no, that horse can't fly. It can't fly.

T: (*I laugh.*)

Their play now has a mutual, relaxed, humorous quality, even as it builds toward yet another aggressive confrontation among the play figures. It is also striking how consistent and repetitive the play theme is, much like a symphony built around a familiar theme with only subtle variations. The recognizable themes here are (a) the need to be hidden, (b) the more powerful need to be found, (c) the aggressive need to penetrate and dominate, and (d) the feelings of guilt and the need for reparation that follow this aggression.

B: (*Inaudible.*)

T: What's going on in this room? I feel like something's going on in this room. (*I've reached the second floor.*)

She uses foreshadowing to help the patient present the next step in the play.

B: He gets angry. Hmmpph. Get out. (*Hits me.*)

T: Oh man.

B: Nobody enters our house. (*The potato man figure is in the room I was trying to get to.*) Oh, what is that brown thing? What you doing here? (*There are two naked dolls lying in the house that he's never noticed before.*) Phhossh. Maybe no. Not that guy, or that guy. It looks gross. With no clothes on. I'm staying here to watch everything that's coming through. Maybe I should use my animals. It's time to go?

The patient notices the nakedness of the figures, but this has much less of an impact than the need to aggress and the need to protect the figures he has hidden from being discovered. He becomes keenly aware of the session coming to a close before he has sufficiently expressed what he feels and goes right to the attack.

T: No, but we're going to start cleaning up in 5 minutes.

B: 5 minutes? Oh man. Okay, let's fight. Attack!

T: We're fighting!

B: No, the rest of your guys have fallen. Attack!

T: Oh my goodness! Well, where are the dinosaurs?

B: You have to find them!

T: Are they on the first floor? Are they in the truck? (*Rumbling noise.*)

B: You cannot find them (*as if commanding me*)!

T: Are they behind the table? Somebody told me, they were *not* in the potato head!

B: Which it is. …

This is an adorable depiction of both his need to hide and his greater wish to be found. On the one hand, he demandingly notes that the dinosaurs (his identificatory figures that must be protected) cannot be found, but then he admits readily that they are in the potato head after all. This sequence is reminiscent of a child playing hide-and-seek with a parent and beginning to giggle as the parent is seen nearby—the wish to be found is almost always more insatiable than the wish to stay well hidden indefinitely.

T: (*Laughing as I try to get to the potato head.*)

B: You cannot go through.

T: Why not? I must go through! I must get through! (*I try to enter, he pushes me away. This happens a few times.*)

T: I gotta get through! (*I try to come in through the back way.*)

B: (*He squeals … laughing. … We're both laughing.*) That's my guy!

T: I'm going to get Mr. Potato Head, over here! What's in here?

B: No, no no, you gotta get one of the guys to do it.

T: I gotta get one of the guys to go? Okay. I want to get to Mr. Potato Head this way!!!

B: You cannot get through.

T: I want to get Mr. Potato Head this way!!! (*I persist in trying to get to him, and he keeps blocking.*)

B: You cannot get through. (*We are both laughing.*)

T: I'm going to get you.

B: Get out, get out.

T: Ahh, lots of hitting.

The play is so mutually exciting and pleasurable that it may be superfluous to use words, but these mutual moments are often an ideal time to make a reflective comment as the child's relaxed but alert state is an ideal time for learning. A comment such as "It's so much fun and so exciting to hide but be found that our fighting feels less scary" may capture the moment well and allow the therapist, at a later moment or later session, to contrast this "fun aggression" with far more scary or threatening "hating aggression."

B: Dinosaurs! Oh, this is okay for the dinosaurs to make them tough. Or you'll get them, they will get tough on you. For real. Rarrrrrrgggh!!! Phooosh.

T: I just want to get inside to see Mr. Potato Head!

B: Gotcha.

T: Oh man, there's so much hitting I can't do anything! Even the good guys hit!

B: We are ready to fight. Oh, no more guys? Oh. No more guys. No more dinosaurs in there?

T: No more dinosaurs in there?

B: Oh yeah. One is stuck.

T: There's one in the shoe? You hid them really well, huh? Is it in there? (*He's struggling to get them out.*)

B: No, that wasn't it.

T: Oh, maybe it was that little piece you thought was a dinosaur, right?

B: Yes. No, I thought it was the dinosaur feet.

T: Is it in there?

B: Nope. All of them is in that guy.

T: Oh my goodness, they all got in there! (*He has stuck all the little pieces into the big Mr. Potato Head.*)

B: We are ready for fighting! Oh, they're all ready.

T: Ready for fighting, huh?

B: Ok, let's go! All the dinosaurs, jump up! Oh, I'm gonna get the dinosaurs. … I have to leave. C'mon dinosaurs, be careful, you watch them. And bam! Whoosh whoosh. You guys need help? Hey, that's it. I got you. Phhhosh. Bam, bam. (*Fighting and hitting ensue.*) I'm Superman! I'm the bad Superman. (*Hits again.*) Oh, that one got hurt.

T: He's hurt. He's hurt. He's hurt. He has no head.

B: He's not hurt. Nobody hurts our friends that take care of us.

Interestingly, he reveals multiple feeling states in this scene: concern and feelings of protection; fierce aggression in his figures' defense; a wish to be the ultimate invulnerable warrior (Superman); the need to label this Superman wish as bad; and the resulting guilt and castration fears when the Superman figure hurts one of the therapist's figures. He then brings in a noteworthy latency-aged theme, that of a fierce sense of loyalty among friends. The emergence of this theme suggests many healthy, developmentally appropriate avenues with which to help this child work through his earlier issues of castration and separation.

T: Okay B, it's time to start cleaning up.
B: Wait, time out. Let me put them in order again. Like before.
T: Let's put. ... This is your guy, right? You want to put those back in the bin? Let's clean up first B. (*He's putting the toys in order. I move the dollhouse back.*) Okay.

We see the return of his latency-aged, somewhat obsessional need to put things in order so that he may leave with his feelings in order as well.

B: Can I keep this guy, because he's broken?
T: No B, I'm afraid not. You know the rules, right?
B: Can I take the toys that are broken? And this one is broken.
T: There are a lot of toys in here that are broken.
B: No, just this one, that's broken.
T: The toys that are here stay here, right? They don't belong to you.

While it is splendid and useful to remain resolute regarding the rules, and while he clearly is reassured more than rejected by her authority in this domain, it may have been more relevant to address the difficulty in leaving with a comment like: "Wanting-to-take-part-of-our-room-home feelings are very strong when it's time to leave."

B: I think I could fix them. Oh, I'm putting them in order with the dinosaurs.
T: Okay, put them back in the bin.
B: Let me put them in order downstairs.
T: (*I'm watching him organize the toys at this point.*)
B: But my mommy's going to get here at 6 o'clock.
T: We meet for 50 minutes, you and me.
B: Can I just play for a little while longer?
T: I'm afraid it's time to go. See, when it gets to 5:50, right?
B: I want to bring this to that room?
T: Do you know the answer to that question?
B: No.
T: What about the toys that are in this room? They stay in this room, right? So they'll be here next time, okay. And I'll see you next week. Like every week we do.
B: I'm hiding all of them. In a place that nobody can find them.
T: Do you want to put them over here?

B: Nope. You can find it still. But they are not going to find it now. They always play with this? (*Opens up Legos.*) Do they spill the whole box?

T: I think so.

B: I'm going to hide them. (*Begins to bury them inside the Lego box, pushing them deep down.*)

T: Okay, time to go.

B: Now, they can't find them. (*Keeps stirring up the Legos.*)

T: Okay, that's enough, B.

B: Now, they never will find them. Never.

"It's so important to keep the dinosaurs safe and hidden, I understand how strong those feelings are when it's time to go" may have quelled some of his anxiety and loss, but leaving can be very hard for children no matter how empathic or thoughtful your comments may be.

T: Let's go.

B: Wait, let me make one shot. (*He discovers a small basketball and wants to shoot it into the hoop attached to the wall.*)

T: Nope, we're done.

B: One shot.

T: B, we're done.

It is impossible to know whether being more "generous" and letting him take a last shot would have been useful here, allowing him to feel more competent in the wake of his loss of control over the therapist and the play, or whether it would have led to a ramping up of his need to extend the session.

B: (*He shoots anyway.*) Why this not up? (*The ball is deflated.*)

T: B, when our time is up, it's up, okay? Those are the rules, okay?

B: I just made the one shot.

It is not surprising, though, that he needs to show a bit of oppositional behavior at the very end of the session to reassert himself in the wake of having to say good-bye.

This session is perhaps the strongest depiction of the power of play as an arena for multiple perspectives to be taken, for multiple and conflicting, even contradictory, feelings to be expressed and as a forum for the balance between feelings and defenses at any given moment. The child when playing vividly has far less need to be defensive; the greater the child's feelings penetrate the play, the delicate dance between affect and defense is increasingly geared toward protecting the child from feeling too strongly. In this session, we see how often the child's resilience can allow the play to continue, but we also see multiple instances when the play is too stimulating, and the child has to shift out of the play and into direct interaction with the therapist. This session is also notable for the shifts in the developmental content of his play; the child goes back and forth between "oedipal/phallic" themes of his power and might and develop-mentally earlier themes of separation and "hide-and-seek." This is a hallmark of treatment in early childhood as the developmental tasks of childhood have a redundant nature that needs constant reworking before the structures become more solidified.

4 A 9-Year-Old Girl

This child had been originally referred due to her refusal to speak in school, an elective mutism that persisted through her first two grades. This is one of the first sessions with her new therapist after 2 years of treatment with a prior therapist.

C: We should clean our box.

T: I think we should, C. I think we should try to figure out what still works and what does not work.

This may be picky, but it is most often useful to avoid "shoulds," even if the patient uses the word. At best, it might be useful to spell out the difference between a "should" and a "could" with a comment like "Should is a have-to-do-it feeling. Are you feeling that we have to clean our box?"

C: Those are stickers, but I took them.

T: You used them all.

C: (*She carefully starts getting all the contents out. She gets the Play-Doh containers out. She opens the first one but it is empty.*)

T: (*I point to the rest of the containers.*) I know that there's some Play-Doh there. But it's so …

C: Dry.

T: Yeah, dry.

C: Yeah. (*Mumbles.*) We should keep the empty containers to use them for the finger paint.

T: For finger paint.

C: That is so dry.

T: Dry. It's like a rock.

C: We should keep this one … (*mumbles*). What is that?

T: Oh, no, that is not good. Hmmmm. (*As C opens the container and throws it in the garbage, we realize that it has mold.*)

It is difficult to discern whether there are affects close enough to the surface in this review of the contents of C's box of supplies from her previous therapy. It is easy to imagine that finding her old supplies damaged and moldy would have powerful real, if not symbolic, significance, leaving me curious regarding whether it might have been useful to note the following at some point here: "I wonder what it feels like to find so many of your supplies in this kind of shape." This comment is vague enough to give her some wiggle room to respond without setting her up to feel any particular content.

C: (*She continues taking the dry Play-Doh out of the containers and throwing it in the garbage.*) What is (*mumbles*)?

T: Hmm, that is hard.

C: (*She continues to get the Play-Doh out using a pencil and banging the container on the garbage bin. Mumbles.*)

T: Oh, my.

C: It's hard.

T: It is very hard.

C: (*She uses a pencil to try to get it out. I watch her, while she struggles to get the old Play-Doh out of the plastic container by banging it on the garbage bin.*) Help me get it out. (*She gives me the plastic container.*)

T: Hmm, I don't think that I will be able to get that Play-Doh out of there.

C: Do you take out the other stuff?

T: Hmm ... let's see.

C: (*Mumbles.*)

T: How about this one? (*I open another Play-Doh.*) It looks pretty ... oops. (*I react to the fact that all of the Play-Doh is in bad shape.*)

C: That is too hard, turned too hard.

T: Hmmm, yeah.

I would now want to amplify her previous comment by saying, "Everything seems too hard," reflecting and building on her words.

C: (*Mumbles.*) When I came out I saw teenagers smoking.

This is a most interesting shift of content on the patient's part, as if the "bad" supplies links in her mind to "bad" teenagers—is everything in this place "bad"?

T: You did?

C: On the ...

T: Where?

C: Outside.

T: Outside the building?

C: Mm-hmmm. Do they always do that?

T: Teenagers? Smoking you mean?

C: Is this college of teenagers?

T: Yes, this is a college for, yes, for students that, hmm, are teenagers.

C: And I saw them smoke.

T: Ahhha. Hmm, how was that, seeing the teenagers smoking?

C: Sometimes they are addicted.

T: Yeah.

The therapist usefully asks what seeing the teenagers stirred up for the patient, but it would also have been useful to follow up on her "addicted" comment: "What would it mean to be addicted? How would they get that way?"

C: (*Quickly turns attention to box again. She carefully starts going through papers, stickers, and drawings.*) We could still use these (*referring to some stickers*).

T: Yeah, those, yeah.

C: Oh, yeah, I know this. (*She takes out her "magic pad."*)

T: Mm-hmmm.

The patient is going through the supply box she created with her previous therapist as one means of coming to grips with her loss. It would be useful to address this directly: "All these supplies are from when you worked with X. I'm wondering about the different thoughts and feelings that go through your mind as you look at these things."

C: (*Mumbles. Gets a Magic Marker out with a plastic pad. She tries to rub marker stains off using her fingers.*) This won't come out. Comes out with water.

T: Comes out with water?

C: Mm-hmmm. (*Stands up and rushes to door.*)

T: Are you going out to get some water?

C: (*She opens door of therapy room. She knows that there is a water fountain that is just next to the room.*) And we need tissues.

T: Yeah. So why would you need water? To take this paint off?

C: (*Mumbles.*) It will come out. (*With the door open, she points to the fountain.*)

T: Okay.

C: (*She gets water and rushes right back, with her fingers wet.*) I don't think it will come out.

T: You don't think so?

C: I don't think it will come out.

T: I don't think it's going to come out with water. Perhaps we should ...

C: With an eraser.

T: Do you think we can use an eraser? Do you think that will work?

C: Mm-hmmm. We have a pencil. ... Where is it? (*Mumbles, something about looking for a pencil that has an eraser. She takes more stuff out of the box, including a 2008 calendar and a bunch of drawings that are folded in half.*) A calendar.

T: Mm-hmmm.

C: That's mine.

T: Mm-hmmm.

C: (*She pulls out a small notebook that looks brand new.*) I haven't used it.

T: Mm-hmmm.

C: (*Mumbles. She tries to unfold some of her old drawings, but they are folded in half, and they are stuck together with paint.*)

T: Oh, my goodness.

C: (*She tries to unfold old drawings that are stuck together because of the paint. I take more drawings out of the box and start unfolding them.*)

Again, it is hard to know if the therapist is showing admirable restraint or whether it might be more useful to comment on this obviously disappointing state of her artwork: "All the paintings are stuck to each other; they're all jumbled up. It must be so hard to see them look this way."

T: I don't know. They are stuck together. Do we keep this one?
C: (Mumbles.) The colors are all stick *(she nods).*
T: Okay.
C: They are stuck together.
T: Yeah.
C: Oh, mm-hmmm *(she is able to open a drawing).* We can keep that one.
T: Okay.
C: That looks good.
T: Mm-hmmm. How about this one?
C: We can keep it inside. Remember these?
T: Mm-hmmm. *(She shows me some watercolors.)*
T: There's a lot of stuff here. It's been a while since you haven't used the box. It must bring so many memories, right?

Here, the therapist gives voice to the memory-evoking process, but by using the word "right" and keeping her comment vague, she is in danger of leading the patient into a yes or no response. I might have directly addressed the issue: "It's hard to know what to feel about seeing all these pictures when they're so stuck together. They're so different from what they were when you first made them a long, long time ago."

C: (She starts opening the acrylic paints.) But it works.
T: Paper?
C: This has a little water.
T: Let's see. Hmmmm. That is dry.
C: I can put water.
T: Oh, use water? You think?
C: I did that with X *(previous therapist).* I think it's too old.
T: Too old.
C: But maybe it will stink.
T: Do you want to throw it away? Do you want to do that?

The patient voices a pull between alternate ideas for the first time as she first wants to try to use the dry paint by adding water, but then calls it old and stinky. The therapist jumps a bit too quickly to the behaviors, while it might have been useful to wonder about the conflicting feelings underlying these behaviors: "One part of you has strong fixing feelings about the paint, maybe because it reminds you of the work you did with X, but another part of you feels they are too stinky and old." The point here is to use the child's own words to validate and help her extend her affective experience.

C: Okay. (*Throws paint into garbage. Inspects more paint.*) That's bad. ... That
     still works.
T: (*I open a container. The paint still looks fresh.*) That still works? Right?
C: (*We get more stuff out of box. She takes more paint and papers out of box.*)
     That's ...
T: Oooohhhhh.
C: Oh shoot. This one still works (*looks disappointed*).

The patient is now coming to express more disappointment. Given her ability to do
this without disruption, I would seek to expand this process: "More and more things
don't work right. What is it like to have more and more stinky, old surprises?"

T: Let's see. Right. Still fresh. Aaaah.
C: But this one is old. Oh shoot, look.
T: Oh my, that is really ...
C: Dry ...
T: How about this drawing?
C: (*Mumbles.*) Oh shoot.
T: Mm, that works. Mmm. This should be fresh.
C: Hmm, yes. But it really stinks. ... Look.
T: Hmm, it does? What do you think we should do?

It might be more useful again to focus on what this process feels like and not
simply on what to do, as throwing out articles from her previous therapy is likely
to stir up a variety of pushes and pulls. The therapist is in a doubly difficult situation here, for not only is she beginning as a therapist, but also she must facilitate
the patient's reckoning with objects from a previous treatment, a treatment toward
which the new therapist is likely to feel like a rank outsider. With this double dose
of vulnerability, it is easy to see why the therapist might feel hesitant to create a
space for the child to expand on her feelings.

C: We should throw it out. Maybe it's going to rot. (*She throws the paint into
     the garbage.*)
T: Hmmm. (*C takes more stuff out the box.*)
C: We have no more tape. (*Pulls out puppy calendar.*) Another calendar.
T: Ohh.
C: That one is for me. X gave it to me.
T: Really?

I would push for a specific memory, if possible: "Can you picture in your mind
when she gave it to you? What do you see, what was that like?"

C: (*Mumbles.*)
T: So this one is from X, and this is from you?
C: No this is from ... ours.

T: Ohhh.

C: That's for me. (*She tries to open some more paint.*) Hmm, I can't do it.

T: Nooo.

C: It's stuck. (*Throws it into the garbage.*)

T: How about these stickers?

C: We can keep them.

T: Ok.

C: There's more stuff here. Well …

T: Hmmmm.

C: (*Mumbles.*) Those are stamps.

T: Mm-hmmm. How about these? (*I point to some cardboard.*)

C: I wonder where that came from? Oh, yeah! We had jacks.

Since the patient appears to have a specific memory, I would again ask: "Can you picture that time when you had jacks? What do you see, what did it feel like?" It is striking that, in the session so far, the patient is engaged in an activity that is so potentially meaningful, evocative, and symbolic, and yet she is going about it methodically, as though it were an inventory. This is a clear and compelling case in which the child is not defensive about, or hostile toward, developing a reflective stance but is simply agnostic to such a position. Helping her conjure up a visual image might help her access her memories in a more vivid, affectively charged way.

T: This is what we were trying to find. (*I point to the scissors.*)

C: (*Mumbles.*)

T: Mm-hmmm. (*We get some more paint out and empty the rest of the contents of the box. We place everything on the table.*)

C: We don't have a … Ohh shoot that still works. It has water.

T: Yeah. What do you think?

C: But it's still working.

T: Okay.

C: It's a little scooshy, okay.

T: Okay.

C: We have a lot of pencils. Can you take this out?

T: Does that still work?

C: That does not have any more tape. (*She inspects it carefully and gives it to me.*)

T: Hmmm.

C: You have to scratch over here.

T: Let's see. Yeah, we may be able to use this. Wow it's been a real, it's been a while.

C: It's been a long time. Really, really, really long time.

It has taken a lot of staying power on the part of both patient and therapist, but the patient can now comment directly and with feeling on the longevity of the supplies she has kept, implying some access to her feelings about her long work with her former therapist.

T: Mm-hmmm. Oh my goodness, and all these things, I am sure you've had these things for so many years, right?

It is most useful to affirm the meaningfulness of how long the patient has kept the items, but a link needs to be made directly from these items to the past therapist and then, it is hoped, to the feelings attached to that therapist: "Each of these things is like a part of your work with X, so I wonder what it feels like when you see and touch each of them?"

C: (*She nods.*) A little dusty. (*She inspects the plastic box and tips it over the garbage bin.*) Look, it has dust.
T: Hmmm.
C: See the dust?
T: Yeah. Oh my …
C: Should we get a paper towel?
T: Do you want to get a paper towel now? Well, we would need to go out of the room for a paper towel.
C: Yeah.
T: Do you think we could do that after?
C: Okay.

This is false compliance on the part of the patient as the therapist feels impelled to stay in the room.

C: But how are we going to put the things back?

The false compliance recedes, and the patient is able to more authentically question the therapist as the need to keep her items intact is paramount.

T: Oh, hmmm, do you see any paper towels here, in the room?

The patient is expressing anxiety about the viability of the objects she has saved and "blaming" their foul state on the box in which they were left. I might add: "It feels important to you that we make your things with X as clean and safe as possible so that they will live a long time."

C: (*We look for a paper towel under the toys and in the racks.*) We should keep paper towels.
T: Yeah, there usually are some.

This is an indirect affirmation by the therapist that the patient's need to clean is a legitimate one.

C: We look for them. (*I see that she hides the puppy calendar under some toys.*) I left it there.

T: You left it there?

C: Yeah.

T: Oh my, the puppies want to stay here in the room, they don't want to go back
to that box.

This is the therapist's first attempt to use metaphor to address the patient's fear of
the further rotting of her supplies from X, a useful and worthwhile effort. Interestingly,
the patient cannot respond directly to the therapist's comment and instead focuses on
her need to clean and repair the other items, a more pressing need.

C: Should we go outside?

T: Hmmm.

C: We can get paper towels and then clean and put everything inside again.

T: Really. Well, we could go really, really quickly. And you really want to clean
that box, right? It means so much. Okay, so let's take a few minutes.

The therapist gets the meaning of the patient's wish to clean and validates the
message in both words and actions. Well done.

T: (*We both go to the bathroom and get some dry and wet paper towels and then
come back to the room.*)

C: (*Mumbles.*)

T: I see it's quite dusty.

T: Hmmm. It's been a while that we haven't …

C: Cleaned it.

T: Cleaned it.

C: What is that? (*She carefully cleans the inside of the box with a wet paper towel.*)

T: Yeah …

C: (*She then cleans the box with dry paper towel.*) Okay. It's dry.

T: It's dry? Hmm, this is interesting, we are going to put some stuff back and
maybe we should think about buying new stuff.

A most interesting moment in the session. The therapist has two paths she
might take. One is to stay with the past, validating its preservation: "It feels so
important to make sure that many of these things from X stay in the box in a good,
safe way." A second path would involve looking toward her future work with the
patient. I'd be inclined to incorporate both: "Maybe there should be keeping feelings for your work with X, and new building feelings for us to work on together."

T: Maybe new Play-Doh. So we have some of the old and some of new.

The therapist speaks to this blend of old and new but could have ideally added
an affective link.

C: This is an old calendar. (*She shows me the calendar with a nostalgic flair.*)

T: Hmm, so many memories, right?

The therapist is definitely on the right track but could be less vague in speaking of C's memories, perhaps saying simply, "So many feelings with X." She needs to more definitively bring the old therapist into the room so the child does not have to feel that she is threatening her new therapist by speaking of her old one.

C: Mm-hmmm. (*We look at the calendar together.*) Where's 2009?

Hah! The patient is bringing up the new therapist and wants to include her.

T: Hmm?
C: There is no 2009?
T: There is no 2009, true. We don't have a calendar for 2009. Maybe we should have a 2009, so we could keep the 2007 and 2008, and then 2009, so we have, hmm, the stuff that you had with X. Put that in the box. And then we can buy new stuff, too. So we can mix everything up. How about that?

An interesting choice of words by the therapist. I'm not sure that the patient is yet capable of mixing her past therapist with her present therapist in this manner. She may need to keep them separate, especially at this moment when she is just beginning to build a relationship with her present therapist. I might comment: "Sounds like you're wondering about how we can keep old things from you and X with new things from you and me. I wonder what that would be like, to keep both?"

C: Yeah, this one. ... (*She stares at contents as if trying to decide what to keep and what to throw away. She throws away some drawings and then selects a couple and puts them in the box.*)
T: Hmm, questions, questions. What should we keep, and what should we throw away? Hmm.

Yes, now the therapist is voicing the patient's indecision in a manner that allows the child to really work on each item.

C: Should we keep this one? Can we keep this one?
T: Sure. Do you wanna keep that one?
C: Mm-hmm (*nods*).

The therapist is now directly validating the patient's past work with X by explicitly expressing her comfort with keeping the "old" items. She might add: "Keeping things from your work with X is a safe feeling in here."

C: (*She shows me the blank notebook that looks brand new.*) I didn't write anything.
T: Basically new, right?

C: Not new.

The patient makes a clear distinction between "new" and not used yet still belonging to her time with X. This reveals her libidinal object constancy and the valid way she keeps X alive and not interchangeable with the new therapist, an important diagnostic finding.

T: Not new?
C: Me and X, hmmm, we did some work in here.
T: Ohhh.
C: We draw, we draw.
T: Yeah. Memories from when X was here.

More than memories, it would be useful to ask about feelings from when she worked with X. Can she explore the feelings?

C: We wrote a story. We wrote stories. (*She shows me a couple of short stories that X wrote in the notebook.*)
T: Mm-hmmm.
C: That's it.
T: That's it. So there are more pages here, for more stories, right? From what X started?

Once again, the therapist is at a crossroads. Does she invite the patient to write more stories with her, or does she help the patient "grieve" for the stories not written with X? Over time, it would seem vital to do both. I would begin with a comment such as: "There are places in the notebook where you and X could have written more stories. I wonder what that feels like?" Then, depending on the patient's response, the space for future stories with the new therapist can be added.

C: Green pens. Did you buy these pens?
T: Hmmm?
C: You bought these pens?
T: Buy?
C: I think you buy them.
T: I am not sure. I don't think so.
C: I think I did. Soo.
T: Mm-hmmm!
C: I think you didn't buy them.
T: No, I think they were bought by X.

In her talk of the green pens, the patient is literally expressing her confusion over where X ends and where the new therapist begins. I would voice this confusion: "It's hard to remember what is part of your old work with X and what is part of our new work together."

T: Except I guess I bought the finger paint?
C: Mm-hmmm. When we found the box it was all messy.

The statement of what the new therapist has brought perhaps frees the patient to acknowledge that her past work with X was left in a messy state.

T: Yes. There was a lot of stuff in there. Hmmm.

I would be more explicit and use the patient's word *messy*: "Yes, the box was in a very messy place."

C: How do you (*mumbles*)? We have some pages. I finished this. Ohhh (*mumbles*), and we found it.
T: Oh my.
C: (*Mumbles.*) Where is this?
T: Where is what? The markers? (*She points out the magic pad, and it seems that she is looking for the Magic Markers.*) Like this? (*I find an orange Magic Marker.*)
C: Yeah, but we had a black one?
T: Ohhh.
C: It's been a long time. (*Mumbles.*)

It is striking how the patient's words cannot be distinctly heard here for the first extended time in the session. It may be just coincidence, but it may also indicate that the feelings evoked by the messy box have dysregulated her, leaving her to go off to a more private space where her need to communicate clearly is obscured. Perhaps the loss of X makes her unwilling to speak with her new therapist. She may even be communicating more inwardly with her introject of X.

C: (*She starts writing on the blackboard. She writes down some multiplication tables: $2 \times 1, 2 \times 2, 2 \times 3.$ …*) 2×1 is 2×2 I already know. Three no no no. I messed up, it's four. I keep on doing … this stuff. I forgot this one. Six.
T: Mm-hmmm.
C: (*She writes down six but erases her answer with her fingers.*)
T: Hmmm, that works. …

The child's retreat to the blackboard is clearly an attempt to regulate herself affectively through a disruption in the play. As we discussed in Chapter 1, this might be a most opportune moment to comment on her defensive operation: "The messy feelings were strong, and then you moved away from the box and to the blackboard. I wonder what made the messy feelings turn into math feelings?"

C: Mm-hmm. (*Takes out the puppy calendar again.*)
T: Stories. Oh my, so many memories in this box. Oh my, all the stories. I wonder. … It's been a while that they haven't been out, I wonder if they. …

C: This is a calendar. Yeah, this is 2009, I think.

The therapist is having trouble finding the words to match the patient's affective experience, leading to some undoing on the patient's part. The patient states that she does in fact have the right calendar, an indirect way of negating her future with the present therapist. Perhaps she feels a bit cut off from the therapist in light of her immersion into her time with X, an experience that is challenging for the new therapist to mirror affectively.

T: Mm-hmmm.
C: (*She pulls out some spelling bee cards.*) Me and X used to play to order and spell.
T: You did.
C: Mm-hmmm.
T: Oh my, I am sure that all of these are bringing you so many memories, and that you remember X.

The therapist now does link the feelings directly to X but is still too vague. This is the precise moment when not knowing the content of a child's mind often leads the therapist to feeling stumped and silenced. It is also a moment when a focus on process could be useful to the child and could even lead to further expression of content: "You seem to be filling up with so many stories and feelings about X, I wonder what that feels like?"

C: We don't have that many paper (*mumbles*). ...
T: We don't. We should put all of our papers in. Some stuff that you had with X and some stuff that we have. ...
C: From us.

The patient now takes the lead in offering to include the therapist with X.

T: From us. Yeah. We keep some of what you did with X and then we have some new stuff.
C: Hmmmm. Ahha. Finger paint.
T: Finger paint. (*We start to put everything inside the box.*)
C: At least we have scissors.

The child's sense of connection to her new therapist makes her more optimistic and appreciative of what they do have: "Even though many things are messy and not right, there are also feelings that some things we do have are good enough."

T: Mm-hmm.
C: (*Unintelligible.*) I am going to? You have to.
T: You do?
C: (*She starts unfolding papers.*) That still works?

T: Mm-hmm, still works. Hmmm, oh my, this is a lot of work. Seeing what still
      works and what doesn't.

The therapist is doing a fine job of keeping a running commentary on the activities of the patient. If she could augment this with further depiction of the child's
mind and its affective states, the child's experience would be enhanced, I believe.

T: (*We continue going through papers.*) What about this card?
C: We keep it.
T: Okay.
C: (*Mumbles.*)
T: Let's see. Let's see.
C: Let's get this out. (*She leaves some markers and paper on the side for us to use
      later on in the session.*)
T: Here we go.
C: We can keep it here. Hmm, this is the finger paint. We are going to use them
      (*refers to empty containers*).
T: Use them for finger paint. How about this?
C: We are going to keep it.
T: We are going to keep it? (*I put some markers inside the box.*)

The child likely feels empowered by the therapist's letting her control what
gets kept and what does not.

C: We are going to use it.
T: We are going to use it now? Aha!
C: (*Inaudible. She gets some paper and markers out, and we start drawing.*)
T: Here we go.
C: (*Mumbles.*)

The child has worked through the objects of the past sufficiently to let herself
engage directly in play with the therapist.

T: Mm-hmmm.
C: What color do you want?
T: Purple
C: (*Mumbles.*)
T: Hmmm.
C: Don't press it too hard.
T: Okay.
T: So can you show me how to use the stencils?
C: You can do it like this.
T: Aha.
C: But don't make it too thick. If it comes out.
T: Okay. (*I start drawing.*)

C: You can (*mumble*).

T: Like this?

C: (*Mumbles.*)

T: What is this? This is a palm tree right? (*We continue drawing with the stencils she provided. We draw on the same piece of paper. She stares constantly at my drawing.*)

T: Oh my.

C: Look. (*She shows me a dog.*)

T: Mm-hmmm. (*We continue drawing. Silence.*)

An important moment in the play that leads us back to our discussion of how play itself is therapeutic. It is often so difficult for a beginning therapist to let play continue, especially in silence. The therapist may need convincing that the play is the thing in itself that allows the child the milieu for creativity, resilience, and working through. After all the buildup and investment of symbolic meaning in the objects and drawings the patient worked on in the past, her silent drawing, especially on the same page as the new therapist, may indeed be sufficient for the work, rendering it unnecessary for the therapist to do anything but play.

T: Ahh, oh my goodness, I think I pushed too hard, right?

C: Mm-hmmm. (*We continue to draw a palm tree and a dog.*)

T: Oh my. That is cool! What is that?

Let the play go. No need to ask.

C: (*Mumbles.*) Oh yeah. ... (*She continues to draw. Silence.*) I forgot, where is X again?

This is a profound moment. The silence of the play is not at all a repression or a defensive maneuver, but rather a holding space for the child to bring her thoughts and feelings about her past therapist to the surface again.

T: Where is X? Lets see. Hmmm. I think that cleaning this box has brought you many memories of X.

A good start by the therapist, perhaps to be enhanced by "Memories are feelings from before that we think about. What comes to your mind when you think and feel about X?"

C: I forgot where she works.

T: Works. Well ... I remember that she told us that she was going to a hospital.

C: To help people?

The therapist might wonder aloud: "What would that be like, for X to go and help other people?"

T: Mm-hmm, to help other people?

C: Ohhh.

T: But I see that you are thinking about her. And you know that you played with
        her for many years, right?

The therapist again validates the child's actions ("you *played* with her for many
years"), but a greater focus on her feelings and her ideas might be more useful.

C: Mm-hmmm.

T: And it is always sad when you say goodbye to someone that you …

C: (*She interrupts me.*) I still have pictures of her in a book.

Ah, now when affect is labeled by the therapist, the patient finds it too dysregu-
lating and interrupts her. It is likely that this is the state of the work at the present,
and that the child is limited in her tolerance for speaking to sadness. I cannot help
but wonder, however, whether a slightly different statement may have provoked
less resistance, for instance: "There are so many different good-bye feelings that
can come to your mind, I wonder what that's like?"

T: Yeah. Hmm, cleaning the box, hmm, I am sure that it has brought many mem-
        ories of her right? Hmm, and we are thinking where is she, right?

The therapist uses "right" to connect to the patient. This is useful to a degree, but it
may also evoke a false compliance that does not quite get at the child's experience.

C: Hmm. (*Inaudible. She starts to draw another dog using the stencil. This time
        she chooses purple.*)

T: You are making the same one purple?

C: Mm-hmmm. (*We continue drawing. Silence.*) Remember when I fractured
        my back?

Again, the power of silent play to allow her mind the space to bring important
issues to the fore is so striking.

C: They are going to check my back I think on Monday.

T: They are going to check your back?

C: I think on Monday.

T: Does it still hurt?

C: Nooo. … They are just going to check on it.

T: Ahha. I remember that was pretty scary. Oh my. It was very scary for all of us.
        Your mom was really scared I remember …

It is vitally useful that the therapist switches from "pretty scary" to "very
scary" to convey the intensity of the patient's experience. I would have stayed
with the patient's rendition of this narrative and not added either the therapist's

own or the patient's mother's reactions as these additions make this important moment in her life more diffuse.

C: (*She continues to draw. Mumbles; mentions that mom is taking her to the hospital.*) And in the hospital she said, hmmm, "They are going to check on your back and you can't eat anything."

Children so often remember trauma through concrete experience, and this is a telling example of that.

T: Oh, that's what she said?
C: She was hungry.
T: Oh, she was hungry.
C: And then I ate.

It is striking how confusing she is here. It is hard to know what is her experience and what is her mother's. It will be diagnostically useful to see whether this pattern of confused pronouns is a systematic indicator of mother-child affective blurring of boundaries, or whether this confusion is rather anomalous and specific to this traumatic memory. In the context of this mother-child confusion, it becomes especially important to avoid speaking about her mother's affective experience while the patient is describing her own experience.

T: And then you ate? After they checked on your back?
C: They had food. And I didn't like it. ...
T: You didn't like it. ...
C: It just tasted like nothing; you could not taste flavor.
T: It was hospital food, right?
C: It didn't have flavor. The other hospital had good flavor from the food.
T: My goodness, that old hospital, I am sure that you miss that old hospital.
C: I am going back to it.
T: You are going back to it?
C: Hmmm, no (*mumbles*). You know 911?
T: Hmm?
C: There. You know 911?
T: Mm-hmm.
C: I went there.
T: You went there? To the ER?
C: And I didn't like the food either.
T: You didn't like the food. ... Sounds like you missed that old hospital where the food was nice and where you have all these good memories. And then there is this new hospital where the food is not so good, and I am sure that you missed the old one, right?

Again, the therapist is effective at linking two different experiences but less effective at exploring their affective underpinnings.

C: I don't go to the old one anymore.
T: No?
C: Don't go there anymore. They gave me toys and stickers.
T: They did? (*Silence. We keep on drawing together on the same page. Silence.*)
C: When she left we had cake?

It is marvelous the way the patient uses the silence to come back to vitally important memories, and the therapist's tolerance of this silence shows what a terrific level of behavioral attunement they have co-created.

T: When X left you had cake?
C: Mm-hmmm. We *had* cake.
T: You mean all your family?
C: Mm-hmm except my brothers. Then we saved them some.
T: Hmmm. My goodness, so X gave you really nice food, just like that the old hospital.

A lovely linking of two warm, oral memories. Again, a statement like "Getting really good food feelings happened at the good hospital and also with X, what was that like?" might have been more useful at evoking a further depiction of her state of mind.

C: Then, hmmm, we, hmm, we, hmmm, gave a present to her, and then she gave us a present.
T: Mm-hmmm.
C: (*Mumbles.*)
T: Oh my goodness, that makes me think that I am sure you miss her.

It is important to avoid such certainty, especially because she may have access to more than one feeling about X, and the therapist's certainty may preclude a further discussion of these other feelings. I would have gone for a more generic opening, such as "Tell me about the present you got for her, what was it, and what did X do when she got it?" Then, depending on her response to this, I might have asked her for a similar visually oriented description of what she remembered about the present she received.

C: Because that was ... because that was. ... (*Silence.*) It's weird. (*She points to her drawing.*)
T: That's weird?
C: Two legs.
T: It has two, four legs.
C: Yes it does.
T: Hmmm.

C: (*Mumbles; refers to a pink crayon missing from the crayon box.*) I had a pink one.

T: You did?

C: Yes, but it ran out.

T: Ohhh?

C: Yes. ... It was stuck. Spell your name.

T: My name? You want to write it?

C: No. You write it.

T: I write it? C and T.

C: T.

T: We made that together, right? We can put that in the box with all the stuff.

The therapist is understandably wanting to create some space for herself in C's box as a metaphor for their future alliance and work together. I would have been a bit more wary to suggest this, however, not wanting to risk false compliance again and wanting C to have the luxury to place or not place their shared work in her precious box, even though C notably requested that the new therapist write their names together on a single page.

C: She made a book.

T: She made one. You mean X?

C: With all the pictures.

T: With all the pictures? Oh my, it makes me feel that you know I am sure that looking in the box it made you miss her. And thinking about how, you know, we can also do stuff that resembles what you did with her. Hmmm.

The therapist is becoming more comfortable specifying a feeling regarding the loss of X and is now also commenting on C's state of mind vis-à-vis doing similar things with her new therapist. This is a definite step toward speaking directly to C's affective life. It is noteworthy that C's response is to think of another activity—braiding—that is inherently interactive, and that involves weaving separate strands together even as they remain distinct. She is clearly making room for her new therapist in her life.

C: Do you know how to braid?

T: Do I know how to braid? I do.

C: I don't.

T: You don't?

C: I think braiding is hard.

T: It's hard. Yeah. It's hard when you do it on yourself.

C: So it's easier when you do it on somebody?

T: It's easier. Oh my, I think that you are trying to see what I can do and what I can't do for you, right? Sort of like thinking of what X could do at some point and what I can do for you. You know, different.

The therapist continues to make links between X and herself and again is no longer limiting herself to similar behaviors between the two therapists but is also including C as a thinking person. The next step would be to speak to affects and not just thinking. I would also encourage the work to be less about seeking C's affirmation ("right?") and more about affirming the possibility that wherever C's mind may go, her therapist will clearly follow.

C: That was in 2007.
T: I know. …
C: And a long time. …
T: A long time. And you know, sometimes you look back on time and you feel sad, like well. …
C: I am using the crayons now.

C shows again that she cannot sit with her sad feelings being labeled. I might have gone for "That's a very long time of feelings about X" and used my tone of voice to express the depth of feeling that was created between C and her former therapist rather than labeling any specific feeling.

T: Hmm.
C: I am using the crayons now.
T: Are you using the crayons?
C: (*Mumbles.*) Space for the pink one.
T: You are right; there is space for the pink one. So there will always be space for the pink one.

A subtle and evocative use of metaphor to give C the feeling that there is room for her in the room with her new therapist.

C: Mm-hmmm. (*Mumbles.*) Mm-hmmm.
T: I think our time is running out soon.
C: It is?
T: I feel that we will have to finish up soon.
C: You finish your drawing. You finished your drawing?
T: I finished my drawing? Okay, so I can put it in the box?

Having both of them finish their drawings and place them in the box that has clearly come to symbolize an experience of permanence serves as an age-appropriate way of concretizing and gaining closure for the session.

C: Mm-hmm. Did you sign it?
T: Sign. Oops, and I am going to draw.
C: That looks like a flower.
T: True. I was going to draw a rainbow.
C: (*She helps me draw the rainbow. Silence.*) What time is it?

T: It is almost close to the hour. Should we finish it, and put our names, like we
         did in your drawing?

C: Okay. (*Mumbles; she writes our names on the drawing.*)

T: T and C. Oh my, what we did today. We cleaned the box, we took out some old
         stuff, we put in some new stuff.

Beginning therapists often put extra pressure on themselves as the session
ends, seeking to find a "perfect" way to bring closure and "neaten up" the messiness of a child session. Here, the therapist resorts to too much vagueness and too
much of an action orientation. An alternative could be "In our cleaning today,
there were many strong goodbye memories and feelings about X for us to think
about as we do more work together next time."

C: (*Mumbles.*)

T: It's sort of like, you know, like when you leave old stuff, you wanna have new
         stuff, but you always hold onto old stuff, too. Always feel like you want
         to have new stuff but also old stuff.

The therapist is trying hard to convey a link between old and new, but the focus
on "stuff" may be experienced by C as vague, so it misses the mark as C goes
back to her mumbling, which is clearly her way of expressing a disconnect with
the therapist.

T: Just painting? Yeah. That is pretty hard.

C: And then (*mumbles*) C and T.

T: Aha. That's right. Are you ready?

C: Mm-hmm.

The session ends poignantly and hopefully with C's affirmation of her link
to her new therapist, a most notable achievement for the beginning of a new
therapy, especially for the beginning of a transfer case. When you are given your
first transfer case, it is difficult not to feel intimidated by the bond that existed
between the patient and a former therapist. You know the child could form this
bond once before, so you feel you should be able to forge such a bond also, yet
the situation also stirs up a certain kind of competition and with it feelings of
inadequacy. Add to this the challenge of being a beginning child clinician, and
you may feel "How could I hope to have the depth of feeling that this child had
with her former therapist, who she saw for years? And I'm just starting out!" In
light of these challenges, the therapist in this session is admirable in how relatively restrained she was. She did not try to force the child to include her, and
she was deeply respectful of her cherished space with her former therapist. The
child rewarded her patience by the end of the session, when the two are working
on projects together and signing drawings with both their names.

5 A 14-Year-Old Boy

Here, the presenting problem was the patient's openly stated experience of "feeling down" and wanting to talk with someone about the death of his father. This is his first session with the therapist.

T: (*Off tape as we entered the room, asking if he had been here before.*)
D: A few years ago.
T: Oh yeah?
D: But then I stopped.
T: Here?
D: Yeah.
T: Why did you stop? Do you remember?
D: I didn't feel comfortable.

After just a few moments in the room, we hear evidence that this patient may have far greater access to his internal states than those we have met until now. He immediately links an action (leaving therapy at the clinic many years earlier) to an *internal* state of discomfort. The therapist thus potentially has a more straightforward path to enhance this capacity.

T: Um ... why not?

This is the most obvious question any therapist might ask, but it is also the most difficult for the patient to answer as a "why" question strongly pushes the envelope of his capacity for self-reflection. I might have gone with "What did that uncomfortableness feel like, can you remember?" This "what" question has the advantage of staying closer to the child's experience and suggests that you, the therapist, are not made uncomfortable by his discomfort. I use his word *comfortable* so my affective inquiry is not extended beyond where he presented it.

D: Sometimes I don't feel comfortable talking to other people about stuff, and so I keep it bottled up, express it some other way.
T: What kind of ways do you express it?

The boy gives a fascinating answer that implies that he experiences emotions at times as physical entities, like a gas under pressure. I would at first go with that expression, asking what it feels like to be bottled up, rather than asking about the behavior that accompanies this bottled-up feeling.

D: I don't know ... just sports or just keep it in.

T: Um, so why don't you tell me, or I mean, about this first experience meeting me and coming here again, you said you were here when you were younger, so … I mean what do you think about coming back here?

The therapist drops the patient's discussion of keeping it in and tries to get at his feeling states about returning to treatment. She focuses on what he thinks, not what he feels, which may keep the discussion too removed but may also allow him to feel more comfortable at first. I would have wished for her to keep with his expression of things "kept in," but she may have sensed that he would not have been able to sustain that line of thought.

D: Um, I was the one that told my mom that I would like to see, I would go, come back again, so hopefully I will open up more and keep things less bottled in. So that is what I am trying to do, be more open.

A striking statement, as early adolescents, especially boys, are less likely to refer themselves to treatment. Clearly, his experience of being "bottled up," a phrase to which he returns, is menacing him. I would try speaking to how difficult a goal it is to be more open: "So a part of you wants to take on the very difficult task of being more open with your feelings, while a larger part of you is used to keeping them bottled up." With a child this advanced in terms of a self-reflective stance, it is most useful to present his inner life as a series of dilemmas, with multiple aspects of the self in a tense, dynamic balance, as this may more fully capture the phenomenology of his inner life.

T: Hmm.
D: (*Smiles.*) That's it

In a sense, he really does not have much else to say as he has succinctly presented his core conflict.

T: (*Smiles and laughs.*) So we can talk, we can play games, we can …

The therapist matches his smile but goes a bit further off base, suggesting games, while he clearly wants to see himself as more "adult."

D: I don't really play with toys.
T: What about board games; we can draw. I think your mom said something like you were going to audition for a musical. How did that go?

This is a striking and most common paradigm in a first session with an adolescent. It is so hard to know how to set a frame for treatment, so the therapist wants to give the standard introduction of what can be done. Unfortunately, this patient is ahead of her on the curve as he has given a more psychological introduction than perhaps she thought he could or would. Thus, her attempts to set up what they can *do,* as opposed to what experiences he can express, fall flat. She then attempts to "make conversation," which would have been a perfectly reasonable approach with a more inhibited patient, but with this youngster pulls them away from his affective life rather than toward it.

D: It went good. I'm in it.

T: You're in it.

D: But um, I don't know the parts yet. The parts will probably be distributed like 2 weeks from now, something like that, so I don't know what I am going to be yet.

T: What musical is it?

D: It's a musical from like a long time ago, from, I forgot what war it was. I think it was either the Civil War or ... yeah I think it was the Civil War.

T: So from a really long time ago.

D: It's about the Civil War, yeah. So, we get a whole bunch of costumes, there are songs that we have to learn, um, the way um there was um like you couldn't, you couldn't um, Whites couldn't interact with other races and if you did you would get killed. So that's mainly what the play is about. They say it was written a long time ago. I forgot what year, but it was supposed to be 3 hours and half, a really long play.

On the one hand, the patient speaks for a long time, so the shift in topic is welcomed as an opportunity to speak about something that is meaningful to him. More important, it gives him a chance to interject race into the room (the therapist is white, the patient African American). I am inclined to respond directly to these introductions of race, class, gender, and so on this early in a treatment as they tell the patient clearly that these topics are definitely open for discussion: "Sounds like the play deals directly with the violent ways in which Whites treated Blacks in this country, and here we are, a Black and a White person. I wonder what role our different skin colors will play in our work together?" I would not necessarily be looking for an answer to this question as race is an unbelievably difficult topic for discussion, especially in a first session, but a statement like this may make the patient feel that the topic is possible to be broached directly.

T: Wow, so do you think that the musical will be that long, too?

D: Yeah, probably 'cause, it's like, he tried to cut out some things so it won't be so long, so basically it is going to be about 2 hours and 45 minutes. It's long.

T: That is long. Have you ever been in a musical before?

D: Um, not a musical, play in the fifth grade and then I did a play at the school I am at now, previously before the musical.

T: So you have some experience?

D: Yeah ... not with a musical though. Play, yes, but I don't know how I sing. I probably sound horrible.

T: Did you have to sing for the audition?

D: Yeah, no just like hit some notes, like ah, just with the piano and that's it.
T: And how was that?

This is an excellent way to ask this question, perhaps with a follow-up of "So what was that like to sit and wait for your turn to sing?"

T: Did you hit them?

This question, however, is too content oriented and gets away from the process of the patient's inner state while auditioning in an area of less competence (singing). His ability to admit vulnerability so early in treatment is striking and suggests a better chance for a strong treatment alliance to build.

D: Some, not the higher ones (*smiles*). So like, you are either going to be the chorus or a leading role, so, probably I'll make the chorus.

Here is another admission that he will not be as successful as he might like. The therapist could explore this: "So what would chorus-making feel like?"

T: How many leading roles are there?
D: I think there is about like four, and then the rest is like the army and then the nurses, 'cause it's girls from different schools that play them.
T: That sounds exciting.

While this comment validates his interests, it may not be in synchrony with his admission of his lack of musical prowess.

D: (*Shrugs shoulders.*) Sort of (*smiles*).
T: Sort of? Not really?

She usefully gets his doubts and does not "rose-color" his experience.

D: I did the musical because I didn't make the basketball team.
T: Hmm.
D: So that's what I initially wanted to do basketball, but musical is a replacement.

Importantly, he now presents the musical in a different light, as a major step down after a great disappointment. A more fruitful way to stick with his affective experience could have been "I wonder what it was like to try and shift from the feelings of not making the basketball team to trying to get up for the musical tryout?"

T: You into sports?

D: Yeah, I like football and baseball. Baseball is in the spring, football is in the fall, I didn't do it because of you had to pay $175 to try out, and my mom didn't want to pay all that money … so I will try out next year.

Now, the patient interjects social class and poverty into the equation. The same directness can be applied to these issues as was applied to issues of race: "So money got in the way of your wish to play; what was that like?"

D: (*Smiles.*)
T: What are you smiling at?
D: (*Points to the recorder.*) It's right there.
T: I know, it's right there. I feel like we should cover it and then maybe …
D: Makes me kind of nervous.
T: What makes you nervous about it?
D: I don't know, being recorded.
T: Mm.
D: Nothing personal right now, but it's not going to be for every session, right?
T: Probably not. No. … What makes you nervous about it?
D: Like I said before, I don't like to talk, talk about stuff, so it will be even more uncomfortable for it to be recorded and exposed to other people.

A strikingly honest interchange. I am wondering to what extent the patient noticed the recorder at that moment as a function of some shame regarding not being able to afford to tryout for football as he noted that they have not touched on personal things yet. He shows great courage in asking if the recorder will be used indefinitely and is most articulate about his fear of being exposed. I might go with that feeling: "Feeling exposed in here would be hard enough, so what would that exposure feeling be like if you felt others were hearing it, too?"

T: Mm. … You know that everything you say is confidential between you and me anyways?
D: That's what they say, I don't know if it is true. I don't know if they tell the parents or other people.

He is so candid and brave in not simply taking confidentiality as a given. Note how he used the third person rather than saying she, the therapist, would break his trust. He is thus candid and yet cautious interpersonally, a person of many social strengths. I would speak to this: "So, even though you've heard about the rule of confidentiality, it doesn't feel yet that you can trust it, especially with a tape recorder staring you in the face."

T: I can tell you that anything that we say in here, I am not going to tell your mom, unless something that, perhaps something I am concerned about, and then I would ask your permission if I can talk to your mom, and then

> you can say yes or no, so. … Believe that whatever happens in these
> four walls stays here.

D: (*Nods.*)

I am most respectful of the therapist's frankness here, especially of the direct
language she uses in her first line. She gets a bit too vague when she speaks of
something she might be concerned about, though. With a child this forthright,
I might have said the following: "The only time I would even think of breaking
confidentiality is if I was worried about your getting suicidal, as your safety has
to come first." Her comments about asking his permission also are not quite correct in that, if she felt he was a true danger to himself, she would have to tell his
mother even if he would not give permission. Her strong statement about keeping
what happens in these four walls does seem to speak meaningfully to him, however, as he immediately asked what they should talk about.

D: So what do we talk about?
T: We can talk about anything that you wanna talk about.
D: I don't know.
T: You don't know. … Maybe do you want to talk about why you asked your
    mom, you know, that you wanted to come back here?

She usefully gets them back on the track of his initiating the treatment.

D: 'Cause like um, you know like arguments and lot of things going on in school,
    at home, just different things, like I did a little bit below like what I
    wanted to do in school.
T: What do you mean?
D: My mom wanted me to get second honors, and I missed it by a grade so, second
    honors is um B+, B+ and below, with the exception of one C+, and I got
    two, so she got a little angry, but not so much. She said but she wanted
    me to get better for the second quarter, and um. … Sometimes just
    like around the house, sometimes I can get lazy and not do something
    when she tells me right away, she has to speak to me, um like, a couple
    of times. So it's just like sometimes we argue. … Just basically those
    kinds of things, normal things.

Three different statements are made by the patient here, making it difficult to
know which pathway to take. First, he speaks about his mom (not himself) wanting
him to get good grades, so one pathway might have been "Sounds like your mom
was letting you know what she felt about your grades. What was that like to hear
that from her?" A second pathway could follow his admission that he gets "lazy."
Laziness and boredom in children and adolescents are often states of mind well
worth exploring, as the dichotomy between the lack of action and the plethora of
feelings that often underlie that inactivity can be most useful for the patient to come
to understand. So, a good start might be "What does being lazy feel like?" The last

statement he made is how "normal" things are between him and his mom, a statement at odds with his desire to come into treatment. This could be addressed as follows: "On the one hand, these arguments seem normal, but on the other hand, they make me think of your bottled-up feelings. What goes through your mind when you think of things being normal or not?" While it is comforting to know that the particular pathway you choose in any given moment does not preclude going down the other pathways at a later time, this is often too abstract a comfort for a beginning therapist, who may feel easily overwhelmed by the overabundance of choices.

T: What kind of things do you argue about?

D: Um, cleaning my room, um, closet and there are things that, um, like, school. When I try and do something, but then like, let's say, making, like, ah, if I try to do something for her, I don't know how I can put this, like, sometimes if I do it wrong or something, I don't know if it is appreciated, I don't know how to put it. ...

T: Can you think of the last time you tried to do something and it didn't work out the way that you wanted it to?

The therapist is most helpful here, as she tries to help him explore his complicated state of mind vis-à-vis his mom by asking for an actual example. I might have prefaced this comment, however, with a note on how difficult it is for him to articulate his interactions with his mom: "Sounds like when things go off track between you and your mom it's hard to put it into words, so can you think of the last time you tried ... ?" This may make the patient feel more affectively connected to the therapist, which in turn may make it easier for him to articulate what it feels like when he and his mother do not connect.

D: Yeah (*nods head*).

T: Can you think of an example when you did that?

D: She told me to clean the kitchen and the bathroom before she got home, and um, I cleaned my room because I had to clean it a long time ago, and I swept up the bathroom and living room and everything. And she got back and the dishes weren't done, but I was like, "I was doing it," and she got mad 'cause I didn't finish the two things that she had told me to do.

T: Mm.

D: So I got mad, 'cause I was trying to clean the whole house, and she got mad at me for the two things that I had to do.

T: Mm, so what did you say to her when you got mad?

The patient presents a most "seductive" dilemma for a beginning therapist here. For the first time in the session, he presents a good deal of content, and as it is related to his relationship with his mother, it appears to be particularly salient content. It would therefore be difficult for a beginning therapist not to do what this therapist did, namely, to ask about what the patient did as opposed to what he felt. However, a more process-oriented question might have led to some depiction of his affective experiences in the context of guilt and reparation, themes that seem salient to his story: "So first you *had* to clean your room, then you *wanted* to clean the whole house, but then you got yelled at for not cleaning the two rooms your mom wanted you to. What did that all feel like?"

D: She just, we just started arguing. I can't talk back to her, she's my mom, so nothing much, just I told her that I was trying to clean the house for her, yeah, that I was trying to clean the house. And she said that she only asked me to do the bathroom and the kitchen, so she got mad, I got mad.

T: Mm.

D: Sorry about my voice, I am losing my voice cause of Thanksgiving, yeah.

T: What happened at Thanksgiving?

This is too abrupt a shift away from his affective experience. It is striking how he dances between using affectively charged words ("got mad," "started arguing") and then undoing this intensity with a rational explanation of why he cannot get angry at his mom. This ties directly to his first comments in the session about how he keeps his feelings bottled up. This might be an opportunity to link these two moments: "So you started arguing, but did your feelings get bottled up because you can't talk back to her? What was that like?"

D: Crazy party.

T: Crazy party? What crazy party?

D: At my mom's house.

T: Oh really?

D: And then on Saturday it was my cousin's birthday, so I am losing my voice.

T: Why are you losing your voice? What were you doing?

D: Just having fun, with cousins, family, so yeah.

T: What kind of things do you do when you have fun?

I worry that the patient might take this question as a statement about whether he is allowed to have fun, almost as if it were a superego-based question. I would be more inclined simply to ask, "What does crazy feel like?"

D: At parties?

T: Yeah.

D: Basically put music on, Spanish music, like meringue, salsa, we start dancing, we um, then we started playing around, like with my cousins, we either watch TV or just fool around, not like kids fool around, but just like fooling around just basically go crazy (*smiles*), acting … everybody is having fun and um some of my family members, they like they do funny stuff during the parties, and it makes it even better.

T: What kind of funny stuff?

Ideally, to have kept in mind the patient's initial stance around feeling bottled up and his frustration/inhibition with his mom might have been useful at this moment in the context of the opposite sorts of feelings: "So going-crazy feelings sound just like the cure for how bottled up your feelings get."

D: Like act all, like um, like either make fun of another family member but in a good way, like to make it funny, or just do something funny, I don't know; it is just random, it makes people laugh.

T: Mm.

D: So that's about it.

T: So you are losing your voice cause you are … laughing so hard?

D: Laughing, shouting, talking while the music is loud, yeah, those things.

T: Sounds like a good time.

A useful affirmation by the therapist, mitigating any feelings of being judged for his playfulness. This gets a smile of confirmation from the patient.

D: Yeah (*smiles*), it is.

T: Does it happen often the whole family gets together?

D: What? Me losing my voice? Or just having fun?

T: Yeah, just having fun.

D: Well, like we're a united family, even though there might be some problems, we always get like resolved, we always have a good time, whatever we are doing, so yeah.

Here again, he glosses over conflict and puts on a good front regarding conflict resolution. The therapist could comment as follows: "So many times you and your family are able to resolve feelings so that they don't get bottled up. That must be a relief." This is affirming yet also pointed at his stated reason for coming to treatment.

T: You all live close, don't you?

D: Some of us live close. Some of us, my father's mother lives right on the corner of us, and my mother's mother lives nine blocks away, and then I have family in the Bronx, family in Florida, family in Georgia, different places scattered … in the Dominican Republic.

T: Yeah, so for Thanksgiving it was …

D: Bronx, at my aunt's house, and my cousin's birthday was in my house.

T: How old is your cousin?

D: She turned five. So the little kids did their stuff and then after the grownups, they partied. …

T: What group are you in?

D: Middle (*smiles*).

T: Middle. What does the middle group do?

A more process-oriented formulation might be "What does being in the middle feel like?"

D: Just, dance, play on the computer, watch some TV, or go outside and play basketball. Lots of sports and I think. ...
T: Sounds like fun.
D: Yeah. It is (*smiles*) ... (*smiles*). What else?

This is now the second time that he seems stalled and turns to the therapist for extrication from his being stuck.

T: What else? I can ask you the same question.

She tries at first to put the onus back on him.

D: About what?
T: About anything.
D: I am not good at bringing up the subject; I am better at people asking me the questions and me answering.

He is again articulate and rational in putting the ball back in her court.

T: Mm. Why do you think that is?

Although a "why" question here is likely to be more useful than a comment on his lack of initiative, this again is a moment when talking about process is even more likely to set a frame for their work that makes self-reflection a worthwhile goal in and of itself: "I wonder what it feels like when you get to one of these places where words don't come? It's not an easy place to get to."

D: I don't know, just when I am thinking, like when I have to think about something, nothing comes to mind, but when a question is asked, I can answer it.
The therapist could help the patient explore this space of not knowing what to say: "So what does that nothing-comes-to-mind feeling make you feel?"

T: What if I don't want to ask you so many questions?
D: Umm. ...
T: What if I just want to see kind of, you know we can sit here, we can be quiet and then you know whatever comes to mind, you can say it.

The therapist is working hard to stay strongly connected to her patient and to keep the onus on him to speak his mind. They get into a tug of war about it, which may be quite productive over time in terms of their feeling "real" to each other. Her allowing a place for quiet is equally useful and important as such a space can often more definitively nourish a "capacity to be alone" in the presence of another (Winnicott, 1958/1965) than can mere "conversation."

D: About what?
T: Anything that comes to mind.
D: Nothing comes to mind, like …
T: Nothing comes to mind, nothing? You are not thinking anything?

Again, however, the way out of this dilemma is likely through an attempt to elucidate what these empty states of mind feel like. Far too often, adolescents are asked to account for their actions, but far less time is spent asking for their affective experience. Going after this affect, paradoxically, is often the most useful way to help adolescents gain self-awareness of their actions. So, rather than questioning whether the patient is thinking anything, it might have been more productive to reiterate "What does it feel like when nothing comes to mind?"

D: About what? There's like (*inaudible*), problems, different things.
T: What do you feel like talking about?
D: Anything.
T: Um. …
D: (*Smiles.*) Um. …
D: Can't think of anything. … Can I have some tissues?
T: Yeah, of course. … Getting sick?
D: Yeah.
T: So sick and losing your voice.
D: Yeah.
T: Not a good combination.

The therapist seems to understand clearly that the child is using somatization as a means of getting away from his inner affective experience. She adroitly links this in a comforting manner to losing his voice after his "crazy" Thanksgiving. I doubt strongly whether the child could have seen the unconscious link between his discomfort with not having anything to say and his asking for tissues. In that sense, I think it was an appropriate "gut" response by the therapist not to suggest a connection between the two at this moment. It would be useful, however, to keep this possible link in mind either for later in the session or for future sessions as part of wondering about what happens physically as well as psychologically when he bottles up his anger.

D: (*D blows nose.*) Sorry.
T: So you were telling me about, um, I guess not getting the second honors, is that what it is called?
D: Yeah.
T: So we can talk about that.

She bails them both out by giving him some content to speak about. Not being in the room, we are limited in knowing whether she was sensing so much frustration in him about not having anything to bring up that this was a truly necessary diversion. But from our luxurious perch, it is easy to suggest that she might have hung in there a bit longer with the ambiguity of not knowing what to say and what that nothingness felt like.

D: Um, I don't think I did so bad. It's like, it's more of a big deal to my mom than it is to me, even though like I do wanna get second honors and first honors. Um, I only went down by one like one grade, from a B to a C+, so hopefully I think that I am doing better this quarter, 'cause what messed me up was I got a C+ in English because I failed a lot of the quizzes, and I handed in the work late.

T: Mm.

D: So that really put my grade down, so now I am doing better.

He's now repeating a dilemma he first identified in describing his interaction with his mother about cleaning the house: What motivates him, his internal state or his mother's demands, and how can he affectively regulate this distinction? The fact that he ends this statement in a positive light presents a challenge for the therapist in terms of how to encourage further exploration of this dilemma.

T: Why do you think that happened … that you were not doing well on the quizzes? …

Inquiring about his role in his schoolwork is a useful move by the therapist, but again she uses her language to focus on what happened rather than what it felt like, making it more likely that he will experience her comments from a "should" perspective as opposed to an affective perspective.

D: 'Cause most of the quizzes were on readings that we had to do, like over the summer, and um, I didn't do it (*smile*).

T: What kind of readings did you have to do?

D: They had summer homework … really sucks.

T: That does suck.

This is a succinct, beautiful, affective affirmation.

D: Yeah. So we had to read books. I'm a good reader, I just don't really like to read, but I read some of the books. And he also gave us a day to, ah, 'cause they are like short stories, 20 pages, but different, different books. So he gave it to us to read it, and like I didn't really focus on reading it, so I passed some but I failed most of them. So that really messed me up. And then I handed in work late, which made it even worse.

T: What work did you hand in late?

To elicit a more reflective response, the therapist might instead say: "I'm wondering what it felt like to have those sucky feelings about so much to read? Handing in the work late, was that related to how sucky it felt?"

D: Like stuff that I had to type, 'cause my printer is not working right now and I had to go to school and print it, sometimes I don't have enough time, so I had to hand it in late and that lowered my grade.

T: That sucks.

While once again she responds affectively to his problem, here I might have not been as willing to go along with his externalizations onto his printer problems without also expressing curiosity about his state of mind: "What happens inside in your head when you're hit with those I-don't-have-enough-time feelings?"

D: Yeah. Other than that, it is okay I guess.

T: What other courses are you taking?

D: Algebra 2, Honors, English, Latin, and everything else is the same from like eighth grade, biology, global, religion, stuff like that.

T: Do you like them? Do you like your classes?

D: Yeah. Yeah they're pretty good, just … yeah.

T: What … you were going to say something. …

D: No, it's pretty good, yeah, I had problems in English, I am doing better.

T: Do you like the teacher?

D: Yeah. … More yes than no, but a little bit of no.

T: What's the little no?

Since this is the first time the patient explicitly expresses mixed feelings, I would have highlighted this state of ambivalence because helping him to better articulate this state will likely be germane to his difficulties with his mother: "What's that feel like, to have 'a little bit of no' and more yes at the same time? That's not an easy state of mind."

D: Uh … he irritates easily, like uh, they say, uh, he is talking or, or, doing something, and you see when someone says "wait" and he says, "What are you going to wait for … my bus?" Like it is funny at times, but when he does it over and over and over again. …

T: Not so funny?

D: Yeah, and everybody asks him why he gets so irritated by that. He says it is a bad habit for people to say "wait." So it's when you try to say something and he stops you, it makes you forget what you were going to say or, you have to rephrase everything, and um. …

T: So how would you rephrase it?

This is an interesting moment as we do not know if this story about his teacher is in some way related to what it might feel like talking to the therapist, that is, to what extent the story is "transferential" in nature. I might have asked: "So he gets irritated and pushes you all to speak differently. What's that like in terms of your feelings inside?"

D: You could say "excuse me" and then say what you had to say, but sometimes he like stops you when you are trying to say something, and he's like, and he just stops you, so you stop yourself or something like that. Overall the teachers are good. A lot of people agree that the biology teacher is not that good.

Again, I would stick with what the English teacher's behavior does to the patient's state of mind as he clearly becomes inhibited in the class and even in his description to the therapist of what happens to his mind in this class. One way to approach this could be to say the following: "There seems to be something about the way he stops you that affects how you feel and then how you speak. What's that like?"

T: Why not?
D: People think that he is lazy 'cause he just sits there, and he like shows us videos and clips and the way he talks to us about the terms in biology and different stuff and like we already know about them, he doesn't explain it, so. ... The only reason I am passing his class is because of labs, reports and stuff, that we have to do every week. 'Cause the highest grade that I have gotten on one of his exams is a 71, and there is a lot of people, even like a lot of kids agree that he is not really a good teacher, those labs are what are helping me. I got 100 on most of them. So that is what is helping me. If there were no labs, I would fail that class.

I might want to get at the larger issue of what it feels like not to have a good teacher as it is often a transferential paradigm for adolescents of what it feels like to be misunderstood, with the "other" being at fault. I might have asked "What goes on in your head when he just plays videos or seems to be poor at teaching?"

T: Mm. What are the exams like?
D: Just like umn, like what he taught, but sometimes we don't understand what he teaches because he didn't explain it well, like he didn't explain it, like the terms, how they can be used, and like osmosis and all of that and what belongs to that. Like he doesn't explain it, and sometimes you have to go and do the research yourself.
T: Mm.
D: So it's frustrating.
T: I can imagine.

D: Yeah.

T: Especially if you are supposed to be going to class and he is supposed to be
    the teacher.

Exactly! Her affective validation of his experience brings him directly to his
superego-laden sense of injustice that the adults do not do their part, and yet the
child (self) has to be quietly tolerant while seething underneath.

D: Yeah. So if it wasn't full of labs, I would fail, I definitely need those labs.
T: (*Laughs.*)
D: Stuck again.

It is diagnostically edifying and prognostically reassuring that he is aware,
even acutely, of his moments of being stuck.

T: It's okay to be stuck sometimes.

This is a most useful affirmation but could be amplified by following with
"What does a stuck feeling feel like?"

D: Um ... what else. ... See I am not good at thinking of stuff to talk about.

This statement speaks clearly to his linkage of not having things to say with
feeling inadequate or disappointing.

T: But there is stuff that you probably want to talk about, right?

Now, the therapist is getting close to framing this situation as a dilemma with
ambivalence at its core. To make this dilemma more explicit, she could follow
with "So a part of you feels like you should have something to say. I wonder what
that 'should' feeling feels like? And does that feeling do battle with other feelings
in your mind?"

D: Yeah, but right now nothing comes to mind, but I'm certain that when we
    leave, something will pop up.
T: Good thing that you are going to come back then probably.

This is a most interesting way for the therapist to begin to create an experience
of their having time together in the future while not binding him to it. His comment also gives her a potential inroad into the nature of his ambivalence: "So I
wonder if there's something about being in here that makes it a battle inside you
to let something get expressed?"

D: Yeah.

T: Does that happen to you, that you can't think of anything to talk about and then, after something pops up.

D: Once, like, not all the time, only when there's a little, like, something to talk about it, um, like this, like discuss about it, like talk about problems, or different things like that. But if it has something to do with something else, I can think of something right away.

This is a way of saying that talking about his inner life is full of resistance, so a comment on the process could be useful: "So problems, or maybe emotions in general, cause something to get blocked up inside you. That makes sense to me."

T: Mm.

D: Nothing comes to mind (*laughs*).

T: (*Laughs.*)

D: It's blank.

T: What does blank look like?

A worthwhile attempt to sit with the "blankness," an experience that can be returned to again and again throughout this treatment.

D: Nothing. ...

T: Nothing. ... Can you remember when you were younger, when you used to come here?

D: Yeah, when I was younger, I didn't really talk I just, 'cause I didn't feel comfortable, I just played games, and just yeah, played games. ... There was this one time that I talked. ... I don't remember what we talked about though. Yeah, just that one time, 'cause I don't really feel comfortable talking to other people. It was like I think 4 years ago, so yeah I don't remember.

It is powerful that the patient can allude to a time when he spoke in his prior treatment but cannot let himself have access to it. This boy so wants to articulate his inner life to someone and is so delicately on the cusp of being able to do so.

T: Now it is different you think?

D: Yeah, 'cause I am more open now. It's not that I am closed up and I am not social. I don't isolate myself, I'm good socializing with other people, but when it comes to personal stuff I don't like to talk about it. Like everything else is fine, just when I start talking about something personal, I don't like to talk about it with other people, 'cause I feel like that is something that has to do with me, and I don't want to talk to someone else about it. But like, now I feel like, if I keep keeping things bottled up, one day it is going to just come out, it is going worse for me.

Here, the boy reveals even more clearly both his capacity to distinguish between an outward socializing and an inner struggle and his fear of his inner state becoming overwhelming. It is important to help parse out these two states of mind: "It seems to me like you're really aware that you have two very different kinds of feelings, those that you can show others and that let you socialize, and those that you keep private, that threaten to overpower you. We can work together to try to understand why those personal feelings feel so difficult to get to." This is the prototype for the creation of a treatment alliance, an alliance formed less around the expression of conflict per se than around building an understanding of the processes by which feelings get expressed or hidden. In other words, it is an alliance grounded in curiosity about affects and defenses in relation to conflict rather than in the simpler notion of the expression of conflict as "curative" in itself.

T: What do you think would happen?
D: I don't know, just like let's say when I get mad sometimes, I tear up, but that's because everything else that has happened that I have kept bottled up just like starts to come out. So because I got mad, or like sad that one time, everything else comes also. So, maybe if I let those things out that won't happen, and I will be able to get through something. So that's why I came.

What a remarkable statement. The patient links the expression of anger to tears and then to the fusion of anger and sadness that he finds paralyzing and ultimately toxic. He then exudes hopefulness that he can express these feelings so that they will not dominate him. Which of the many pathways he evokes here would be the most worthy to follow at this time? Do you go for the physical, somatizing quality anger produces? If so, you might ask the following: "So there's something about angry feelings that makes your body tear up. I wonder what that feels like?" You could go back to the notion of things feeling bottled up: "Once again you're telling me that somehow feelings get lumped together inside you so that they are almost too big to squeeze out. Where does that squeezed feeling take you?" You could go toward his interesting yet nonsequitor statement that he was sad that one time: "Tell me some more about that one sad time. What did that feel like? And I wonder what it feels like inside when sadness and anger gang up together?" Or you could follow his path of hope: "There is a strong part of you that believes that somehow you can get that lump of feelings to pass through you, and that's why you're here, but it's so hard to know how to get that process started." There is no one pathway that is better than the others, and the hope is that over time, all these roads will be followed. You should simply allow yourself to be guided by your best intuitive sense of which pathways feel most reachable affectively in the least amount of time.

T: Do you talk to anyone about your problems? Your personal ones?
D: No.
T: Not your mom?

I am not sure why the therapist would bring mom into the mix at this point as it may only dilute the developing connection between patient and therapist, creating a triadic conflict when there may not be one.

D: No, 'cause like about some things, I feel that um that if I talk to her, it might bring back some memories that I don't want her to remember, like not bad things. ... 'Cause my father passed away, and some things that happened, like most of the things revolve around that, so I don't want to talk to her about that 'cause I don't want her to feel bad or start crying. So I would rather, like I told her that I don't want to talk to her about that kind of stuff because I don't want to hurt her feelings or make her feel bad about it. Because when that happened she also came to therapy and she still does now, so I don't want to make problems for her, so that's why I don't want to talk to her about that stuff ... 'cause it had a big impact on us. ...

The patient's need not to be a burden, and the loneliness of the burden he then puts upon himself, is poignant and courageous.

T: I can't imagine. ... Does she know that you don't want to talk to her about your dad?

The therapist senses the power of this burden and asks a legitimate question.

D: I told her, probably when I told her that I would probably want to come back, I told her, at first she thought that, when I said I don't want to hurt her feelings, she thought it was something bad about her, so she started laughing. And I told her that it wasn't about something bad but it was about my dad, so she was like, "Oh, okay." I don't want to bring back mem-, not memories, because memories can be brought back for good reasons, but just I don't want to put pain back in her heart or whatever.

It is also striking that the youth can bring humor to this exchange between himself and his mom in the midst of this intense topic, a sign of great ego strength on both their parts.

T: And you think that that's what will happen if you talk about your dad?

An adroit connection by the therapist.

D: Yeah.
T: Have you, when you were younger, did you try and talk to your mom about your dad?

Here, however, I wish the therapist had stayed in the moment with the patient rather than letting them both off the hook by shifting back in time. One way to do this could be through a comment like "It makes me wonder about how powerful and complicated your feelings are about the loss of your dad, and how we will have to walk slowly through these very strong feelings."

D: No, 'cause like I never kept things bottled up, up until then. I didn't fear things up until then, like now I feel it, or something is going to happen, I am always thinking about that kind of stuff, so. ... That's been ever since that happened, so ... I don't want the same thing to happen to her.

This is a most evocative, phenomenological definition of the trauma of his loss: how the fear and helplessness it evoked originally have not yet been sufficiently mitigated and thus powerfully remain in the space between him and his mother.

T: So you think the same thing is going to happen. ...
D: Yeah, ever since that, I think that something can happen to her or to my sister, to somebody else in my family, so like, like say somebody takes a plane (*beginning to cry*) I would fear that the plane might crash because my dad passed away and I am always thinking that something bad might happen to somebody (*crying*).

Now, the patient shows us so viscerally how close to the surface and "unbottled up" those feelings really are. When he expresses sadness and apprehension, the feelings can be experienced fully, but when anger is fused with those experiences, he becomes blocked and "bottled up" again. This provides valuable diagnostic information about which affects can tolerate direct intervention and which are less available to him at present. I might say the following: "Those sad feelings can so quickly get attached to deep worries about the people you love that they come right to the surface."

T: Must be really scary to think about that all the time.

Well done. I might have used the word *feel* instead of *think*, but here the therapist's affective connection makes the particular word usage less relevant.

D: (*Nods head, still crying.*)
T: I think that it is really great that you came here, and that you want to try and help yourself and possibly also help your mom and help your sister. You know, it's like you are not keeping stuff bottled up. ... Do you want to talk a little bit about how you are feeling now?

The therapist provides three vibrant pathways all at once and then decides for herself which one to follow. She comments on the value of his decision to come back to treatment, of his wish to help his mother and sister, and of his not bottling up his sadness. She then follows the pathway that has the most affective charge, and he is most willing to go with that as well.

D: Feel like sad, like remembering, so … 'cause I don't know what happened. I don't know if my mom knows or if anybody else knows, but I don't know so. I don't know how he passed away. He went on vacation, and I don't know what happened. He died 2 days before my birthday, which made it even the more worse. …

T: Wow. … That must have been really hard.

Again, the therapist's affective validation of his experience is dead-on.

D: I would like to know what happened, but I don't know if I would be able to handle it or if my mom would think it would be good for me to know what happened. 'Cause I know he didn't die of natural causes; he was so young, so like I know something must have happened, so I don't know. …

The boy is so torn between his wish to know and his fear that he is not strong enough to handle it and the fact that his mom has not told him makes him that much more likely to feel that he could not handle it. I would go for that dilemma: "So, a part of you so wants to know, but another part of you feels so unsure of whether it would be safe to know."

T: How do you think you would feel if you, if you knew how he died?

A perfectly fine question, especially as the therapist keeps it within the realm of feeling for the first time.

D: I'd cry, but I'd think, I don't know, I think I might feel better if I knew what happened. But when it comes down to it, I don't know, I think I would react well, but sometimes you think something will go a certain way but it ends up happening like the exact opposite. So I don't know what would happen, I don't know if my mom would feel comfortable, if she does know what happened, telling me what happened … so. …

The patient voices his ambivalence, his mom's ambivalence, and their overlap. I might articulate the complexity of this situation: "So there seem to be two big parts of this that make you unsure. You're not sure whether your feelings would go badly or whether your mom's feelings would go badly. That must make it doubly confusing to figure out what to do with your feelings."

T: Must be pretty confusing not to know what happened.

She sticks well with one aspect of the ambivalence and picks his, which I think would be the preferred choice.

D: Yeah … it is hard. Like I say, I am always scared that something bad will happen to somebody. I tell myself, "Oh don't think about that, 'cause if it does happen you will feel guilty because you said that it was going to happen. …" So I think I say, "Oh don't think about that, don't think about that, think about something else," and it is just because of that, those kinds of things come to mind (*crying*).

Once again, the patient speaks achingly about how his defenses only serve to tie him in knots. To get at this dilemma, I might try a comment such as "So you seem so trapped by your feelings, because if you dwell on something bad happening and it does, you'll feel responsible, but when you push yourself to block it out, it somehow comes charging right back at you." I try to use active verbs like "charging" to convey my understanding of the depth of a patient's feelings.

T: Do you think that if you knew you wouldn't, you wouldn't be worried about everyone around you?

While this comment certainly applies continuity to the therapist's line of thought, it misses the push-pull of the patient's defenses. Over time, she will be able to help him tease his magical thinking about the "bad" consequences of dwelling on his apprehensions apart from his wish to repress his loss, but for now focusing on the intensity of his dilemma would be closer to his experience and hence help him feel less alone.

D: I am not sure, because it's still that he did pass away that makes me, because it was unexpected. Like I wouldn't think that he would have passed away at that time, me so young, him so young, and it made me think if anything that death is unexpected, and you never know when it is going to happen. So like that makes me scared … so. …
T: What was your dad like?

I certainly understand the temptation to flesh out his experience of his dad, but this question takes him away from the ongoing horror of a shocking death. To stay with his experience grappling with this horror, I might comment as follows: "So if a terrible loss can happen once and so out of the blue, then nothing feels like it could be safe, like you can't take anything for granted."

D: He was, he was good, funny, and he was good to us you know, he wasn't a bad person.
T: What kind of things did you guys do?

Again, I'd focus on his affective connection to his father, asking "What feelings come to mind when you think of him?" rather than what they did together.

D: He took me to a basketball game and um the New Jersey Nets.

T: Cool ... first time at an NBA game?

D: Yeah.

T: Pretty cool?

D: (*Nods head.*) Different things. ... He used to have a sneaker store, and so I would have new sneakers and stuff and we would spend some time together. That's just basically it, like a normal father and son. The good thing is that I remember him, and I don't know how much my sister remembers him.

T: Yeah, she is younger than you. ...

I might add: "Remembering him allows you to have a different set of feelings than your sister. What is that like?"

D: Yeah, so I think she was like 4 years old, or 3, 4, 5, between those ages, I don't know how she remembers. ... There's something. ... Like I remember the day that he left I don't know if I said good-bye to him or was I at school, or like where was I, so. ... It's hard just to think about him and not cry, and think, wish he was here. When that first happened, I sort of didn't believe in God a lot. I was saying that if there is God and he tried to help you why would he take a person that you love? I was just ... I was just thinking that to myself, and like why would that happen, why would it happen to me? And so just, and then I started thinking like God probably needed him or something, I don't even know. ...

Two pathways seem relevant here. One would involve the boy never having said good-bye: "Part of what feels so painful is that you never had a chance to say good-bye, and you wonder what it would have felt like to know he would not come back." The other pathway involves his wish for a sense of meaning to his father's death and his confusion over his belief in God: "You seem to be wrestling so hard with all the confusing feelings about how to make sense of his loss, and what meaning there could be to losing someone you love so quickly."

T: Sounds like you miss him a lot. ...

A strong and necessary statement.

D: Yeah. ...

T: Must be pretty hard to not have him around. ... (D *nods head.*) ... Well, I think that it is really great that you came in, and you know we can meet again, we can keep talking about anything that you want. ... How does that sound?

Again, she offers him a place and a person to speak with and gives him control over whether that happens, a most respectful act of kindness. I do have some concern about talking about how "great" it is that he has come to therapy since he is talking about how pained and sad he feels speaking about these things. Framing his decision to come in as "useful" rather than "great" might be closer to his felt experience.

D: Good.
T: Yeah? ... I think we are almost out of time. ... How are you feeling?

She artfully checks in with him about his affective state before leaving.

D: Good, and sad. Good that I told somebody and sad about my dad.

His capacity to acknowledge mixed feelings is again evident, and his ability to feel "unbottled" vis-à-vis sadness is also clear.

T: It is a mix of emotions, isn't it? Feeling one thing and feeling another thing at the same time. ... (*D nods.*) Okay.

The therapist ends the session with a validation of the nature of ambivalence in a most nonjudgmental, helpful manner, giving them a clear path toward reconsidering his many feelings as an ongoing part of their work together—an excellent, helpful beginning to treatment. This case is also instructive in the way it addresses the role of *working through* painful experiences. A useful treatment stands at the crossroads between "catharsis" at one end of the spectrum and a largely "rational" understanding of past dilemmas on the other. Simple stirring up of intense affect without stoking the processes for regulation is a most dangerous mode of treatment. On the other hand, an exclusive focus on how the child "thinks" about such a painful loss is prone to a more superficial handling of his experience without helping the child further develop a process by which he can acknowledge, understand, and eventually have greater empathy for his own emotional life. It is this last goal that I feel is most worthy for a treatment in which inadequate mourning is a paramount concern, as in this particular case.

Section II

Responding to Challenges to the Frame

In each of the next four cases, the child is not only agnostic to the notion of self-reflection but also overtly antagonistic to such a frame. The task for the therapist then becomes one of containing this overt defiance while actively attempting to help the child consider what these feelings feel like internally and eventually linking this visceral experience to behaviors and ideas.

In Chapter 6, a 9-year-old girl relentlessly attacks her new therapist for failing to replicate the behavior and presence of her previous therapist. In Chapter 7, the same 9-year-old girl presented in Chapter 4 is presented again, several months later, after a traumatic injury that necessitated a long break from therapy. One of the sequelae of this injury was a more overt challenge to the framework of a reflective stance, so she is included in this section as well. In Chapter 8, a 5-year-old girl blatantly resists "conversation" with the therapist, holds on to special "secrets" that cannot be told, and uses the session to engage in a "dance" between hungry yearnings and vehement withholding, all within a resistant stance. In Chapter 9, a 9-year-old girl is repeatedly and all-too-easily flooded by impulsive, destructive behavior that provides a most profound challenge to the creation of a link among self, other, and affect.

6 A 9-Year-Old Girl

This patient is beginning a new treatment after 4 years with her previous therapist. She is the third child in her family to be in treatment, originally referred because of her great stubbornness and defiance.

T: There you go, it is working now (*speaking about tape recorder*).
E: Yeah, what are we going to do next, fly out the window?

In this case, right from the start we have a child who is not only uninhibited around aggression toward her therapist but also in fact seems to be organized around the expression of this aggression. The challenge for the therapist is not only setting a frame but also finding a way to respond to overt challenges to any frame in which self-reflection might flourish.

T: Fly out the window, why?
E: No, I am not joking, what are we going to do next?

The problem of what to do with ambiguity is "solved" by this child impulsively, with an overt challenge to the therapist to supply an activity.

T: Whatever you want to do, I mean this is just …
E: (*Cuts my sentence.*) Oh, I am going to talk to your professor.
T: Okay. Go ahead.

The child feels that the therapist's words can be cut off at any time, that the therapist is not allowed any space or boundary but can be intruded on at will. How can this pattern, this violation, be brought into the therapy between them without damaging the child's need to control the session? The therapist starts off with an easy, flexible shift, allowing the patient to use the space to talk to the third person in the room, "the professor."

E: Hmmmm. She hates me. She wants to kill me (*giggles*). Okay. I am just kidding about that. But she gives me crackers that are too small. We don't go down to the second floor to get soda, and worst of all she gives me bad presents. Like for Christmas, guess what she gave me, she gave me four barrettes and a Japanese sticker and that was very hurtful. By the time I got home, I cried until my eyes got red. Now you tell him your little problems.

What a provocateur. She is trying to deal with her anxiety about the tape recorder, which she experiences as a particular type of violation: She, the patient, is subject to scrutiny by the "professor" listening to the tape. It seems from the start that this patient uses turning passive into active as a way to cope with anxiety. Is there any room in her to reflect on this approach? She begins with murderous projections, although importantly she can giggle about them and retreat from this extreme. She so readily carries with her, however, past injustices, remembering insufficient presents or inadequate "oral" supplies. In marked contrast to the previous case, in which anger had to be repressed and only sadness was available, here the converse is true. This is potentially far more problematic for a beginning therapist as coping with a patient's "attacks" without personally being thrown is difficult.

T: My problem is, Professor, with E I can never do anything right, I can never
please her. Whatever I do is wrong.

The therapist pointedly takes on the metaphor of using the professor to voice grievances, a strikingly courageous choice. At its best, such a stance lets the child know both that the therapist is aware of the child's aggression and that she is not afraid of this aggression. In doing so, she attempts to detoxify the aggression, for if it can be directly voiced without retaliation, then the therapist cannot be "killed off," and the child feels less dangerous. It begs the question, however, regarding whether the therapist's comments are felt as retaliation on some level. A possible alternative might have been to comment on how "hurtful" the presents she received were: "I hear how hurtful the presents felt. What was that like, what went through your mind as you cried on the way home? Can you remember?" This focuses the session on the child's inner experience as opposed to the interaction between patient and therapist.

E: Because she, we don't go down to the second floor and get soda, first of all.
T: That's the big thing. I don't buy her things, and I think I now discover that I
think she thinks I don't like her, that's why …

Another courageous, powerful leap by the therapist, who shifts from acknowledging her "insufficient" provisions to putting on the table that the child may interpret this as the therapist's hate for her. I might have been inclined to take on the same subject, but in the more cautious form of a question: "I wonder what it feels like when you don't get bought things by me that you really want?"

E: (*Cuts my sentence.*) She doesn't. She doesn't like me period. Wait a minute. Is
this thing on?
T: Yeah, it's on.
E: It's on high.
T: No, it's okay. It's turning.
E: Professor, I want just to tell you something. She is ruining my life. I can never
sleep, I can never eat, I can never even have a snack. I can't even eat
breakfast in the morning.

I am struck by how important it is for the patient to make sure the tape recorder is on and that her grievances be as exaggerated as possible in part because she is making a case to this "other." I might have commented on this process: "It seems especially important that the tape recorder work so that my professor gets to hear how badly you're in pain because of what I don't do right. I wonder what makes telling him so important?"

T: Oh, my God!

E: Be quiet! You see I am talking to the professor.

T: Okay. Sorry. Go on.

E: We can never do anything fun like my (*inaudible*). Let me tell you this. Let me tell you about my old therapist, Miss X. Now with her, she was (*inaudible*). We would go down to the second floor and get soda, something to drink, and come right back up. She would give me parties, a (*inaudible*), like about maybe four presents. Once we played an electronic game when, when she said we weren't, she wasn't supposed to. Like one time we went down, we went to every floor and said hello to everybody on the, we said hello to some people on every floor. But Ms. T, what she does is to sit around, always looking at me, always looking at my brother and she got evil eyes, evil eyes. You know one time what she did to me, you know what she said to me Professor, she said that my eyes were so big a whale could pop in it (*reference to a previous game we played*). And that wasn't fun. What I said to her is that, what was it again, yes, I said to her that her earwax is so sticky that she can use them as glue. Now that's funny because her earwax are (*inaudible*) yellow and she always wears the same shirt every single day. She said that I have got issues. She said that I am mentally retarded. Now just kidding about that. But she is mean. Take it from here Miss T.

Perhaps what is most remarkable is the pleasure E appears to be deriving from her put-downs of her therapist, even to the point of inviting her therapist to give her "rebuttal" at the end of her diatribe. Can it be possible to get E to reflect on this pleasure, or is it too ego syntonic? I would want at least to test out whether she could reflect on her behavior: "What does it feel like to get a chance to record so many ways that I've hurt your feelings?" One could also go down the path of bringing her former therapist into the room: "Ms. X seemed to make you feel very different inside. What were those feelings like?" Anger and ridicule are just so easy for this child, to the point of caricature, and they mask a sadness and deprivation that are profound.

T: Oh, E, E, I think that I don't do anything right, and as I understand it I don't like you at all. The fact that we …

This is a patient with whom word usage is extremely important, almost as if you had to defend yourself on the witness stand in front of a prosecutor. When the therapist says, "as I understand it I don't like you at all," she sets herself up for the words to be twisted. A comment such as "My not doing anything right toward you, what does that make you feel?" while far simpler, may be more useful in the attempt to help E shift away from actions and toward her inner affective experience.

E: (*Cuts my sentence.*) She admitted, wait, hold it, she admitted, she said that she
    don't like me. She admitted it.
T: You are taking my words out of context again.
E: You see that now she is (*inaudible*). (*Pretends to cry.*)

The dramatics, the use of the tape recorder to "bear witness," the notion of the therapist "admitting" her badness, all are acted out with minimal ability to self-reflect. It is a most formidable challenge to setting a frame of self-reflection.

E: (*Bouncing a ball on the windowsill.*) See, I'm not joking. And I like to joke,
    Professor. That's why I'm joking you. I'm just a kid, and kids have
    rights. I mean kids can't sit around cooking in their house all day. If
    you can't, if you can't live the past, you can't go to the future.

Her thoughts are flying between a drive for autonomy above all else, to a sense of being trapped by her house and by the past. A picture is developing of a child with strong sadistic features, who enjoys messing with the therapist's and the professor's minds, who feels powerless at her core and is fighting to convince herself otherwise. I would ask the following: "I'm wondering about what these jokes feel like inside your mind because they don't feel like jokes."

E: (*Makes a gesture for me to speak.*)
T: Talk to my professor?
E: Yes, talk!
T: What should I say to him?
E: Don't ask me!
T: I could say I made a big discovery. A discovery that I now understand why the
    soda downstairs is so important.

The therapist is trying to validate the importance of E's sense of oral deprivation, but it feels too removed from the patient's comments. Perhaps instead say, "It would be very hard to tell my professor what I think because it's so hard to know which of your feelings are most important for us to try to understand right now."

E: Because every single Tuesday and Thursday it's apple juice and crackers, apple
    juice and crackers. And some days there ain't nothing.
T: There are some days we are …

E: (*Cuts my sentence.*) Next day is apple juice and crackers, apple juice and crackers, and I want to have something different.

T: A variety?

E: Something to drink like soda.

T: Why do you think I don't get it?

An interesting approach by the therapist, asking E to reflect on her state of mind.

E: Because you are lazy.

T: Uhmm. What else?

E: Ha! You hear that Professor. She admitted it. She is lazy.

Again, the importance of precise language emerges as E turns her therapist's language against her and uses the third party (the professor) to bear witness to her inadequacies. At the same time, her therapist's "admission" and lack of retaliation detoxify E's comments.

T: What else am I?

E: You are sick of me.

T: That's the point. You think that because I don't get you some things that you want, I don't like you.

A powerful linkage is made by the therapist that ties her behavior to E's feelings of being worthy of hate.

E: You can't deal with it, anyway. You can't deal with it.

This is a striking projection because the therapist's comments show that she indeed can deal with E's aggression and neediness.

T: This is an important discovery for me.

This response, though, appears too distant again from the patient and too focused on the therapist's gains in awareness, which would mean little to E at this point. I am reminded of Klein's paranoid position and Winnicott's notion of the depressive position as the age of concern. This child is acting at the moment as if the depressive position has not been adequately attained as she portrays a ruthlessness about her therapist's experience that feels more paranoid than depressive. I might have gone in the direction of speaking to this ruthlessness: "You don't believe that I could ever handle how mean you feel toward me when I don't give you things you need and want."

E: Don't move your legs like this, you are man or something? Close your legs miss.

This feels like a powerful projection of being different from the therapist and needing to exaggerate these differences in a self-protective way.

T: Okay. I open my legs, my butt is up all the time (*reference to previous sessions; when I bend to pick something from the floor, she makes this comment*).
E: I never said that her butt was up all the time. She is, I don't know what she is talking about. She is just trying to make me (*inaudible*) so I could go somewhere where I don't have to be with my parents. She just wants me to separate me from my mom and my dad and my whole family.

Almost on cue, the patient reveals a deeply frightened, paranoid fantasy of being taken away from her family. She likely is not aware of this prior reference to the therapist's butt, so takes the comment as an attack to be warded off.

T: Do you want me to help you with that? (*Trying to open her juice.*)
E: No, I don't need no help. Every single day apple juice and crackers, apple juice and crackers. Even that room key looks like a cracker.
T: (*I smile.*)
E: I can't stand it, and it's not funny.

A telling interchange. First the therapist offers help despite the animosity between them, and the patient must deny her neediness even in so trivial an arena as opening a bottle. The bottle, in fact, leads us back to the monotony and inadequacy of the therapist's oral supplies. It should also be noted that the child is African American and the therapist is White, giving a doubly negative meaning to the word *cracker.* With so many levels of hostility present, it would be difficult to choose racial differences to focus on at this moment, but it certainly will be a theme in future sessions.

T: Okay. Everything is so boring, isn't it?

I think it would be more accurate to say that everything is infuriating.

E: You. At one time I made an airplane, she wouldn't let me, a paper airplane and she wouldn't let me take it out of the room. 'Cause she wants to let it stay here so we can see it every Tuesday and Thursday. Well I tell her I can see it every single day when I am not here in this junkyard. I can't do anything I want.

It is remarkable how the girl uses the third person to speak of her therapist, so that the tape recorder allows her some distance from her enormous aggression, protecting both the therapist and the patient. I would not comment on this at this point as she clearly needs to have some means of limiting her rage. As a way of getting back to the linkage of behavior to affect, despite how much projection E is employing, I might say, "You take my wanting to keep what we work on in here together as another sign of how mean I feel toward you."

T: I am open to all the suggestions.

E: Oh, yeah, it is the same thing about the soda. If we had soda, hour after 'til we get apple juice and crackers I bet she would have said no, too. That's the thing that I don't like about Miss T. She don't know how to be nice.

T: I am so boring, huh?

E: You are boring me. I mean why are we doing this? Let us just go right now to the professor right now. Tell him what. We ain't saying anything now. Can you turn this thing off so we can like say little crazy things? Is it recording right?

Here, the patient reveals a wish to say something crazy that cannot be recorded. Is this a wish to be kinder, to repair with her therapist? Or, does crazy mean more hostile, and the tape recorder serves as a superego prohibiter of still more aggression? It is impossible to know without being in the room. I might ask the following: "The tape recorder seems to bring out two different kinds of feelings. It allows you to tell someone else about all the ways I feel mean to you, but I wonder about what feelings you have about wanting to stop the tape?"

T: Yeah, it is recording.

E: How can you hear it again?

T: Towards the end I will turn it off and we will hear it again.

E: The whole thing.

T: Not the whole thing, but some parts of it we can hear it again.

The therapist validates her wish to hear the tape, and she feels less powerless, which interestingly …

E: All we have is apple juice and crackers, she can't even turn a rope.

… allows her to be diminishing of the therapist again.

T: I try my best.

E: You hear that she can't turn a rope. She is always going from up to down, up to down, up to down, up to down.

T: I try my best, Professor, I try my best.

The therapist allows herself to be placed in the masochistic position, even to the point of tacitly admitting her inadequacies to the professor. The advantage to this approach is to validate the patient's sense of injustice. The downside of this approach is that it keeps the patient's sadism ego syntonic. I might have noted: "You so want the professor to know what you feel like inside when I don't do what you need me to do, as if you don't think he'd believe your feelings." This puts the girl's affective experience "on the table" yet enlists the third person in the room as a way to soften the blows of her rage.

E: (Simultaneously.) Talk, talk, talk, talk. The recorder is playing chiching, chi-ching. Now why don't you talk, talk to your professor, tell him how you feel?

Her sadism is so belittling. She so needs to denigrate the process of self-reflection, probably because she is so prone to feeling that her mind can be invaded, and this must be defended against at all costs.

T: I feel frustrated.
E: Frustrated.
T: I feel frustrated because I don't know what to do, whatever I do or say is wrong.
E: She said, she said frus-rated, it's frustrated.
T: What did I say wrong?
E: Frus-rated.
T: Oh, okay. I pronounced it wrong.
E: Go talk to your professor, talk to your professor.
T: Well, I will talk to him when I have something to say; I don't have anything to say.

The therapist is caught in a horrible bind: The patient is so belittling, it is extremely difficult not to feel defensive, yet the extent of the child's vulnerability is in direct proportion to her ruthlessness, so some measure of containment must be created. The therapist is trying to create this containment by establishing a limit regarding what she would say or not say to her professor.

E: You can talk to him about how you feel, why are you here, yeah why is she here, Professor? She doesn't do anything to help me, I have a miserable life, my dad is upstate, my mom, my brother drives my mom nuts, I can't do anything, true.
T: So you feel frustrated, too.

In hindsight, this was not the most useful thing to say as it pairs up therapist and patient, something the patient desperately wants to avoid at this point. If they have the same feelings, the patient is likely to believe, they risk becoming fused psychologically at the very moment the patient most wants to establish autonomy and a defiant aloneness. Yet, she tells the therapist of the many injustices in her life in a way that feels real and heartfelt, so something might be said to address her real-life pain: "With so many miseries, it's hard to believe that talking about your feelings with me would do anything but make you feel worse."

E: Don't feel frustrated, I am not on your little team.

T: What do you feel, then?

E: You don't, you don't need to know what I feel.

T: Okay. That's the problem Professor ...

E: (*Cuts my sentence.*) She is always minding my business; I don't mind her business.

T: You don't give me any clues.

E: I can't, I am not supposed to give you clues. You are grown up.

These last four comments speak tellingly of her need to provoke distance and her experience of the therapist as a hostile, intrusive force. The therapist could comment: "You're telling me and the professor so clearly that anything I try to do feels weak and useless to you."

T: So I am supposed to understand without you saying anything.

E: You are supposed to know that you are not supposed to know my business. Then you may report it on the news.

The tape recorder and the professor are thus part of a split. On one side, the recorder signifies E's fear that her privacy is being violated. On the other, it represents her use of the professor to bear witness to the deprivations she has experienced in the treatment room as a metaphor for her deprivations in the rest of her life.

T: You think I will talk about, oh, so you don't talk to me, you think I will talk about ...

E: (*Cuts my sentence.*) I don't trust you period.

T: Do you think that I will talk about your business without ...

E: (*Cuts my sentence.*) I don't trust her, Professor, I don't trust her period. I don't trust her at all. The only people that I trust is my family members, and my best friends, and my teacher, and my principal (*mumbles*). You think that I will tell Miss T my secrets. I tell Miss X my secrets. And she don't even, she don't even tell nobody. Like my last therapist Miss, Miss X, she gave me her phone number, she gave, I gave, she gave, her, her, she gave me her phone number so I could call her any time I want to.

Now, the splitting becomes oriented toward good versus bad people, with the former therapist becoming the good object who maintains her privacy and gives her time and her phone number, while the depriving new therapist gives her neither. The pronoun confusions between E and Miss X are striking and speak to the girl's wish to be fused with someone while she fights so hard to stay far apart from her new therapist. In hindsight, the use of a tape recorder may have unnecessarily exacerbated her paranoid experiences.

T: Really?

E: Really. But Ms. T, I have been scared to ask her. I don't feel like asking her. The next thing is she is going to hang up on me. I mean Miss X talks to me for like maybe 30 minutes, and Miss T she may just talk to me for 5 seconds.

T: You know this all boils down to the same thing.

The therapist is trying to get in a word edgewise without getting cut off, but speaking under these conditions is nearly impossible, and sticking with the patient's experience under these conditions would be daunting for even an experienced therapist. All the patient's ego resources are directed toward keeping her new therapist as depriving, inadequate, and distant. The only thing one might be able to say would be to validate how painful the loss of her former therapist still is to her: "Sounds like you have such strong missing feelings for Miss X, like you keep thinking about her and wishing she were here to help you now instead of me."

E: He can't hear you, he can't hear you.

T: He can't hear me, why?

E: Because you are not speaking up close?

T: Okay. I will now talk up close.

E: Don't repeat what I say. See, Professor, don't repeat what I say. It ain't good on my nerves.

T: (*I smile.*)

E: It is not, she thinks it's funny. She is laughing like (*imitates a laugh*), and it's not a joke. So, you talk.

The therapist is drawn again into enacting her inadequacies behaviorally and not being able to respond affectively. She might say, "It feels to me like you can't feel anything I say is helpful."

T: Okay. So the conclusion I draw from all what you say is that I don't like you and I don't care about you. Is it that? I don't give you my phone number, I don't take you to the second floor, I don't buy you expensive presents (*a reference to previous sessions about presents*), that means ...

E: (*Cuts my sentence.*) I never said that she has to buy me expensive presents. All I want to do, I just want her to buy me a decent, beautiful present. Not expensive, or cheap, or something that can break easily. Last Christmas, last Christmas before my, my old, my old therapist Miss X she gave me three presents. She gave me this Harry Potter Quidditch game, she gave me a Hula-hoop, and she gave me a piñata, a piñata with candy and Harry Potter books. Miss T, no, she wouldn't give me that, all she is gonna give me is apple juice and crackers, apple juice and crackers.

T: What about the birthday gift? You never mention that.

I would rather try the following: "From me you fear that you'll never get anything different or fun or useful like Miss X gave you. You must miss her so much."

E: What birthday gift, what birthday gift?
T: You forgot about the Barbie doll?
E: That was just a Barbie doll; I can't even find her clothes.
T: Why?
E: Because it is cheap, too expensive. And first of all did I ask for a Barbie doll, no I asked for a piñata. And where is my piñata from Christmas first of all?

Much like a small child, a gift is not a gift unless it matches the wish of the child. A young child finds it impossible to "appreciate the thought" behind a gift and can only focus on her egocentric wish for a gift that concretely matches her fantasy. The therapist is again the "badly attuned mother" whose gift only further alienates.

T: I said that it is not possible to get everything you ask for.
E: No, you said you are going to give me the piñata.
T: I just said that I will try to do my best.
E: Yes, you said you are going to give me the piñata.
T: Oh, well.
E: You did it again, you ruined my life, you made my life miserable, and next thing you know I will be poor, I will be crying.
T: You will be what and crying?
E: I will be crying. I have been crying for Miss X, I have been crying for her. Shoot! I don't even like this therapist. First of all, when the first time we met, and we are playing this game she said d-a, she said a curse word d-a-m-n, she says d-a-m-n i-t word. (*She has been saying for a while that I said "damn it" in our first session.*)

Again, the child shifts from first person to third person, using the tape recorder to validate her rage by now accusing her therapist of saying a "bad" word as a concrete way to keep her bad. She needs to keep T bad so that she does not have to be angry at X for leaving her. The connection to her father "upstate" may suggest that getting angry at X would leave her enraged at her father as well, something she is not yet capable of owning.

T: So how can I become a better therapist, how can I be better?

I would have focused on her crying for X: "The more I fail to be of help to you, the more you feel the loss of X."

E: First of all by taking me to the second floor and get soda, second of all by being nice and giving me more than one present. There you go. We should have some fun. All we do is stay cooped up in this so-called playroom. And I am bored, feel like throwing (*inaudible*).

T: It seems to me that …
E: (*Cuts my sentence.*) I don't even know why I want to go to City College. City
       College is boring to me. This place is so boring I can go to sleep. First
       of all I have to say, Professor, that she is giving me a headache. She
       gives me stomach cramps.

The patient is now feeling so undone that her sadistic verbiage no longer soothes her, so she resorts to somatization and complains of feeling bored
(empty). I would continue with "Missing X hurts so much, it may even make your
body hurt."

T: I make you sick.
E: I didn't say you gave me stomach cramps; you don't listen. You could talk to
       your therapist now, I am done. I bet that's all you want to hear from me.
       Next thing you know it will be 2005, still going to be here you didn't
       graduate. I will be moving. In 2010, I will be a decent lady, you still be
       in City College, Professor, dumb therapist.

The girl appears to be speaking, in a confused fashion, about her past therapist X, her possible explanation for when X graduated, and feeling trapped while
therapists come and go and leave her behind.

T: So, I, you will go forward, I will be just here at this place doing the same things.

Exactly the opposite of what E fears.

E: Being stuck like glue, I am going to beat you, you can speak to your professor.
       Don't be looking at me; I said don't be looking at me!
T: Where should I look?
E: Wherever you want to except around me.
T: Okay.
E: Why don't you talk to your therapist, I mean your professor?

Here, the confusion becomes striking, for now the patient seems to make the
professor into her therapist's therapist and thus gives the meaning of the therapy
a different cast: Therapy is a place where you feel weak and inadequate, so T can
play that demeaning role while E will have none of it. The therapist might comment on this process: "It is confusing, this idea of my talking to my professor so
that I can be more helpful to you."

T: Well, I will talk to him when I have something to say.
E: You can talk to how you feel, your feelings, your emotional expression.
T: My feeling is of frustration, I told him that before, I don't know what to do. I feel
       like frozen, I feel like paralyzed. Whatever I do doesn't go anywhere.

The therapist has been so thwarted that she can only eloquently voice her powerlessness. While this may confirm a "victory" of sorts for E, it is a pyrrhic victory as it confirms that E can be truly toxic and rejecting. I might have been inclined to say, "My feelings don't matter very much now, Professor, what matters is how angry and hurt E is by losing X." This approach stays within the metaphor of using the tape recorder as an outside validator but makes the validation about E's affective state and not about T's behaviors, which is a no-win situation.

E: Yeah, this dumb picture. (*Looking in her folder, a reference to a picture X took of me, her, and her mother, which she threw in the garbage a few sessions ago.*) And she ruined the whole picture first of all.

In the midst of this rage at T, E takes out a picture that links T to herself and her mother and indirectly to X. It is striking how E has not directly said that she wants not to see T.

Indeed, we can see, if perversely, how attached, in a dismissive way, E is to her new therapist.

T: I ruined it?
E: Yes, you ruined the picture; you don't even have a smile. So I threw it up in the garbage, you don't believe it. To me she is just like a stranger.

The use of the third person ("she is just like a stranger") could simply be her speaking to the recorder as a witness again, but it also may be a reference to X.

T: So the way to get close to you ...

Better to avoid behavior again and move toward process: "I feel inside like a stranger to you, that fills you with what kinds of feelings?"

E: (*Cuts my sentence.*) What do you mean close, I need to be far away from you.
T: Okay. You know if I want to be closer to you ...
E: (*Cuts my sentence.*) I don't want to be closer to you; I want to be somewhere farther away from you. Don't keep looking at me!

The patient's inner state is so vulnerable that she needs to make her therapist avert her gaze, again reminiscent of a dismissive baby who averts its glance from a mother she deems intrusive or worthy of rejection.

E: (*Bouncing a ball on the windowsill.*) Yeah, and something else, Professor. If it was between Miss T and Miss X, who will be the best therapist, some contest, I would give Miss X a 20 for being good, I would give Miss T zero, no, 30 minus! She is the worst therapist I ever had. The second therapist I have ever had.

Responding to E's loss could be useful here: "It's terribly painful to have two therapists when you never wanted the first one to leave."

T: It occurs to me that you don't remember any of the good times we had.
E: We never had any good times!
T: Okay. I thought that sometimes we played, and we liked playing and had fun.
E: I had to do it because I had to go to this place. Not doing it for you. (*Bouncing the same ball on the windowsill.*) Oh, aren't you going to talk to your professor? Are you having sad feelings?

Now, the patient is projecting sadness instead of anger. The therapist could reflect this: "I wonder if the real sad feelings are inside your mind when you think about missing X."

T: Why do you think I am sad?
E: Because you are mad at me.

Her confused blurring of sadness and anger is striking and indicative of why she is so confused and enraged about X: If she feels sad about X, she cannot dismiss anger at X, so she must split the two feeling states and project the anger onto T. I might try the following, with no real feeling that it could be heard now: "I think you have a very strong mix-up between what makes you sad and what makes you mad, and it seems like it's hard to keep them separate."

T: I am mad at you, why?
E: I didn't say me.
T: Why should I be sad?
E: I didn't say you are sad. Don't make me throw this at you. Hear, Professor, one time she threw a ball at me. A basketball. It was really hard, and it hit my head.
T: Oh! So I hurt you, too.
E: Yes, hello, you remember over there that corner, you said let's throw a ball at E and see how she feels (*reference to a previous session*). You were smiling, too. So, don't play.

To connect E's present anxieties with her feelings of having been attacked, I might say, "So that was another big mix-up, you took my playing as attacking you. No wonder you feel like I'm bad."

T: I thought that you would like me to throw the ball back.
E: That wasn't a game. I was mad. Hello.
T: But you know whatever I think, whatever I do, whatever I say is wrong.
E: Bad.
T: Wrong and bad.
E: Wrong, (*inaudible*), dumb, and pitiful.

T: Painful?

E: I said pitiful. We never play games.

T: Why?

E: Because you don't listen to the rules. What I am doing, Professor, is writing on the chalkboard. We are going to play a game of hangman. Now watch how she is going to leave. You could do whatever you want.

In the midst of utter rejection, E finds a way to start to play! Perhaps in getting to her sadness, even in a projected form, she is freed a bit from her dismissive needs and can move, albeit tentatively, toward initiating an activity with T.

T: (*First time we are playing this game.*) We are playing hangman.

E: Da. That's what I said. See Professor, she doesn't listen. So smart and all.

T: I am so smart?

E: There is just a little bit of writing chalk.

T: Okay. I will bring some chalk next time.

E: If there is next time?

She has to throw her therapist off balance again, just as she moves toward her a bit. Their to and fro is not like the peek-a-boo or hide-and-seek of Chapter 3 but rather one of a more ruthless dismissal and a wondering if the therapist can survive E's hate. It is, as stated, more like the play of a 5-month-old than of an older baby who has attained mastery of the depressive position.

T: Oh, you are not coming on Thursday?

E: I said I may not.

T: (*Board is slippery, can't write on it.*) We can play on a piece of paper, if you like, or we can play it over here (*the small chalkboard*).

E: Be quiet! I am waiting.

T: A hint?

E: I am not giving you. Forget about that. Move, move! (*We are in front of the small chalkboard, sitting side by side, very close.*)

The contrast between E's body language, which establishes complete proximity, and her verbal language, which pushes T as far away from her as possible, is simply astounding. It is a powerful example of how much children use their bodies to express their deepest wishes and conflicts.

E: Professor, we are going to show you, I am going to, well I am going to show you, how Miss T plays hangman. She plays really, really deep.

T: Is there an A?

E: First result she asks me a question, is it A? She is just supposed to say the letter.

T: A.

E: Result two. She is just saying it in a question; I don't want her to say it in a question, I want her to say it in a regular voice that she has.

T: A.

E: See how she says it; she says it in some a grown-up voice.

The girl's sarcasm and taunting while using the third person make the contrast with their sitting side by side all the more stark. It is as though no "food" the therapist gives is right, and each must be rejected.

E: Where is the chalk? We have numbers in it, too.

T: Numbers?

E: Yes.

T: A.

E: Wait. Result three. She asks me is there any numbers in it, and I just said there is numbers in it.

T: Two?

E: Result four. As I was saying result four, she asks me a question again, or should I say result five.

T: Two.

E: Result six, she is asking a question again.

T: Two.

E: Result seven, she is asking me another question. I said that she has to answer it in a regular voice.

T: Two.

E: That's doing it in a result voice like she is a grown-up around here. It is making me feel sad.

I might have tried to pick up on the patient's use of sad: "Your sad feeling seems to carry a lot of other feelings, too. I wonder if you noticed that?"

T: Okay. C.

E: See, she is doing it again.

T: This is a long word. What can it be, both numbers and letters. Thinking about F, is there an F in it?

E: Wrong! She is doing it again.

T: No hint, you will not give me any hint?

It may well be that asking for hints is stirring up E's sadism. I might have tried to voice my own process here: "There are a lot of pressured feelings I have, trying to come up with the right answer and feeling worried about looking stupid." It is likely, however, that this comment may stir up more taunting. The therapist would be on safer ground to the degree that she can successfully mirror E's state of rage and longing rather than trying to model a reflective stance. Unlike in the first four cases, modeling is less useful when a paranoid rage is so prominent. It is likely that the patient is organized around being furious about having to take care of others' moods, so that modeling would be experienced as a further imposition on and lack of attunement to her.

E: I can't give her a hint because this is a game with no hints in it. I am the one who made up this game in the first place.

I might wonder aloud about E's choice to create a game with these particular rules: "Yes, you've made up a game where I'm on my own. I wonder why?"

T: Okay. M. I think there should be an M in this.
E: She is right, finally.
T: Let me think. I think there should be an E in it.
E: Right again.
T: This is very difficult to guess. Thank you for holding the tape for me.
E: You are unwelcomed. Look at her ears is red, her whole face is red. It is making me die.
T: In what way is it making you die?
E: Hurry up.
T: Okay. I am trying. R. There should be a R in it.
E: She is right again. I can't believe it for the first time.
T: I can't guess the first letter, though, what could it be? A P, is there a P in this?
E: No! Wrong, again!

It seemed for a moment that E was pleased that T was getting things right and thus was identifying a bit with her instead of away from her, but this identification ends so quickly.

T: Okay. Is there an O in it?
E: She is speaking loud. Do you see! She, she is going up on my face spitting on me. That's why I am having a cold. She has stomach cramps; I was throwing up because of her.

The quick loss of her affective equilibrium (perhaps related to her brief connection to T's prowess?) results in a confusing blend of somatization and fear of being attacked and invaded. Anxieties about a blurring of body boundaries also appear to be stirred up, as E locates her somatic symptoms in her therapist's body ("she has stomach cramps") as well as her own.

T: (*I look bewildered.*)
E: Next.
T: What could this word be? So strange. Ca, ma. … I can't guess the first letter. No hint, E?
E: No hints.
T: It is so difficult. Is there a number around here?
E: No.

T: So this is the only number?
E: Yes.

Again, we have a brief thaw in their verbal connection, as she is giving T some hints.

T: Can you just tell me the type?
E: No, I am not telling!
T: Okay. D? Is there a D?
E: Wrong!
T: Okay. Is there an L?
E: Wrong!
T: Okay. B. Is there a B?
E: Wrong!
T: Oh, my God! I can't guess what this word is?
E: Thinking about the vowels?

Another hint. It is poignant how a part of E wants her therapist to succeed. I don't believe it would be useful at all to comment on this, however, as it would only stir up distance and rage in E.

T: U?
E: Wrong! Wrong!
T: I?
E: Finally right.
T: What kind of a word is this, I can't find it. Okay, there is a V, this is a movie.
E: Finally!
T: Okay. Scary Movie 2.
E: Finally she got it right! This is, this is, too, that's just, I didn't say anything.

E stops herself from wanting to attack her therapist, an important moment that again is too fragile for a comment.

T: Is it your turn now? Okay.
E: Make it quick, I'm losing my makeup here.
T: You are losing your makeup?
E: Just go on.
T: All right. Okay.
E: You have to give me a hint?

E's need for her therapist to give to her and not retaliate for E's cruelty is transparent here.

T: I have to give you a hint?
E: Yes.

T: Why? You didn't give me any hints?

Unfortunately, the power of E's sadism has worn her therapist down at this moment as she needs to retaliate in the form of this question.

E: That's because people under, over 9 years old you can't get hints. People under 9 or 9 get it.
T: So, the grown-ups should give direction.
E: The grown-ups should do it by themselves. Little kids should try their best, and they are permitted to a hint.
T: Okay. Grown-ups should give direction, grown-ups should give help and support. Okay.
E: The kids should get that always. Because we are the kids in America. Da.

It is poignant how E uses her sense of injustice to affirm what all young children should get from adults. She gives it a "cultural" rationale, however, as it would be too precarious for her to ask her therapist directly for what she personally needs when she is in the vulnerable position of not knowing what the word is. I might add: "Yes, all kids should have adults to be supportive when they don't feel safe."

T: All right, the hint is this is an animal.
E: A tiger?
T: Won't you say the letter? It is not a tiger.
E: Give me some vowels, A, E, I, O, U?
T: Pick a vowel.
E: I'm saying A, E, A.
T: There is one A.
E: E? A jaguar?
T: There is an E there.
E: A humpback whale?
T: Humpback whale, no.
E: Give me a hint, give me another hint. Does it have four legs?
T: Yes, it has four legs.
E: Does it run?
T: Yes.
E: An elephant?
T: No.
E: You are sure?
T: Yes, I am sure. It is a, it eats plants, and it runs, it is a land animal. It lives on the land.
E: Tiger, leprechaun.
T: No.
E: Give me another hint.
T: Well, it is tall, a tall animal.

E: Giraffe.

T: There you go. This is a giraffe!

E: She writes sloppy.

Getting the "gifts" of hints from T is far too difficult for E to tolerate, so she immediately has to be dismissive and push T away by commenting negatively on her sloppiness.

T: I write sloppy?

E: Yes, I just said that. She writes sloppy. She writes (*sounds*) it is so sloppy to me. It is making me look bad. It is like she is abusing me, not like that, it is like she is torturing me?

What is so remarkable is that E *is* tortured in relation to her new therapist: She is tortured by her wish to move closer to her while having desperately to push her away at the first hint of this closeness. One could also say that at this moment E is so overidentified with T that T's writing becomes E's writing; therefore, T's sloppiness is E's as well, causing shame and humiliation: "So one second you get the right answer, and the next second I'm getting criticized, and the third second you feel tortured. I wonder how these feelings can change so fast."

T: How am I torturing you?

E: By your sloppy work, like sloppy (*inaudible*), and this is how she is playing music. That is how she plays music. This is how I play music.

T: You know, E, I feel awful. You know I feel awful, and I feel sad, and I feel at a loss. Because it is so hard to do something good, and everything is wrong.

The therapist is beaten down and feels her only choice is to admit defeat, as if E's sadism may only be breached by T's admission of defeat. I see how relentless E has been and thus understand this response. On the other hand, in perfect hindsight, I wish she might have said, "Now your feelings are not changing fast at all; they are resting in an angry place again toward me."

E: Forget about that now.

T: Are you playing music for the professor?

E: (*She nods.*)

T: That's great.

E: (*She makes a face.*)

T: You know you can't even take any compliments.

E: (*She makes another face.*)

T: Why don't you accept anything good?

This is a most important pathway to take, but it might be enhanced by framing it as an internally oriented question: "I wonder what it feels like inside when I give you a compliment and you have to push it away?"

E: Taa-taa! I mean, taa-taa!
T: (*I clap.*)
E: No clue. Here is my other song. Play when I start saying go, okay?
T: I play?
E: Yes.
T: Okay.
E: You play good. That's the thing.

Incredibly and unpredictably, E reverses herself and now compliments T. Perhaps this child's vast hunger for any sort of sustenance was sated for a moment by T's compliment after all.

E: (*We are playing together.*) Oh, yeah, I want you to hear something else, too, hold it near the ground, hold it like this.

This connection continues, as they play mutually, and even moves expansively, as E wants T to hear more.

E: (*Inaudible.*)
T: Okay. You are quite performing for the professor.
E: I want to show you how smart, talented, and wonderful I am. Now let's do it again five, six, seven, eight.

The remarkable turnaround continues, as she now performs for more "applause" without inhibition or shame. The all-or-none quality to her experience is simply remarkable as suddenly E is able to witness T turning her into an all-good cheerleader.

E: (*Doing cheerleading figures.*) Taa-taa!
T: It's great!
T: I guess this is now time to clean up. So I'm turning this off, bye Professor, you want to say bye to him?

Now the session ends with the "professor" as witness to their "reconciliation."

E: Bye, Professor, and I want to meet you one day. Maybe not, but. Tell your student that she needs to be more kind to a child and more persuade.

Fittingly, E tells us that although she might be tempted to meet the professor, she has some ambivalence and uses the professor as a benevolent object who can make T continue to act in a kindly way. I might end the session with "So we end today with hopeful feelings that maybe I can be more kind and you can have more hopeful feelings inside."

T: Persuade.
E: Bye.
T: Bye.

Reflecting on this session as a whole, both the therapist and the patient seem brave. Especially for a beginning therapist, it takes such strength to be able to stay with a patient who is so disparaging and not to retaliate, but this therapist does so beautifully. And on the patient's part, while she seems at first like a child who lacks a capacity to play since she is so caught up in belittling back and forth with her therapist, it shows a surprising supply of resources on her part suddenly to be able to recover and to create a play space for herself and her therapist at the end of the session. When she creates this play space, she at first creates a dynamic in which she is telling the therapist, "You aren't getting anything, you aren't getting any hints, you're an idiot." But then, as the therapist begins to get some answers right, the patient's merger with the therapist allows her to begin to feel that *she* can do things competently, allowing her to switch gears and ask the therapist for hints. Thank goodness the therapist does give her hints because if she had refused, the game likely would have broken down. Each hint the therapist gives feels almost like an attempt to spoon-feed a baby, and finally, instead of the baby turning away, she accepts the food, and the two can connect. This speaks to the tension in this session between violently pushing away intimacy and, in moments, beginning to accept it.

Finally, the ways in which the patient uses the tape recorder in this session are striking and resourceful: At times it bears witness, at times it is a safe person to resort to, at times it is a sounding board. This raises questions about how this session would have gone if the tape recorder had not been in the room. On the one hand, it made the patient more paranoid and contributed to much of the aggression between her and the therapist early in the session. But on the other hand, it served as a relief and as an opportunity for her to give testimony and therefore to feel that she was being heard and held. Also, unlike another person, a tape recorder never retaliates or criticizes, so it can shift from being a persecutory object to being a safe object. In this case, the recorder becomes safe enough by the end of the session that the patient says she might even like to meet this once-threatening object.

7 A 9-Year-Old Girl

This session is with the same child discussed in Chapter 4 but a month later, during which time the child suffered a serious injury that caused her to miss several weeks of treatment. The injury was not at all life threatening, but serious enough to have warranted emergency room care.

F: (She notices that I am using a different tape recorder.) And the other one?
T: Which other one?
F: (Inaudible) for tape?
T: Oh, because I used another one last time, huh?
F: (She starts arranging the pieces so we can play Connect Four.) You think this is going to fall down? *(She wants to know if I can guess if the pieces will fall all the way down to the table.)*

The session begins with the patient alert and focused. She notices a change in the tape recorder and begins playing a game (Connect Four) in which the possibility of the checkers all falling down unexpectedly is suggested. A parallel with her sudden injury seems likely. The emergence of this parallel creates an interesting set of questions for the therapist: How conscious is this connection to the patient? Would it be useful to make the connection explicit, or would it be better to let her expand on her play to see where it goes? Although it may be difficult for a beginning therapist to wait to comment on such a connection, it nevertheless seems vital to stand back and let the child do her work. One reason to wait lies in knowing that it is so early in the session that there is much time to let the play unfold and gather affective depth. A second reason for waiting is grounded in the idea that if the child is aware, even unconsciously, that she is bringing her injury to her play, then she will present in a manner authentic to her, giving a far more meaningful feel to the process that unfolds during the session.

T: Which one?
F: This.
T: Hmm. Should I guess?
F: Your turn. Okay. Go!

The child anxiously wants the therapist to place her checker in the slot so that it can fall through and does not want her to guess ahead of time as that would presumably spoil the "shock" of the checker falling. I would be inclined to voice the "experience" of the checker: "Whoa, here I am the checker about to drop down the slot. Will I fall but get safely caught, or will I crash? It's a worried feeling not to know." This at least sets a frame for reflecting on an affective experience of falling without warning.

T: Hmm, yes!

F: It fell. You are black.

T: Oh, I am black. Okay. Aha, let me see. … Where should I put my token? Ohhh. I know that you know all the tricks for Connect Four!

F: Oh really, if I go here. Here.

T: Yeah.

F: One, two, three, four.

T: Ah, I see. Hmmm. So that is a possibility, and another possibility is that you would try to get me here. (*I point to three tokens that are lined up.*)

The therapist is trying to create a running commentary on the game. In general, I find this most useful in this sort of strategy game as it allows the child to know what I am feeling and thinking and models a reflective stance.

F: What time is it?

If used too much, however, creating a running commentary can disrupt the play by breaking a communicative silence that may be most useful for the child at that moment. Here, the child gets distracted from the game and focuses on the clock. Like noticing the new tape recorder on entering the room, getting distracted by the clock seems to convey a highly vigilant stance. This being the child's first day back in treatment, her vigilance is understandable, yet it may also reflect a reaction to the trauma of her injury.

T: Hmm, it's 5:20, but I think that's wrong, it says 4:20. (*I pull out my phone to check the time.*)

F: I just fixed it! (*She had set the time last week and apparently the clock is running out of batteries.*)

T: I know. Maybe it is running out of batteries.

F: Maybe somebody is changing it. What's the time?

Her hypervigilance now extends to a brief thought that someone is changing the time, that is, intruding on their space. I might comment, "Things feel different in here today, a new recorder, the time is not right—I wonder what that feels like?"

T: Oh, let's see. 5:20.

F: That is right.

T: Yeah…that is.

F: Ten, 15, 20, …

T: That is 4:20, right?

F: (*She assiduously changes the hour on the clock.*) I can't do it. Oh, this is the hour hand.

T: Right.

F: Can I see your phone? (*She wants to check the time.*)

T: Let's see, ... it's 5:26.

F: Five, 10, 15, 20. Twenty-four. It's still on the five, right.

T: So that is 20.

F: Five, 10, 15, 20, 25. ... Twenty-five, 25, 26. Hmm. Okay. Your turn.

T: Now that we have the time set up correctly, let's see.

F: Hmm.

T: Hmm.

F: I'm making my plan.

After this long exchange about the time, she can finally go back to the play.

T: I know that you are making your plan. You are really thinking ahead of me, huh? Hmm, let's see. I guess I need to, sort of, let's see.

F: Nice choice.

T: Nice choice? I see now. I am thinking that you can get me here or here. Wow, this is a game where you really need to think ahead of what people will do, huh? Hmm.

F: Guess what? My friend cut her finger, right here.

This sudden shift by the patient brings her still more directly to the topic of her own injury, albeit once removed.

T: She did?

F: Her meat was showing,

T: Oh, my.

I appreciate the affect behind this statement, but I would have tried to turn the remark toward an examination of the child's witnessing of the "meat" as it resonates with her visceral experience of her own injury: "I wonder what looking at the meat felt like?"

F: By accident. Hmm, she was, hmm, cutting wood and then she, I don't know how she did it, but she cut, hmm, right here (*points to her middle finger*). And then she was crying.

T: Did that happen at school?

The common tendency to respond by asking for particulars is understandable, but experience distant. I might instead try, "So the meat was showing, and she was crying. What do you think was going through her mind?"

F: Are you ready to go?

This moment speaks to the delicate "art" of psychotherapy with children: How do you continue to play a game and remain available to its vicissitudes while sharing a psychological space with the child that addresses the affects stirred up by the injury? The therapist continues playing, which is crucial to not interrupting the child's flow.

T: How did that happen, was that in a class?
F: No.
T: How did she cut herself?
F: At art.
T: Oh at art, I see. … That seems pretty scary, I guess, I guess you can get hurt. …
F: Thank you!!! (*She wins the game. My interpretation ruined. …*)

I do not believe the interpretation was "ruined." However, as the therapist continues to ask content questions about what happened as opposed to what was felt, the child is able to pull away from the material and can break the flow of the therapist's words by focusing defensively on the triumph of the game.

T: Oh, no!
F: Okay, next. …
T: Oh my goodness, I didn't see that coming. I was thinking of your friend, and you got me.
F: I am filling all the Connect Four.
T: Aha.
F: I am the yellow ones, too.
T: Okay. So you are red and yellow, and I am the black? (*We start playing.*) Hmm, I was trying to think about your friend and then puff, it's difficult to think and then play, when you have to concentrate. …

These are two lovely attempts by the therapist to describe and model the impact of the injury on her capacity to think and concentrate. It might have been still better to say, "The feelings about getting cut were so strong in me that I couldn't concentrate on the game. Sometimes worries are so strong that you can't think right."

F: (*She pulls out a measuring tape and starts measuring the Connect Four board.*) Here at 95.
T: 95?

The child drops the play and uses other, more obsessional defenses to further distance herself from the injury. Whenever that dramatic a shift away from play occurs, it is a direct challenge to setting a reflective frame in treatment. At this point, it is usually worth a try to comment on the shifting process: "Oh, one second we were filling the board, then I tried to tell you about my feelings about your friend, and now we're measuring. I wonder how we went from feelings to measuring?"

F: That looks like an iPod. It's a phone?

T: It's a phone.

F: We are going to try something?

T: Sure.

F: I am not going to do anything bad. Wait, I can't do that, I am going to get something. My pen. (*She inspects my phone, tries to turn it on.*)

T: I wonder what you are going to do? Let me guess, is she going to take her battery out?

F: Oh, I see. With the finger? No battery (*she tries to switch it on*).

T: I guess that I don't have much battery.

F: I locked it.

T: Yeah.

F: Oh, let's just press this button. (*She grabs a faceless puppet that she has referred to in prior sessions as "the clone."*)

The child has apparently used playing with the therapist's phone as a bit of respite from the feelings stirred up by the injury to her friend. She now can resume symbolic play and goes to an "old friend" in the room to re-engage.

T: Oh, is that the clone? Is that Mr. Clone? I remember him.

F: He is somebody else.

What seems like a lovely move by the therapist to readily accept the shift into puppet play is refused by the patient, raising questions about the meaning behind this act of autonomy.

T: Somebody else? Who is he? Is he … mm … Mr. Clone's friend, no? Mystery Man.

F: My name is Mystery Man.

Here, the patient adopts her therapist's words, perhaps reflecting a bit of false compliance after an attempt at autonomy.

T: Mystery Man, who are you?

F: I'm a clone.

T: You are a clone?

F: Yes!

T: Whose clone?

F: Someone's clone?

T: Does that mean that you are exactly like someone else?

F: Yep. Look. Watch this. (*She puts the puppet in a plastic box and pulls out a Playmobil figure.*) I am somebody else.

T: How did that happen? He is another person.

F: He disappeared.

T: He disappeared? How did that happened? He was a person, and then another person, and now he disappeared. It's pretty confusing to me. ... I wonder why they call him Mystery Man.

A most useful review of the changes in the puppet, but rather than focusing on these changes as confusing to the therapist, I might have stayed with what "disappearing" itself might be like: "I wonder what it would feel like inside to first become someone else and then to disappear?"

F: (*She starts playing with a small house and a couple of Playmobil figures. Knocks on door.*) Oh. I am home. Okay. Did we pick up the spongy thing?
T: Yes! Our spongy thing that we hid last time. Where is it?
F: (*She looks for the foam that we call the "protective costume."*)
T: It's the foam pants or the foam costume, right? Ohhh, still there. No one saw it, hmm?
F: No one ever looks at the games. (*She organizes the house and starts assembling a gun with wooden blocks and sticks.*)
T: What is that?
F: A laser.
T: A laser? So is that guy going to use the laser?

The child is clearly using play and its preparation to reveal something about her experience. In light of this, the therapist may be asking too many questions. Given this child's tendency toward false compliance, it is imperative to let her lead the way.

F: Oh, wait. ...
T: Okay. He is scared I am sure. (*F points laser at a Playmobil figure.*)

The therapist is speaking directly to a powerful affect, but it may not be useful to be so sure. Better to let F articulate the feeling for herself: "With that laser pointing at him, I wonder where he goes with his feelings?"

F: Look. Bye-bye. Gosh, that was a tan. ...
T: He is getting a tan? Who is he?
F: I don't know. I just made him up.
T: I see. I'm wondering what will happen. ...
F: But we don't have any money. ...
T: Oh no, so what should we do?
F: Stay in our house.
T: Okay.
F: He is wondering where is the kitchen. You don't eat.
T: Oh my goodness, they don't have any money, they don't have any food.
F: Or toys.
T: Oh my, need and needs, and more money, no more food, no more toys?

A lovely following of the patient's lead, affirming their poverty.

T: What do you think? Do you think it measures like this?
F: (*She pulls out a measuring tape and starts measuring the Playmobil figures.*)

But again, speaking of deprivations (a link to sadness?) is too disruptive, and she must shift the play from fantasy-laden to concrete action. In so doing, she tells us again about the nature and degree of her affective tolerance and suggests that a central goal of treatment should be to enhance this capacity, at least around sadness and loss.

T: Hmm, smaller? Hmm, yeah. Are they? Did I guess incorrectly?
F: Almost.
T: Almost, so many things to guess. Oh well, about these people.

I might comment on this process of guessing and uncertainty: "When you don't know something, it's a very hard feeling and not comfortable at all."

F: (*She gets distracted with some markers.*) Don't tell me somebody put water?
       (*She inspects the markers.*) Yep (*looks disappointed*).
T: Someone put water on the markers? Oh my goodness. … Someone has moved
       the hour on the clock, and someone is messing up the markers?

The therapist echoes the behaviors but again does not speak to the affect. To encourage a reflective stance, she could add, "All these moving-around and disappearing feelings, I wonder what that feels like?"

F: No, they didn't put any water on the markers. Why did they put water? It
       doesn't make sense.
T: Yeah. Oh my goodness, someone is messing with our stuff here. That is
       pretty annoying.

The therapist expands on her previous verbalization about behavior to include an affect: "annoying." This is an important precursor to the stance I have suggested throughout the book, namely, that we want affect to play a central role in the session, and that we ideally want to locate this affect in the patient's mind to enhance her curiosity and hence her reflective capacities. This will, in turn, broaden her ability to tolerate and express affects.

F: (*Again turns her attention to the dollhouse.*) Help me, I am sick! Take this.

The acknowledgment of negative affect appears to help organize F and gives her the ability to let herself play. Interestingly, the play episode involves an inversion of roles, with F starting out by being sick herself but quickly delegating this role to her therapist instead. It appears that being the patient herself would hit too close to home, so she must put herself in the healer role with her therapist as the patient.

T: Would that make me feel better?
F: (*She takes my temperature with a toy thermometer.*) It's really high. ...
T: Does that mean that I am going to be sick, that I am going to be hurt?

Here is an opportunity to see if the child can use play to symbolically and metaphorically depict her own injury. I might approach this by asking, "So I have a high fever [and then in a whispered voice, as an aside], what do I feel like inside when I am this sick?"

F: You are going to sleep.
T: Okay, would that make me feel better?
F: Yes! Okay. I am going to get some food (*she pretends to leave the house*).
T: Okay. Please do! I am hungry. And I am sick so I really need you to take care of me.

Another excellent first step by the therapist, who readily takes on the role of an ill child who needs help. I might have tried to see if F could tolerate a depiction of the separation fears she seems to present by her character leaving the house: "I am feeling hopeful that food will come soon, but being-left-alone feelings are very strong, too."

T: You locked it, he locked the house?
F: So that nobody gets in.
T: We really want to get that guy protected, hmm? Especially if he is sick.
F: That is a girl!
T: Oh, that is a girl. We want to get her protected.
F: Shhhh. He took all the money, and now he is going to another house.

F's play shifts to the addition of an aggressor who, instead of getting food, steals money and leaves.

T: Oh, he is going to leave her there?

To try to make sense of this shift is most difficult, but this might help: "One moment he's going to get food, and now he leaves her behind. I wonder what feelings are going on in his mind?"

T: So where is the new house?
F: Nowhere?
T: Nowhere? (*F seems paralyzed.*)
F: Guess what?
T: Yeah, tell me?
F: Nothing!

T: Nothing. Oh my goodness, so many things that I have to guess today.

F: You always use this (*referring to my bag*)?

F is clearly brought to a halt in the play by the intrusion of her aggressive, stealing fantasies, as evidenced by her attempts to focus concretely on her therapist's bag to gain some distance from her experience.

T: Mm-hmm.

F: (*She sort of gets paralyzed looking at house.*)

T: Okay. Hello, hello, is someone there? I think someone. Is someone there? Someone locked the house, and I am still here.

The therapist adroitly attempts to help F resume the play by taking on the character of the abandoned child.

F: (*Inaudible.*)

T: Okay. I was feeling sick, but I am feeling much better now, and then I found the house closed. I was really worried that you would not come back for me.

This may be a premature attempt to ease F's anxiety by having the aggressor end his abandonment and return. It seems important to give the child the space to extend her fantasies about whether she can truly count on others for nurturance or whether betrayal will be the dominant theme.

F: Sssshhhh.

T: Ahhhh. Where I am going? (*F takes figure as if flying.*)

F: You are going to live in a new house.

F cannot tolerate her therapist's attempt to reverse her aggression but instead creates her own Pollyanna-ish solution, magically allowing the sick character to fly away to a new house.

T: Oh, wow. A new house!

F: I bought a new house (*she moves the house*). This is our new house.

T: Oh we have a new house. Uff. That makes me feel much better.

F: No it doesn't! You spent our money!

But F cannot let go of the aggression so easily. She instead "blames the victim," holding the sick child accountable for using up all the supplies and causing the deprivation.

T: I did? No.

F: Him!

Now F must undo her placement of the blame on the child and goes back to blaming the adult character. I might comment on this shift as follows: "It's so hard to know who should have the spending-all-the-money feelings and who should be the one to blame." This puts the focus on the defensive shifting and allows the balance between affect and defense to be a central feature of the play.

T: What did he do?

F: He spent the money. ...

T: How?

F: To buy a house.

T: Oh, to buy a new house. I am sure that this girl, she feels pretty safe knowing that she has another house. And. ... Oh.

F: (*She grabs a wooden stick and starts pushing it through the windows, while the figures are inside. I am not sure what is going on.*)

T: Hmm, I wonder what that is? Is that ...

F: Shooo, you *shrinked*.

T: Ah, what happened just now?

F: You *shrinked*.

T: Oh my goodness, I am smaller? What happened? I don't understand. First we didn't have money for a new house, now we have a new house, and now I am smaller. It's so confusing, what is happening? He feels really very confused. ... Oh, now he is getting a beat in the head. Where did that come from?

F: (*After beating the hell out of the figure, she places the figure in the bed.*)

Here is a beautiful enactment of the power of play to allow a "thing" and its opposite to coexist, much like in the dream of an adult. F's figure flits from being the provider of a new house to the violent aggressor who makes people shrink and then attacks them. I appreciate the therapist's use of the word *confusing* to describe the process.

T: I have to rest.

F: You are locked.

T: I am locked forever? How come? I am pretty confused then, oh. And now there is something coming in from the window? Oh my!

F: Shooooo, shoooo.

T: There is something coming out from the roof, from the window.

F: I'm trying to make you fall (*she starts shaking the house*).

T: You are trying to make me fall from the bed?

F: Don't look (*she shakes the house*).

T: Ahhhh, what is going on, what is going on? I don't understand.

F: You think he fell down?

T: Oh my goodness, let's see? Do I think that he fell down? (She asks me to guess if the figure will still be in his bed or if he fell down after she shook the house.)

The child is presenting two sets of confusions, one metaphorically and one literally. In the play, she metaphorically presents the fear and bewilderment of the locked-up child. When she begins shaking the house, however, it becomes too intense for her to express and maintain this extreme violence within the flow of the play. In an attempt to reduce the affective charge of such "violence," she turns to creating a form of guessing game with the therapist. Thus, in her interaction with her therapist, she presents a more literal set of confusions by asking the therapist to guess what happened to the character in the play. I might try to speak to this duality by noting: "My figure is so scared and confused by this scary shaking house, and now I'm confused about what will happen to her."

T: Tough call. He is going to be … still in his bed. Did he fall down? Oh, he did? Oh.
F: Massage (*she starts beating up the figure*).
T: Massage? No, that massage looks pretty harsh.
F: It feels good!
T: It feels good? That beating up feels good?
F: It's not beating up. …
T: I understand. Well, you know, I am confused because. … Ohhh, I see. Oh, that is nice; I am more relaxed now. Now I can be calmer. So many things going on today. (*She pretends to give the figure a massage.*)

It would be useful to articulate the ambivalence and unpredictability that F is expressing through her play: "That man has two kinds of feelings toward the girl, hurting feelings and massaging feelings, and the girl is not sure which feeling is going to win out."

F: Now you are living here.
T: Now I am living there? (*F puts the figure inside a puppet.*) Oh my goodness. I am living inside. Oh no. Then I was in a house, then I went to another house, and then I got beat up and then I got a massage and now I am living inside. …
F: (*Inaudible.*)
T: That is pretty confusing.

While "confusing" is an accurate description, I would try to be less vague: "So many opposite things happen to her, it must be so hard to know whether to feel safe inside or whether to feel afraid."

F: Don't move.
T: Okay.
F: Whoever moves loses. Ready, set, go!
T: Okay. (*We stay in our chairs motionless. She tries to make me laugh by making faces.*)

F loses her capacity to play symbolically for the moment as she is thrown by the rapid shifts in her characters, which express the unintegrated aspects of her own aggression. It may well be that the play tapped her feelings of abandonment and terror while in the hospital with her own injury; these feelings were at a level that she could no longer tolerate. She then breaks the plane of the symbolic play and shifts toward having them play with their bodies instead. Fascinatingly, she introduces a game in which being the most willfully paralyzed wins, turning her moments of becoming "paralyzed" (according to the therapist's description) in the play from a vulnerability into a strength.

T: Can I speak?

F: No.

T: Okay. I feel that you are trying to make me laugh so I can lose, hmm?

F: Mm-hmm. Hmm, I got bored.

Boredom is the state most opposite to the capacity to play. It implies that the child cannot conjure up a space of inner vitality from which play can proceed, and she cannot use her defenses well enough to let herself become immersed in a toy or object or person outside herself. She is emotionally in a nowhere land that causes a restless agitation that must be soothed. F tried to gain respite from her affectively charged play by her "paralysis" game, but even that could not provide the sanctuary she needed, with boredom the temporary result.

T: I know that was long.

This is an excellent affirmation by the therapist that F's symbolic play was long and taxing. I might have been a bit more specific: "All that play was so long, with so many jumbled-together feelings that you became tired of it all and bored instead."

F: (*Knocks on door.*) I have a TV that says that (*referring to the Sony brand on the tape recorder*).

T: Oh, Sony. Who's there? What is that? There is something coming in from the window.

F: Okay (*shakes house*).

T: Oops, it came out. Oh, ahhhh, where did he go?

F: It's a she.

T: Oh she is a she. I keep forgetting. ...

F: I am trying to balance (*she places figure on a stick and tries a balancing act ...*).

T: Will he fall? Oh, wow.

For a brief moment, F tries to regain her ability to play symbolically, but she gives this up quickly and returns instead to an active, interactive game. While this is a notable resiliency and a significant recovery from her boredom, it is also a definite sign that she got too far ahead of herself in creating a highly charged symbolic play space.

F: Let's play the throwing game.

T: The throwing game. Which one?

F: The one that you throw like that. …

T: Ohhh, I remember. (*This game entails my throwing the Connect Four tokens from one side of the room and her catching them on the other side.*)

F: (*Inaudible.*)

T: Okay.

F: (*She puts token on the table.*) Okay, ready, go! Okay, oh, oh. Oh, okay, true!

T: Are you ready!?

F: Mm-hmm.

T: Ready, set, go!

F: Ready, set, go!

T: Ready, set, go. Almost! Ready, set, go! Again? Ready, set, go. Ready, seeet, go. Oops. That slipped out from your hands, how is that possible? Ready, set, go!

F: Just pick it up. Just pick them up and do it again (*referring to the pieces she cannot catch that are on the floor*).

T: Okay. Go! Ready, go, oh wow. Let me get that. Ready, go!

F: How is that possible? I had it. Oh, here it is.

T: Did that fall down?

F: Yeah. There was a black one in the floor. I'll get it.

T: Wow. (*We continue with throwing game.*)

F: Catch!

T: You want to throw it back to me?

F: Frisbee.

T: Like a Frisbee. Should I try that? If you throw it like that it is going to go faster, right?

F: (*Inaudible.*)

T: Yeah, okay. How is your foot healing?

A long period of interactive play is ended when the therapist asks a direct question about F's injury. Ideally, I would have let the play proceed, as this question could be too easily answered with a black or white, one-word answer. Such an exchange could set up the potential quagmire by which the therapist keeps asking questions and the child keeps giving one-word answers, so that words become burdens instead of catalysts.

F: Good.

T: I see that you are starting to walk again, hmm? That is pretty exciting!

While this is a perfectly benign conversational tone, it is still a tricky tactic by the therapist because although F's improvement may seem notable to the therapist, it may be a different experience for F. "I wonder what it feels like inside for you as you start to walk again?" might be a more adaptive, open-ended approach, giving F the emotional room to complain about her recovery if she needs to do so.

T: One, two, go! That is hard. Without looking is hard.

F: Okay. Ready, set, go.

T: That is going to be impossible (*I refer to catching the tokens without looking*).

F: You did it.

T: Without looking? Almost! Oh yeah, that could count.

F: One, two, three … twenty.

T: Twenty, wow.

F: How is that possible for us to throw that many?!

T: I guess it requires, not only requires me throwing it to the right place, but you also need to catch it, so it's a two-people thing, oh!

F: Oh nice.

T: Ready? That's harder?

F: Keep throwing!

T: Okay. You are about to catch them all. Both. (*I continue throwing the pieces to her.*) Should I come to you? Oh, no!

F: Okay, go!

T: Wow. We are almost done with every single one, wow. Oh wow. Oops they are … now there is a. … They are falling off my hands. … One, two. …

F: I am falling. …

T: Good catch. Wow.

F: Oh, shoot (*she misses*). That is it?

T: That is it! You caught them all! Do we have more? We have 50 more tokens in here. I had forgotten about that. Oh, wow. (*We start using more pieces, while we throw them at each other faster.*)

The play between them is smooth, full of mutuality and appreciation and, notably, of many supplies that do not run out. The game is satisfying on many levels: (a) It avoids and gives F a distance from her scary fantasies of violence and abandonment when vulnerable; (b) it is inherently interactive, a "two-people thing" to use the therapist's expression, and thus soothes F's feelings of abandonment; and (c) it allows both to feel athletic and competent, an especially vital feeling given F's recovery from her leg injury. This last point might have been worth articulating, "I wonder how all these good-catching feelings make you feel about your foot?"

F: That is too low.

T: It's too low. You know what, I see that our time is over, and we will have to stop. You caught all those tokens.

F: Let's put them back.

T: Let's put them back?

F: One, two, three, … thirty-one.

T: Oh, wow.

F: Thirty-two … fifty-nine.

Counting all their "supplies" is a most useful way for F to feel sated and hence is quite an antidote to the losing feelings of having to say good-bye at the end of the session.

F: (*As soon as she put everything back in the box, she wanted to turn the tape recorder off.*) I want to press it.
T: You want to press it?
F: Which one? (*Wants to know which button to press.*)
T: Meaning that we have to go, so you should press this one.

The therapist gives F a final experience of control and autonomy vis-à-vis the end of the session by letting her shut off the tape recorder.

This session illustrates the difficulties inherent in how to help a child connect with overwhelming feelings about a traumatic event when these feelings are so strongly avoided through the child's self-imposed breaks in the play. It also brings into focus both the necessity of attunement on the therapist's part and the moments in which attunement alone may not be enough to foster a reflective stance. This therapist is deeply empathic and attuned to her patient's feeling states, and this repeatedly allows the child to feel understood, no small achievement indeed. However, the next phase of the treatment will need to involve helping the child to internalize this attunement and to carry it with her when she leaves the room. Sometimes, it can take months and years of work before a child trusts your empathy enough to truly internalize it and practice it outside sessions. Yet, it will be your precise use of language, and your persistence in building a frame for self-reflection, that will, over time, allow your patients to develop this capacity for themselves.

8 A 5-Year-Old Girl

G presented with an ongoing history, diagnosed first at age 2.5, of expressive language delays, social-emotional difficulties (low self-esteem, frequent crying spells, highly avoidant/withdrawn behavior in group situations, difficulty expressing her emotions and needs to parents or teachers), and odd behavior (clenched teeth and fists, walking sideways, frequent refusal to eat, falling to the ground when upset, and daytime enuresis).

T: G has brought a lunch box, telling *T* there is a secret inside. The therapist puts G's snack down on the table. She sits down to eat her snack at the table.

The session starts magically, as the patient lets the therapist know there are secrets to be found. The child thus begins with a hide-and-seek game, in which she holds all the cards.

G: I'll tell you after we play.
T: Only after we play you'll tell me.

Unlike the therapists in previous chapters, this therapist's style is to begin by mirroring the child's words, without in any way challenging or questioning the child's stance. I might add, "I wonder what it's going to feel like to wait," as a means of noting not only that I am willing to wait but also that my waiting has an emotional impact on my mind.

G: Yes.
T: Okay.
G: But no conversation.
T: No conversation.
G: I'm not opening this.
T: No conversation and you're not opening it. Huh. Well, what does that leave for us to do? What do you think?

The therapist is exceptionally patient and mutual ("what does that leave for us?"), but I would focus on the impact on their states of mind and not on their actions: "Well, what does that leave for us to *feel* while we wait?"

G: Not yet ... (*inaudible*).
T: I have to be very patient and wait.
G: (*Inaudible.*)

T: What do you think we should do? That's a hard one, let me open it (*juice can*).
G: No conversation.
T: I'm sorry, can I talk with my hands?
G: No conversation, even with the hands, even with our heads, even with our
    mouths, even with our eyes, even with our whole bodies.

Here, there is a clear and ego-syntonic prohibition against conversation, a challenge to the development of a frame for self-reflectiveness. The task becomes one of providing a means by which the child's mind may become accessible. One way to do this would be to comment on the fact that even when the two of them are not moving or speaking, they still have feelings inside: "While our whole bodies stay silent, our feelings are still moving in our minds. There are still so many things to feel."

T: What do we do then?
G: Wait until I finish eating.
T: Be a statue?
G: Or just go to sleep.
T: Go to sleep.
G: Or just ... go to sleep.
T: Wait quietly and go to sleep?

Here, I might try to stretch the boundaries of a reflective stance to include sleep as well: "I wonder if we still have feelings when we sleep? Oh yeah, we have dreams that have all kinds of feelings."

G: Or go to sleep.
T: Or go to sleep. What do you think I should do?
G: You.
T: I can't help it; I want to keep my eyes open. So why shouldn't we have any
    conversation?

The beginning therapist has to be careful about her own impatience. The child has come in with a secret after all, and the waiting for the secret to unfold seems to be a more useful way to stay with the child's experience.

G: 'Cause I don't like to.
T: You don't want to?
G: I want ... (*inaudible*). ... So no conversation, I said.
T: Are we gonna play later?
G: (*She nods her head.*)
T: Yeah. You like to play, but you don't want to talk.
G: Not yet.
T: Oh, okay. (*She chews dramatically.*) Very quiet. When you chew it sounds like
    a little conversation. (*I make chewing sounds. She has her feet on the
    table.*) Do you talk with your feet? (*We laugh.*) Hmm, no?

The therapist is most attuned to the child; her sounds and her posture all are in play, and the child seems to appreciate the attunement. This bodes well for the ability of the therapist to help the child become attuned over time to her own affective life.

G: Not with nothing.
T: Not with nothing.
G: Even your eyebrows.
T: Even my eyebrows? It's hard to be so still.

The child is equally attuned to bodily experience as it is most unusual to focus on eyebrows. The therapist usefully speaks to how difficult it is to keep her body still. As an attempt to establish an awareness of the connection between body and mind, the therapist might add, "And keeping my feelings quiet enough so that they don't make my body move is really hard."

G: But, you're sleeping.
T: Oh okay. Should I sleep with my eyes open?
G: I have a dream I think about, and that all ... you.
T: A dream you think about? Okay, you tell me what the dream is.
G: I'm thinking of it.
T: You're thinking about it.
G: It's just an imaginations.
T: Uh-huh. You don't want to tell me what it is?

The therapist backs herself into a bit of a corner as she has perhaps allowed a potentially rich discussion of the child's dreams to be subsumed under the "secret" (withholding) umbrella. I might have gone with the following: "I wonder where imaginations come from and what they feel like inside?"

G: No, you have to guess yourself.
T: I have to guess? That sounds hard. Hmmm.
G: Like a guessing game.
T: A guessing game?
G: *Like* a guessing game. Like!
T: Okay. A dream about ... the rain?
G: Nooo.
T: Nooo. Ummm.
G: Make your own dream.

This child is strikingly able to switch gears from an initial wish for the thera-pist to "find" her dreams to wanting to keep herself private and have the therapist stick with her own dreams. I am struck here by the way in which this patient speaks to a valuable quotation by Winnicott (1963/1965) from his article on com-municating and not communicating: "The patient's most important experience in relation to the good or potentially satisfying object is the refusal of it. The refusal of it is part of the process of creating it" (p. 182).

T: Make my own? I thought I was guessing yours. Make my own up?
G: Mm-hmmm.
T: It's hard to make up a dream.
G: I dream of ... the sky.
T: What kind of sky?

The therapist is now fully submerged in a guessing game. If Winnicott (1963/1965) is correct that "it is joy to be hidden but disaster not to be found" (p. 184), then she and her patient are on fragile ground here. I might be inclined to sit and wait patiently and let the patient "hide," or say something like, "I wonder what a dream about a sky feels like?"

G: The sky ... (*inaudible*). Just a sky!
T: Just a sky. A sunny sky or a cloudy sky, or a rainy sky, a dark sky?
G: What is a weenie?
T: What is a what?
G: What is a weenie?
T: A weenie?
G: A weenie sky.

The child's nonsequitor response is reminiscent of the way a youngster of her age might respond to inquiry on the Rorschach. Five-year-olds can be so egocentric in their thinking that the notion of justifying their perceptions can seem absurd, so they often answer with an irrelevant response just because they know that *some* response is called for to remain connected with the adult.

T: I don't know. Rainy, rainy. With rain in it. A sky like tonight?
G: Nooo.
T: Nooo. What kind?
G: (*Inaudible. Laughs.*) Make your own dream.
T: Make my own. Hmm. It's hard to make up a dream. It takes a lot of imagination to make one up.
G: No, it doesn't.
T: For me it does.
G: Yes, but put on your thinking cap, and that's all.
T: Put on my thinking cap. Do you remember your dreams when you have them at night?
G: Yes, I do.
T: Haa. ...
G: I'm ... you're talking. Remember no conversation.

The patient catches herself just in time. Just before she is about to reveal the "location" of her dream, she reminds the therapist that silence is golden.

T: I broke the rule. Do I have to wait until the whole cookie … ? Huhhh. I feel like I want to talk to you, but I just have to sit here quietly?

A useful step toward framing her affective experience, but it stops at her behavior, which might set her up for a battle of wills with the patient that she is bound to "lose." Instead, I would try the following: "I feel like I want to talk to you, but these no-conversation feelings are very strong in my mind and are fighting my talking feelings." This frames her mind as engaged in a push-pull battle and places the parallel battle going on between patient and therapist in a secondary role.

G: I'm barefooted.

The child interestingly shifts the discussion away from the therapist's laments.

T: You're barefooted. Huh, look at that.
G: Now … (*laughs*).
T: Where did your boots go? … Those boots look like imagination boots.
G: No they aren't.
T: To me, they look like something from a story. (*The boots are made to look like purple ladybugs.*)
G: They're raining.
T: They're raining.
G: They're galoshes.
T: They're good luck?
G: Those are galoshes. That's boots.
T: Boots.
G: That's how they say it, and that's another way to say it.
T: Galoshes.
G: Yes. My rain boots.
T: Your rain boots. You have a Band-Aid on, too. That looks like. … What's on there? Another purple …
G: I don't know my father got it.
T: Did you hurt your finger?
G: Yes.
T: What happened?
G: It got stuck in that … it got in that escalator.
T: An escalator.
G: The handle you know.
T: Oh.
G: The moving one. It was old 'cause … it was old 'cause it was made a long time ago.

T: Oh, and it hurt your finger?
G: Mm-hmm.
T: Were you scared when that happened?

This is a most opportune moment to present a question about the child's mind-body connection: "I wonder what it felt like in your mind when you felt the pain in your finger?"

G: Nope. My mom ... heard me say, "Oww, oww."
T: She heard you, and she came to help you?
G: No. She pulled it out! Do you think that would hurt?
T: Yeah, I think that would hurt.
G: No conversation!

This child has many tricks up her sleeve when it comes to protecting her inner experience. She finds herself wanting the therapist to acknowledge the hurt she felt, so she asks her a question, but as soon as the therapist acknowledges the hurt, then the patient reminds her that silence is the law here.

T: Oh. ... How do I keep breaking those rules?
G: (*She laughs.*)
T: I'm gonna button it up (*I gesture*).

The therapist beautifully responds to the challenge by using humor and her own body to affirm the child's need for space and silence.

G: I'm zipping mines up.

The child tells us that this was a most useful intervention by mirroring the therapist.

T: Okay. I'm gonna put a padlock on mine. Mmmm, mmmm.
G: No conversation!
T: (*My hand is covering my mouth.*) Are you almost done with your cookie?
G: No conversations! (*Her feet are on the table. I pretend to be putting mine on the table, too.*) And no putting your feet up.

The child lets the therapist know here that she does not want to be mirrored. It feels too exploitative of her sense of autonomy.

T: What about your feet.
G: Or my feet.
T: (*Inaudible.*)
G: No. 'Cause yours are too big, and they might kick me in my face.
T: I might kick you?

G: In my face. 'Cause this is a little table.
T: So I can't talk or put my feet up.
G: It's a little table and …
T: Can you eat with your feet?
G: Rabbo … rabbo. …
T: Is that a song?
G: No questions … (*we laugh*). You forgot.
T: I can't help it. I want to talk to you.
G: Okay.
T: Okay … what are we gonna. … Do we get to have conversation?
G: Nooo.
T: Nooo. No conversation! Do we get to play?
G: Yes!

Now that the child seems willing to play, it would be most useful if the therapist simply used silence to allow the child to set the scene for their play.

T: Yes! What are we gonna play?

A little too much impatience by the therapist here.

G: (*She grabs the lunch box from the table and hides it behind her back.*) Hmmm.
T: Uh, oh. What do you have there?
G: Nothing.
T: Nothing?
G: And I'm not opening it yet!
T: Okay.
G: Only when I get you.
T: It's hard to wait. I'm so curious.

The therapist does make a link between waiting (an action) and curiosity (her mind). I would try to make this link more explicit, framing it again as a push-pull: "My waiting feelings are not as strong as my curious feelings, so it's so hard to wait."

G: I know you are.
T: You want to make me wait.

The therapist is able to articulate the patient's desire to make her wait, and this allows the patient to become free to reveal her "secret."

G: So let me get my package. Yeah! (*She opens the lunch box to reveal some very hot Barbie attire.*)
T: Oh, wow. Look at that. Wow, you brought all that.
G: Mine is this one.

T: Wow, look at all that.

I would want to accentuate the specialness of her secret and hence its need to be hidden: "No wonder you wanted to keep it secret!"

G: And look what I get to eat (*taunting*).

The taunting tells us that this act of keeping things secret has a powerful aggressive component. Would the child be able to acknowledge this aggression, and would that lead, much further down the road, to an ability to speak to the vulnerable feelings that may lie underneath this bravado? I might want to toss out a comment about this state of mind to assess her ability to recognize it. If she does acknowledge it, a new direction opens for affective exploration. If it does not, it might still be referred to in future sessions as part of a creation of a scaffold to help prop up her tentative abilities to acknowledge her aggression. Thus, I might say, "I wonder if having something special to eat when I don't creates some strong and powerful feelings inside you."

T: What do you get?
G: A cupcake.
T: You get a cupcake.
G: A little one.
T: A little baby cupcake.
G: It's not a baby cupcake.
T: Just a little cupcake.
G: It's a cupcake for Barbies.
T: Just a little …
G: For Barbies! And a pie for Barbies.
T: And a pie?
G: For Barbies.
T: Look at those pants.

While there is certainly nothing wrong with engaging the child in the clothes she brought, I might have waited to see where the child would go next. I say this because the evocation of oral supplies in a taunting manner is a powerful dynamic, and I would like to see if she could sit with this power or, if she changed direction, what themes she would evoke in her play.

G: And I'm not sharing with you!
T: You're not sharing with me. Okay. Can I have this old dress?

The patient declares her space aggressively, and the therapist initially complies but then asks to play.

G: You have that dress and this dress that has a little dark spot.

The child easily takes this invitation and gives her the far lesser dress, in "Cinderella"-like fashion.

T: How come I don't get a pretty dress?
G: You can't. They're in the store now. ... The store is closed.
T: Oh. All I have is this old, ugly dress to wear.
G: That's not even a dress! It's not!
T: This old ugly skirt.
G: And?
T: And a shirt. They're both ugly. I want new clothes.
G: You can't get new clothes yet. You didn't even go shopping. We're going shopping together. You didn't even go shopping. Already.
T: We get to go shopping.
G: When we go shopping you use this (*hands me the lunch box then takes it back*). Now we're gonna. ... You can use this one.
T: 'Cause it's broken. I get a broken shopping bag.

A fascinating stretch of true play. The child easily engages the therapist in a play scenario in which she gets all the special things, and the therapist is left to lament her secondary status.

G: You could fix it. Look.

This is a subtle shift as the patient's character shows a trace of concern and is no longer the controlling, depriving protagonist.

T: Okay.
G: It's easy. You get the big food, and I get the little food (*taunting*). Okay? You could get those, I just want the cake (*clearly the most enticing piece of play food of the bunch*).
T: I want the cake. I don't get the cake either? I get nothing!

Quickly the play shifts back to taunting and diminishing the therapist's character.

G: That's chocolate ice cream. (*Hands me a chocolate milk.*)

Again, a trace of guilt and some reparation by the child.

T: I don't want it.

The therapist pushes the play in a new direction by having her character not be satisfied by the "leftovers." This is a most interesting moment. The therapist has created a new pathway in the play, one in which the patient, if she stays in character, must either acquiesce and give the therapist more or become more dramatic in her sadistic withholding. I might have stayed where the child was and asked, in a whispered voice, "Should I like this ice cream or not?" This gives the child far greater autonomy in deciding where the play will go.

G: That's chocolate ice cream!
T: I want the cake.
G: I'm not letting you have the cake; you have the chocolate ice cream.
T: It's not ice cream; it's milk.
G: Chocolate milk. I get a big cake.

The child initially tries to placate the "demanding" therapist by claiming it is ice cream, but then quickly returns to her aggressive stance in which she does indeed enjoy the spoils of war. I would want to comment on this indecision as follows: "A part of you first seemed to want to make me feel better by telling me it's ice cream, but now another feeling part of you wants to make sure I know I got the milk and you got the big cake."

T: I never get anything I want. Look at her, she has a big cake, and I only have a
        stupid ice cream and an ugly dress.
G: Stupid is a bad word.

The therapist's playing out the role of the aggrieved goes too far for the patient in her use of the word *stupid*.

T: A bad word?
G: A mean word.
T: A mean word?
G: 'Cause would you like people to call you that?
T: I called the ice cream stupid.
G: Would you like people to call you.
T: No, I don't think I would like people to call me that.
G: It's a mean word, so you never could say it. Even grown-ups can't.
T: I didn't think the ice cream had feelings, that's why I said that. That might hurt
        someone's feelings?
G: Yes. That's mean.
T: That's mean.
G: That's a mean word to say, don't say that.
T: Did you ever say that?
G: Okay. (*Gives me the cake.*)

A fascinating glimpse into the mind of this child and perhaps a window into superego formation at this age. The child goes to great lengths to proclaim the immorality of the mean word *stupid* while oblivious to how mean she was acting in her doling out of her supplies. This depicts how in play a child has far greater access to a wide range of behaviors and feelings that would simply be unacceptable in the "real" world. When the therapist uses the word *stupid*, it has such an overlearned cache of "badness" that it disrupts the frame of the play. Once the child is out of the play, she is far more vulnerable to superego pressures, and she places all "meanness" onto the therapist. When the therapist then asks if the patient ever used the word, the brittleness of her projections collapses; she becomes guilt ridden and immediately offers the therapist the cake as reparation.

T: Oh, she gave me the cake. Thank you for giving me the cake. What's that little
    piece over there? Is that a corn?

If the preceding line of inference has some validity, it would now make sense to comment on this shift in the child's behavior on an affective level: "So one minute I was having mean, angry feelings about not getting the big cake, but then you gave it to me. I wonder where those cake-giving feelings from your person came from?"

G: A corn for a Barbie.
T: A corn for a Barbie. Where are you going?
G: To my house.
T: Your house is awfully far away today.
G: That's where it goes.
T: Oh.
G: Let's see what you're going to put in your home.
T: A whole piece of cake.
G: And aren't you going to have toast or something?
T: I think I have enough.
G: All you've got is a cake
T: Well, that's all I wanted.
G: You can't have just that to eat 'cause you'll never ever grow.

The child seems to still feel guilty and therefore wants the therapist's figure to have more to eat. I might add, "Sounds like your guy is having worrying feelings about whether my guy will get enough to eat."

T: I won't grow if I just eat cake?
G: No.
T: You have a cake, too.
G: Yes, but I have more than one cake.
T: But you have a cupcake and a pie. That's not very healthy, is it?
G: Yes … but, it's healthy because I have a pie because it's a pumpkin pie, not a
    chocolate pie, and I have a corn.
T: And a corn.
G: So my … treat.
T: Okay, I'm going to take this one.

G: If you want, you can have a ...
T: A banana.
G: Now that's enough. Now we shop for our clothes.

The child feels that she can go on to shopping because enough reparation has been made.

T: Ooooh.
G: I take this, and this. There's more clothes here. You can have this.
T: Okay. (She takes all the dresses and gives me a skirt and two shirts, the least stylish I might add.) Look at all those clothes. I only have two, three clothes.
G: No you don't.
T: Three clothes. These are my old yucky clothes.
G: You can have these of mine. (*Takes clothes off the doll in the playroom.*)
T: Those are old.
G: These are not old; these are brand new.
T: Brand new?
G: They're brand new. ... Put it on.

Again, the therapist takes on the role of the deprived one, and again the child tries to convince her that she is not being deprived. Significantly, the child does not give up the "good" clothes. There is no altruistic surrender in the face of the therapist's protests, only a desire to placate the therapist.

T: Okay, okay. (*I start to change my doll.*)
G: You could still wear them. But you're not even home yet so people are gonna see you.
T: I'm in the dressing room.
G: There's no dressing room here.
T: Ahhh. There's not. I thought there was. Well, you're changing, aren't you?
G: No, I'm not changing ... my clothes. Are you having my clothes or not?
T: Thank you.
G: Bye, bye. You're not even home yet. There's no dressing room.

A humorous lapse into prudishness by the patient as again her capacity to let her imaginative play flow freely is curtailed. Is it the guilt that limits her? I might have gone along with this inhibition just to see if the child would expand on it: "Oh my, I can't let people see me with no clothes on. What would they feel, what would I feel?"

T: Okay.
G: And I got a big ...
T: What's that?
G: A big thing. Is this. A nice dress. ... And then we put the stuff up.

T: What kind of stuff?

G: I don't know.

T: What is that? Is that …

G: No. Just an ugly blanket.

T: A blanket.

G: It's ugly and has stains.

T: Oh. It has stains.

G: You don't want one that has stains, do you?

T: No. I want a nice one.

G: I don't have any more nice ones. I can't get my pants on. That's for Christmas. (*She takes my clothes away from me.*)

T: What are you doing?

G: You got your own Christmas clothes. (*She has decided that we are shopping for each other, and I'm doing everything wrong, wearing the pants I'm supposed to give her for a gift, etc.*)

T: I got my own clothes, and I can't wear them.

This would be a useful moment for the therapist to expand on her affective experience: "It's so hard to know what to feel when I'm not sure what clothes are safe to wear and what clothes don't belong to me, especially when I so want to have so many clothes right now."

G: This is Christmas clothes.

T: Do I have to wait?

G: It's not old. It's new.

T: Are you buying your own Christmas clothes?

G: This one's for a teenager. I keep mine.

T: What's the name of the teenager?

G: Like 15, like something teen. That's my house! I got a minibroom to sweep. Get your own.

T: Why do you have a mini …

G: I love that pink.

T: You love pink.

G: It's my favorite color. That's my teenager. Not yours.

T: Mine, mine, mine.

The therapist expresses, in the most basic language possible, the core feeling of the session: the child's wish to possess fully and completely.

G: Ahhh. I won't share my clothes with you anymore. You won't have anymore clothes. You won't have this clothes and …

T: You'll take all my clothes away from me?

G: Yes and …

T: You'll punish me for that.

On some basic level, the child hears the therapist's core comment and has to psychologically run from her own acquisitiveness by becoming the depriving, withholding punisher.

G: (*Inaudible.*)
T: I want my clothes.
G: (*Inaudible.*)
T: It's too hard to wait.
G: (*Inaudible.*)

Much as in Chapter 7, the child's words do not adequately serve her in the face of this affectively charged, hungry-withholding dynamic. The boundaries in the play between self and other have become too blurred: Who is the punisher, and who is the needy person? In the face of this conflict, she is left to mumble until she can recover.

T: How can I wait?
G: You have to wait now. ... I won't punish you from now on.

She begins to recover by making her character less punitive.

T: Okay ... you won't punish me?
G: No. I'll punish you if you don't wear those clothes.
T: Okay.
G: See. She's not wearing your clothes.

The child is trying to justify to the therapist why her character should not be outraged, telling her that her play figure is not taking clothes from the therapist's figure.

T: She'll be mad that I took her clothes.
G: (Inaudible.)

Again, when the therapist voices her character's anger, the patient cannot respond audibly. I might add, "My guy's angry feelings seem to make your guy feel so many things that I can't hear what she said. I wonder how she is feeling?"

G: A towel and a ...
T: A what?
G: A thing to sleep.
T: A thing to sleep?
G: A blanket.
T: A blanket.
G: Or do you want a daughter?
T: A blanket or a daughter? That's a hard choice.
G: Pick one.

T: Pick one? I'll take a daughter.

G: Then you won't have no blanket.

T: I'm being punished for having a daughter.

The therapist again brings the punishing-deprived dynamic to the fore.

G: You're not punished. You don't have a blanket.

T: I don't have that one.

G: Not this one. This one is not the right color for you. This one is mine 'cause I
   don't have a bigger head.

T: That one's yours.

G: I don't have a big head.

The child is able to respond to the therapist's dynamic by rationalizing why her figure gets to have something the therapist's figure cannot, and the therapist wisely does not challenge this rationalization. It seems far too early in the treatment to challenge this patient's obvious vulnerability around such a conflictual arena.

G: So my daughter can learn. ... I have a computer. A laptop computer and a book.

T: You have a book and a laptop computer.

G: So she can learn.

T: Does she like to learn?

G: Yes. She does.

T: How is my daughter gonna learn?

G: From school. Do you think it wouldn't be fair for your daughter?

T: It wouldn't be fair.

G: Do you think?

T: If she didn't have a book or a laptop?

G: If she did not go to school?

T: I don't know.

Now, the question of fairness is made explicit by the patient. I would now try to shift the plane of reflection from what appears to be a blatantly superego-oriented domain into the arena of affect and defenses, that is, an ego-oriented approach: "I'm not sure what's fair, but I do wonder what my child would feel like going to school when she didn't have those special things and other kids did."

G: This is mine.

T: This is a new voice for you. Who's voice is that? When you're talking. That's a
   new play voice.

G: No (*laughs*).

T: Yeah. It sounds different from one of the other voices. Doesn't it?

G: (*She laughs.*)

T: That's a pretend voice, right?

G: Yeah (*laughs*). Okay. All right.

Here is a moment when the remarkably attuned qualities of this therapist to even subtle shifts in behavior, voice, or posture may have gotten in the way. If indeed this voice is so new, it might have been useful to let it develop and see what pathways such a voice could allow the child to explore. Instead, in compliance, the child gives up the voice and goes back to her play without it.

T: Is it Christmas yet?
G: No.
T: Ahhhh. I can't wait anymore.
G: Did you forget? It's Christmas already!
T: It's Christmas?
G: Yes.

On some level, the child so appreciates the therapist that she cannot bear to keep her in deprivation any longer and makes it Christmas right away.

T: Right now.
G: Yes. What did I got for Christmas. ... Because I still have to go to school. I don't need to go to school anymore!
T: She doesn't have to go to school anymore. She's got ...
G: A laptop.
T: She got a laptop.
G: And a book.
T: She doesn't have to go to school?
G: No 'cause I got a laptop and a book. Yeah, yeah, yeah. What does your daughter got for Christmas? And I got a room.
T: And you got a room, too? My daughter got a ...

Although its quite likely that the child could not be dissuaded from her focus on the relative bounties each child figure gets from her mother, I might have tried to see if she could expand on the internal experience of getting the presents: "I wonder what the daughter feels inside with getting a laptop, book, and her own room?"

G: Cake.
T: A cake.
G: What do you have?
T: And a new sweater. We have a little time left, okay. We have five more minutes.
G: Okay.
T: And your mom's gonna ...
G: Okay. This is my sweater. I think. ... What does my mom have for Christmas? What did you get for Christmas?
T: What did you get?

It is a useful approach by the therapist not to answer this question but to let the child provide the next shift in play. I might add, in a whispered aside, "What should she get?"

T: Look what I got for you.
G: Ohhh. It's lovely!
T: Do you like it?
G: Yes.
T: What did you get for me? I've been waiting forever. Oh, wow. Look at those. Oh my goodness. I've always wanted this pair of pants. Can I put them on?

Perhaps because the end of the session is voiced, the play becomes about mutual gratification and gratitude, an understandable way to give a positive closure to the hour.

G: Yes, but you have to wear this ... put it on her.
T: Did you get what you wanted for Christmas?
G: It is so lovely! I didn't even know what I wanted for Christmas.

It is unclear whether the child is answering the question "in character" or has lost the plane of the play and speaks about herself.

T: You didn't even know what you wanted. I wonder what would have happened if she didn't get anything for Christmas? I would have been really mad.

The therapist creates a new path late in the session that deals with direct expression of anger at a deprivation. I am not sure if I would have gone in that blatant a direction. I also think it might have been more useful, if she wanted to generate this theme, to keep the feelings more open-ended as the child may have felt more sadness or hurt than anger. For example, "I wonder what different feelings might have come to her mind if she didn't get anything?"

G: What did you get for my daughter?
T: For your daughter, I got your daughter ...
G: No, not a sweater.
T: Where is your daughter?
G: She's ... taking a bath somewhere. Okay?

The child shifts back to the play as the direct expression of anger was too much to take on. This is a typical example of why beginning therapists usually need not fret if they "say the wrong thing" on occasion—the child will simply ignore it. If the therapist's comments disrupt and end an episode of play, that is an important sign that the comment was inadvisable. But, if the child ignores the comment and returns to the play, as in this example, there is little to worry about.

G: You, smell my feet.
T: She kicked me in the nose.
G: Now you smelled ... my feet.
T: I smelled your foot.

The child loses the play space again and resorts to a more anal, domineering, "smelly" stance. I would comment on the shift: "Oh, one moment we were wondering where your daughter is and the next minute I'm getting a lot of smelly foot feelings, I wonder what happened?"

T: What did you get your own daughter? Did you get her a present?
G: She doesn't need a present from me.
T: Why not?
G: 'Cause of Santa Claus.

The child is placed on the defensive by the therapist's comments, speaking to the guilt she has been wrestling with all session long regarding who should get and who should give.

T: I did it wrong. (*We're putting our new clothes on.*)
G: Yeah.
T: You did it right. Wow, look at that.
G: Don't even think about looking at me.

The child becomes strikingly hostile for the first time, as if comparisons between the two figures stir up such need and envy that she cannot even bear being looked at. I am quite doubtful regarding whether the child could hear any comments about this, but I might have tried: "Wow, even looking feelings can get dangerous sometimes."

T: Haaa. I'm not looking at you.

The therapist handles this hostility with humor and respect for the child's space, a most useful approach.

G: I'm not gonna wear it. I'm just gonna hang it up, 'cause this doesn't even fit me. It doesn't even fit my daughter.
T: It doesn't fit her either?
G: Hello. What did you get me?

Returning to the play, the child's character repudiates the "bad" supplies she has received and then demands to know what she has been given.

T: I got you this sweater.
G: Oh.

The child seems mollified by getting something from the therapist's character.

T: Is that your room?
G: Yep.
T: She got a room for Christmas? How did she do that?
G: No she didn't.
T: Oh, I thought you said that.

Now she denies having gotten a special present of her own room. It is confusing regarding why she rejects this present; is it because of guilt? I might have said, "It's so confusing to know what to feel when sometimes people get what they want and sometimes they don't."

G: ... My fairy god dress.
T: Wow, look at that.
G: ... and I bought it.
T: Wow, a beautiful dress. A fairy dress.
G: My fairy god dress.
T: Your fairy god dress.

The patient and therapist again "reconcile" by both admiring a gift the figure bought for herself: "Buying things for yourself is a very strong taking-care-of-yourself feeling that pushes away worries about not getting enough."

G: How long do we stay in here?
T: Hmm?
G: How long do we have in here?
T: How long do we have left?
G: How long do we work here?
T: Uh. ... How long have we been in here? Uh, 45 minutes.
G: 45 minutes?
T: We stay in here 50 minutes.
G: We always do?
T: Uh-huh.
G: But not today?

The child shifts out of the play one last time but carries the residue of her deprivation worries over to whether she is getting her full time from the therapist in the session.

T: Yes, today. I usually tell you about 5 minutes before we go. I always tell you.
G: (*Sings to self.*)

This singing appears to express her contentment in knowing she was given her full supply of time by the therapist.

T: I'm gonna change back to my old clothes 'cause we have to go.

G: (*Inaudible*) … that snack.

T: You like the snack?

G: Yes, I really like that snack. Nooo. Nooo.

T: I'll bring it every time.

G: What?

T: I'll bring you that snack every time.

G: Nooo. (*Pretends to cry.*)

What a remarkable ending: The child acknowledges loving the supplies the therapist brings but responds to the therapist's affirmation that she will always bring the supplies by mock crying. It is as though the dream-come-true quality of an always-bountiful, nondepriving relationship must get mocked as it stirs up too many wishes.

T: Every time.

Wonderfully, the therapist affirms her commitment to an oral supply she can produce, providing both a real and symbolically gratifying end to a most powerfully focused session.

This session is notable for several reasons: (a) It accentuates the vital importance of body language in young children and how extremely important it is for the therapist working with a preschool child to use his or her body to express emotion every bit as much as, if not more than, words. The child at this age processes what is most affectively vital through his or her body, and the greater the degree to which the therapist can be both attuned to the child's bodily states and rhythms and to their own use of their bodies to convey understanding, the more meaningful the treatment is to the child. (b) The case provided a terrific example of how one can use a whisper as an aside both to maintain the frame of the play and yet to step outside the play for a moment to ask the child to tell the therapist where the child would most like the play to go. This highlights the "transitional space" (Tuber, 2008; Winnicott, 1958/1965) nature of play in that play is simultaneously both real and imagined, and the child can therefore tolerate "asides" from the therapist as brief interludes of reality sitting next to the play space created by the child and the therapist. (c) Last, this session also highlights how easily young children can tolerate interpretative "mistakes" by the therapist as long as the basic atmosphere in the room stays benign. A young child will simply ignore your "interpretations" if they are wrong and go on playing. As long as you do not experience their dismissal of your comments as a personal affront (not always easy in one's first cases), the child will usually allow you back into his or her play quickly as the process of playing is far more important to the child than any specific moment of content.

9 A 9-Year-Old Girl

H's parents observed changes in her mood and behavior following their separation. She became uncharacteristically rebellious at home and at school as well as tearful, clingy, and needy in the months after her father's departure from the family home.

T: Again, twice already, you're really noticing things today! (*She remarked on my new haircut on the way to the room, as well as the appearance of a large piece of white drawing.*)

H: Do you have tape?

T: Do we have tape? Let's find out—let's look for some. Let's see. ... Do you remember that last time we didn't have tape either, what did we do last time? Yeah, do you remember? I remember that we did something like this, we hung it over the, I think it's big enough that we can do that.

The therapist begins the session by linking a past lack to the present one, a useful way to build continuity in the earliest phase of treatment. The therapist is essentially saying that even difficult moments from prior sessions can be remembered without the need for denial.

H: I wanted to put it here. (*She presses the paper to the chalkboard.*) I wanted to tape it. (*She yanks the basketball hoop off the chalkboard rim.*) Did I do that wrong?

T: Hmm?

H: Did I do that wrong?

T: What, did what wrong? No, what happened?

H: Forget it.

T: Forget what? Are you looking at that thing?

H: Hey, why doesn't this glue come off? Dumb, dumb, dummy, dummy. Why are the paper clips there?

The patient lets the therapist know extremely early in the session that both of their experiences will be under hypercritical review: First, she quickly admits wrongdoing that the therapist had not even noticed, and then she calls the glue dumb. The therapist may want to attempt to see whether this behavior is subject to self-reflection: "Wow, first there were some doing-something-wrong feelings and now there are dumb and dummy feelings. I wonder where those strong feelings are coming from?"

T: Why are they there? Ooh, I hadn't seen that there. Had you?

H: Can I use one of your keys to open this thing?

T: Let's see, do we need it, let's see. I think it's open. ... See, I don't think it's going to work. Wow, I must be really disappointing today. No tape, now the glue won't work!

Rather than focusing on being disappointing to the child, which may or may not be true yet, I would suggest that the therapist take the last phrase and wonder aloud about it so that the child can expand on whatever she feels: "No tape, now the glue won't work, I wonder what that feels like inside?"

H: Do you have tape?

T: I don't think so. I think today's gonna be ...

H: I mean in your room. We could go before we started. ...

T: I think it's important that we stay here and play.

H: I wanna get some tape, some tape!

T: Do you think you can do without it this one time, and next week I'll bring tape? Let's do that, next week, H, I will bring some tape. (*The child responds by knocking her forehead twice on the chalkboard.*) How do you feel about that?

Critically important information about this child's capacity for affective flooding is evident here. The child becomes demanding, the therapist tries to have the child defer gratification until the following session, and the child enacts her fury in a self-punishing way. At that moment, asking the child how she feels may no longer be sufficient to stem this flooding. We learn that appealing to the child's capacity to delay is not going to work, so we are almost left with no choice but to respond empathically and reflectively: "You want some tape so badly, it's hard to get those wanting feelings to stop."

H: And now this won't stand up—it's gonna fall. I don't know what to do.

T: You don't know what to do? (*The child begins to draw.*)

Her words suggest a frantic desperation, but she quickly shifts to drawing, as though her words, which suggest being easily overwhelmed, are not synchronized with her behavior, which suggests far better defenses. I would comment on this: "A part of you seemed to feel so stuck, but another part of you can let yourself draw."

H: I'm leaving June 25.

T: You know it's really important that you say that. I was going, I wanted to talk to you about that. You're leaving on June 25th. ...

H: To Z.

T: To Z.

H: (*She tears the front cover off of a small notepad attached to the paint/drawing kit.*) I just broke this. Why is this so ...

Her unusual pattern of impulsive, sometimes destructive, behavior, with a quick sense of blame (either toward the self or the object), continues. This is extremely difficult for any therapist, much less a beginning therapist in her fourth session with a patient, to handle. The behaviors are so immediate that the therapist is liable to feel constantly on the defensive, having to be reactively "putting out fires" rather than able to step back and make sense of what is going on in the child's mind. Although less verbally assaultive than the other patients discussed in this section, this child so far presents the most difficult challenge to the creation of a frame for affective mindfulness.

T: It's taped on there. It's a notepad, so you can move it like this. Do you want to take it out?
H: It's broken.

The patient completely ignores that she herself broke it. The therapist is left with a dilemma: Does she pursue the pathway toward the patient's "breaking feelings" or the path the child created about leaving the country? The therapist decides to go with the child's departure, which makes complete sense to me.

T: It's just the top anyways. So you're leaving, H, how are you feeling about that?

A subtle point but worth mentioning here is the significance of word choice when you are trying to help a child develop a sense of her mind. Asking, "How are you feeling about that?" with a child this nonreflective will almost always elicit a one- or two-word answer. An alternative might be, "I wonder what leaving feelings feel like in your mind?" Obviously, there is no guarantee that such phrasing will inspire a more reflective response, but this second phrasing may speak to the child on a more visceral level through the use of action language ("leaving feelings") and leaves room for the idea that feelings exist in a place in the child's mind.

H: Happy!
T: You're happy?

Asking, "What does the happy feeling look like?" may help the child explore this state of mind.

H: 'Cause I could go anywhere I want.

Because this child feels far more comfortable in behavior, it is possible that none of the suggestions may be useful.

T: Where are you gonna go?
H: I could go to the beach; I could go to the store by myself.
T: Really?
H: There's a lot of thief.

T: Thieves?

H: Yeah.

T: In Z?

H: It's a dangerous place, but I still take care of myself.

T: You do take care of yourself. How do you take care of yourself?

Here, the child strikingly juxtaposes her love of freedom, on the one hand, and on the other, her awareness that the place where she is free to roam is unsafe: "So one part of you looks forward to feeling those go-anywhere-I-want feelings, but another part of you has some strong danger worries."

H: I don't know. Can we play Candy Land? (*She slips out of her chair and slowly falls to the floor. She's sandwiched between the chair and the air conditioning unit.*)

Her rapid shifts away from her inner experience are remarkable and so difficult to track.

T: Whoa, there you go, slipping away! Where were you sitting? Are you okay?

The therapist does a lovely job of commenting on her slipping away while still being protective.

H: Yeah.

T: Okay?

H: The first time that's happened to me.

T: I know, the slipping. (*She gets up and finds the Candy Land boxes on the shelf.*) There we go. There are two. (*The patient grabs at the board games and several fall to the floor, scattering boards and cards all around her.*) Oh wow! There's a lot of stuff going on today, things are falling, you're falling!

The therapist is adept here at linking her patient's behaviors with her own vibrant, nonjudgmental affect. I might have gone with the child's surprise at slipping: "So many slipping, surprising feelings so far today, as if your mind is feeling so many different things one right after another."

H: Oh, look at them. (*She has taken out both Candy Land boards and placed them side by side.*)

T: Look at the people.

H: Let's play both of them at the same time.

T: All right. Both what? Both Candy Lands at the same time? One on the floor and one on the table?

H: No, both of them on the floor!

T: Both on the floor? All right!

H: It's gonna be exciting.

This is clearly a child who lives for action. On the negative side, we can see how hard it is for her to delay gratification and to stop herself from careening from thing to thing. On the positive side, we can almost feel her zest for playing and her ego-syntonic love of excitement.

T: Gonna be exciting. Ooh, are they different?

Better might have been: "Ooh, exciting feelings are so strong sometimes."

H: No. But they're different because one of them is big and the other one is little.
T: Oh, they must have been made at different times.
H: Which one do you want to be, green or blue?
T: Why can't I be both since we're playing on two boards?
H: Hey you stinking chair, move away!
T: So Z. You're happy about going to Z.

I would have preferred to let the child's play develop rather than go back to her departure, although it is so tempting to return to this theme because of its immediacy. It is through play that we are most likely to see the child's affective life come to the surface; thus, we need to utilize the power of play to allow the child to move forward rather than to focus on content. This is most difficult for a beginning therapist, for whom "just playing" can seem frivolous or confusing compared to a focus on content.

H: I'm going to fix these cards. They go with that one (*pointing to the Candy Land board game closest to me*).

The child lets her know that she is not going to be deterred from her play.

T: Which one? They go with this one? Okay.
H: Okay, this is going to be exciting!
T: So is that you over there, H, the yellow? That's you? Okay.
H: You could put yours right next to it.
T: Right here.
H: Let's put it on purple. I want to be red on the other one.
T: Okay, should we set up the other one, too?
H: Yeah.
T: All right. Here we go. And, I'll be green.
H: Can you pick up this one please? (*She leans on the table and accidentally knocks over the digital recorder.*) Oh, look what just fell.
T: Everything is falling today, H!
H: Today is Falling Day.
T: Falling Day. Today *is* Falling Day. We have officially named it Falling Day.

To link this acted-out experience of precariousness with the child's inner life, I might comment: "I wonder if so many falling feelings are going on inside you while things fall outside you at the same time."

H: Everything is falling. (*She falls on her back and stomps her feet on the floor dramatically.*)

T: Did you just fall? Again? That's a good make-believe fall.

H: I do this every single time I go to sleep.

T: What?

H: I'm asleep, like that, and then I do this.

T: What is that?

H: I don't know. Aaah!

T: Did you just fall again? (*This time I'm concerned she's hit her head intentionally.*)

H: Oooww, my head!

T: Oh, we have to learn how to—what are we going to do to protect ourselves on Falling Day? (*H looks at the stuffed animals on the shelves.*) Pillows, lots of pillows, right, we need lots of pillows, and stuffed animals.

What a great idea by the therapist! She acknowledges "Falling Day" in so creative a manner that there is no negative judgment at all. In fact, she creates the possibility that falling behaviors can be protected. Would it be possible to create a parallel protection regarding H's feelings? I might wonder about this aloud: "We need lots of pillows for your falling body, but what can we do to keep your falling feelings safe?"

H: Not hard animals. Whoo. (*Another set of board games topples from the shelves while H is taking stuffed animals from there and placing them on the floor.*) God, I wonder …

T: Now that's not a surprise—on Falling Day something would fall. How cushy! Oh, this is so cushy!

H: That could be our couch. We could turn this like this. (*She arranges the two board games so that they can be played from the couch.*)

T: Oh perfect. I'm going to sit right here.

H: You go over there with the other one. Get the other cards.

T: Alrighty. Let's see. …

H: I just took the ones from here.

T: Okay. Oh, you mean those? This game takes a really long time to set up, I've noticed. Well, we are playing two, right?

H: This is my pack of my cards, and this is your pack of cards. So, if I take green, I move two greens in both of them so I don't have to take double cards.

T: So do you want me to use these cards?

H: Yeah. Two yellow. Am I blue?

T: I don't know. I can't remember which one—blue or yellow? You're yellow?

H: Oh, I'm supposed to go on that one, too.

T: Oh, right, this is going to be confusing. You're right, okay, good. And then my turn? Yellow. Yellow. This is a double Candy Land. So it's actually Candy Lands. Green. They're going on a trip, too, right? I wonder if that's to Z. Wait, now I'm getting confused. This is confusing with two boards. Okay. Purple.

The therapist again makes a brief attempt to link the play to H's departure but wisely focuses back to the game.

H: You're supposed to be on yellow. Look, my tooth came out. (*She shows me.*)
T: Oh wow, when did that happen?
H: Yesterday, mi tia me lo saco. [My aunt took it out.]
T: Te lo saco? [She took it out?] Y como te sentiste? [How did you feel?]
H: Eso no duele. [That doesn't hurt.] The only part that hurts es cuando te lo estan metiendo por la na-, por el medio de eso, por la. [The only part that hurts is when they're sticking a thing in the middle here.]
T: El molar? El de atras? [Your molar, the one in back?]
H: No, cuando te lo estan cogiendo por el medio, y te lo amarran y le hacen asi. Pero cuando a ti te lo halan no sientes nada. [No, when they're taking it in the middle, tying it up and then going like this. But when they're just pulling, you don't feel a thing.]
T: Entonces te lo halo tu tia. [So your aunt pulled it out.]

It is so striking that H resorts to her "mother tongue" to describe a painful, scary experience. The therapist wisely stays with the use of Spanish, justifying and normalizing its use to describe something important. I would have been inclined to ask, in Spanish: "So the pulling feelings were okay, but the tying feelings, what were they like?"

H: Hmmm.
T: Cual tia, X? [Which aunt, X?] (*She stares at me with disbelief.*) Cual tia? [Which aunt?]
H: Eh, la que me cuida. [The one that takes care of me.] How do you know that one of my tia's name is X?
T: You remember telling me? We were sitting right over there. It was like, maybe the second time we were here.

The therapist expertly tries to create a link from the immediacy of the moment, where H seems to dwell, to prior sessions, attempting to create a history between them. It is a most useful and worthy effort as it tries to help the child establish libidinal object constancy for their work and play together.

H: I don't remember.
T: Okay. So, on Falling Day, we have two Candy Lands, en route to, where are they going?

H: Oooh, you're getting close to Plumpy. I passed Plumpy. Plumpy, look at Plumpy right there.

T: Plumpy. Is Plumpy happy? Plumpy's happy.

H: He loves grapes.

T: He loves grapes. He absolutely loves them.

H: Grumpy, grumpy, grumpy, Plumpy. Rainbow Trail.

T: My turn? Purple and purple. There we go. Amarillo.

H: Ooh, my hand. Plumpo, plumpy.

T: Double, double, double.

H: You're close to me.

T: Which one did you do? Purple? My turn? Ooh, what does this do? (*I've gotten a lollipop/princess card that moves my gingerbread man very close to the finish line.*)

H: (*She looks at me with mock shock, then buries her face in her hands.*)

T: Oh, no. Are you sad? What's going on? (*She's turned her back to me and is quickly flipping through all of her cards, looking for one in particular.*) Are you going to let me in on that play?

I would focus on the "mock" aspect of her dramatic behavior: "Well, H, your body just looked like it was feeling so, so surprised and sad, but I wonder what your mind's feelings and ideas were?"

H: Yea.

T: Or is it going to be a secret game?

H: I wanna go here. ... Secret game!

T: Secret game!

H: I passed it? Yeah. I wanna use a card that's perfect, that's perfect, that's perfect! (*A short burst of nonsensical sounds.*) I found one! I found one!

T: Yeah what did you find?

H: It's a secret.

T: It's a secret game. All right. So what should I do with this one?

H: Play.

T: I'm going to play it, all right. I have a hunch you have something up your sleeve.

H: Perfect. (*Another short burst of nonsensical sounds.*) I'm missing a card.

T: Really, how do you know that? So I'm going to go, I'm traveling, I'm traveling, I wonder, is he going, are gingerbread people, how are they traveling?

H: (*A set of completely nonsensical sounds.*)

T: You've never made that sound before, what's that?

H: (*A set of completely nonsensical sounds.*)

T: I can't tell, I can't tell if you're happy or excited. ... (*The child leans back and topples over and is now lying on the ground, face up.*) Did you fall again? It's incredible, all this falling.

A remarkable sequence in which the child's aggression and competitiveness is stirred up massively by the therapist's advancing past her. The child resorts to "stealing" an even better card ("the secret game") but is so affectively flooded by this behavior that her words become gibberish. The therapist gamely attempts to follow this inexplicable play by labeling her as happy or excited, but this only leads to the child falling again in the enactment of her flooded state. It may well be that the therapist's approach, which is so noncritical yet demonstratively aware of the falling ("it's incredible"), is the best that can be done to stay with this child emotionally during these enactments. As an alternative, I might have tried, "These secret game feelings are so strong that real words couldn't match how strong they were—and maybe not even falling feelings can match how strong your inside feelings are about your secret playing."

H: You went?

T: Okay, wait, there, Mr. Blue Man, Mr. Blue Man has to go here, right?

H: Very nice.

T: That's, oh wow, the same. Wow!

H: But I'm gonna win.

T: You're gonna win. Alright.

H: But we're in the same Lolli … Princess Lolli. She looks pretty. (*She is pointing at the picture of Princess Lollipop.*)

T: She's pretty. She's wearing, are those lollipops in her head? Oh wow, she's got a lollipop crown. Green. Okay. I'm green, right, green and green. (*She coyly hands me a card she's picked out from the rest.*) Queen Frostine. So the secret game, I think I know how the secret game works.

So the "stealing" of the most powerful card is both so exciting yet so guilt producing that H has to give it to the therapist to use instead of her. I would comment on this sense of power: "The secret game is about this superpowerful card and what to do with the superpowerful feelings it builds up inside of you."

H: I'm gonna get a card.

T: Is it my turn now? Or you just went? Or I just went? No, I just went? No, you just went? This is very confusing.

H: I just went, now you go.

T: Double red.

H: Yes, the perfect day of my life!

T: This is, this is, okay. Yellow.

H: I'm so happy.

T: You're really happy—you're falling down on the floor happy. I wonder why you're so happy?

The therapist uses the child's body to describe the feeling, a lovely use of action language and a reflective stance.

H: (*She is lying on her back on the floor with her legs still crossed.*) Can I get a little help?

T: What's going on?

H: I feel air. I need help!

T: Really, do you need my help? Or would you like me to just pull you up? Because that would be fun, but I think you could get up on your own.

H: Can I hold something?

T: That's, you're like in a pretzel? Are you stuck?

H: No.

T: Do you need a hand? Here we go. (*I help her out of her pretzel pose.*) Oh, why did H get so weak?

The patient's mercurial shifts from euphoria to despair in seconds, combined with her use of her body to enact her inner experience, continue to create a most difficult challenge to the creation of a reflective stance. There is no way this child is yet capable of answering the therapist's question, so we are left with the approach of creating a scaffolding for future reflectivity: "I think your body is letting us know that you have so many different feelings inside, and they keep busting out all over. I wonder if we can someday help your body's feelings get to know your mind's feelings?" Future sessions could refer to this moment: "Remember that Candy Land falling time we had? Then your secret game feelings were so strong you were falling and falling. Today feels a lot like that, did you notice?"

H: (*She is searching through a bunch of scattered cards.*) Hey, hey you owe me one, you stupid cards! You owe me a hundred buckets. Or I ain't gonna use you no more. Losers.

T: Oh, no, were those cards bad? What did they do?

Instead of asking what these cards did, it could be useful to ask, "Those cards are full of loser feelings. I wonder what that's like?"

H: Hey you sticking whatevers. … You go.

T: Alrighty. Purple.

H: Two green.

T: Two green. Are you back to the secret game?

H: I'm just taking these over here.

T: You're taking cards there. My turn?

H: Yep.

T: What is this? Check this out. Oh, no, Mr. Green Man gets to go all the way back here. All the way back to the Plumpy Land. And Mr. Blue needs to do the same. …

H: I give you permission. (*She hands me a card that would place me very close to the finish line, but still behind her gingerbread man.*)

T: Oh really?

H: Take it. Take it.

T: Hmm. What's this for? Wow! This is very interesting, H.

The therapist adroitly wants to pause the game and to find a way to help H note her reparative wish to have the therapist succeed at the game as well. She might try: "So now we both get to have winning feelings. Those losing feelings must really feel bad inside."

H: Can we go now please? You just went?
T: I just did, then you just did. This is very interesting.
H: Twice purple.
T: You just gave me a card that made me …
H: Oh-uh. (*Another nonsensical noise.*)
T: Oh, but it seems like someone still wants to win, even though you gave me this card.

The therapist is usefully addressing the behavior, but by not framing this behavior in affective terms, she is not meeting the child where she is. In a sense, the child needs to be *primed* emotionally before there is a chance that she can make note of her behaviors: "So a part of you has strong winning feelings, but a part of you doesn't want me to have strong losing feelings. It seems like those two kinds of feelings are arguing with each other."

H: Where's the lollipop one? Es una enanita. [She's a dwarf.]
T: She might be a little elf, right? Es chiquita. [She's small.]
H: Como de este tamaño. [Like this tall.] (*She measures a height of 2 feet.*)

Again, a fascinating shift to her mother tongue is inspired by the intense feelings generated by her aggression/guilt dialectic.

T: Look, compared to the lollipops. And what's her name, Princess Lolli. All right.
H: Double orange. (*Another nonsensical noise.*)
T: An orange and an orange. Wow!
H: And purple. (*She moves her gingerbread man to the finish.*) Yeaaaaaaa!
T: Oh wow! Look at that. …
H: Yeaaaaaaaa!
T: Yay! (*The child falls down on her back in a wooden, robotic manner.*) Whoa, what happened? So what happens when you win? (*The child is frozen where she fell, on her back, her legs in a W.*)

The great pleasure in winning almost immediately stirs up a bodily enactment of guilt: The child is *frozen,* simultaneously suggesting a denial that she could have done something aggressive if she cannot move or asserting that she must be punished for her aggressive/winning behavior by immobilizing herself. This is a simply remarkable process. Again, the therapist does a beautiful job of addressing her behaviors ("So what happens when you win?"). To speak to her affective experience as well, I would add the following: "So those wonderful 'Yeaaaaaa!' feelings stir up other falling, stuck feelings."

H: Can I get a little bit of help over here?
T: What's going on H, what do you need help in? Are you stuck again?
H: Aowwwh. Can someone get me up? I'm stuck.
T: Stuck? I think, are you play stuck, frozen stuck?
H: Frozen stuck.
T: Are you frozen stuck? (*The patient throws a stuffed animal across the room.*)
          Ooh, you don't seem stuck anymore. How did you do that?
H: I threw it with this arm and like that.
T: You got a little unstuck.
H: Can you give me this? This please.
T: What?
H: The bunny.
T: Where do you want me to put it?
H: In my hand.
T: Which hand?
H: In this hand.
T: Okay. All right. Will it help you get unstuck?
H: No.
T: No. How does it feel to be stuck?

The therapist has helped to cocreate a warm, playful experience for the child, in which she shifts from frozen to thawing to being unstuck. The therapist then feels the time is right to ask H about her affective experience behind being stuck. Unfortunately, she frames it in a manner that is likely to elicit only a one-word answer. A more open-ended approach might be, "These stuck feelings have lasted a long time; we've almost forgotten that they came right after your 'Yeaaaa!' feelings. I wonder why one feeling came right after the other?" The goal of this type of affective comment is to prime the child to think about her affects and the connections between them, to reflect on the "how" of inner experience, not the "what."

H: Fine.
T: Fine? I know, you're smiling, you're the happiest frozen person I've ever seen.
          Oh, but wait, look, wait a second, there's some movement there. Oh, I
          think you're melting a bit. I think that you're getting unfrozen.

The therapist is again right on track in pointing out that the child's facial expressions do not match her frozen stature. Ideally, these astute observations about her bodily states could be used as a bridge toward wondering about her inner feeling state.

H: Give me that one.
T: What?

H: Will you help me!

T: Which one? It's really hard to get what you want when you're stuck, isn't it?

H: That one.

T: Oh, look, oh my gosh, she's moving!

H: My foot!

T: Oh, look, wow, oh, look, there it is! You're unstuck a little. This is a really interesting game. What should we call this game? I just realized, you kind
of look like one of these stuffed animals, just lying here on the floor.

H: Give me all of my animals! Oh my god. ...

T: You want your animals?

H: I want to be frozen. ... (*She grabs several stuffed animals and brings them
near her.*)

T: Oh, look, there's movement, there's movement! The "I'm frozen game." (*The
child throws one of the stuffed animals violently at the wall behind
me.*) Oh wow!

The play sequence seems to be building in a new and stronger direction. The
contrast between the child's stated wish to be frozen and the vehemence with
which she throws the stuffed animals right past the therapist suggest a new, more
intense enactment of aggressive/regressive themes.

H: (*She lays back down again on her back, sticks her feet up in the air, like a baby
in her crib or a dead insect, and begins squirming around.*) Gurgles.

T: What is this? Well, obviously not the stuck and frozen. I'm confused. What's
going on? I don't understand what you're saying. You seem, you're
smiling. It's like a little baby. That's what it is, that's what you remind
me of. It's like you're a little baby, and your feet are up like a little
baby. (*The patient squirms around madly and bangs her head on the
air conditioning vent.*) Be careful, H, I don't want you to get hurt.
Okay, H? So is this your baby game; I'm going to call this when H gets
in her baby game. I wonder what brought on the baby game. We were
playing Candy Land ... and you won and then. ... The baby's pointing, hmmmm. What does that mean? This is hard, I don't know what
you're talking about. Maybe we can figure out a way to communicate.
How do babies communicate? (*The child is pointing at an area filled
with toys.*) Point. Foot? Shoe? Car? Yeah, you want this? (*I hand her a
stuffed animal.*) All right.

The therapist expertly finds a way to make sense of the child's play. She recog-
nizes the regressed qualities and labels them as a game, allowing H to continue playing out these themes without feeling shamed. The therapist then comments in an
equally nonjudgmental way on the "baby's" wish to nonverbally communicate.

H: (*She suddenly gets up on her hands and knees and begins crawling.*) I'm going
to crawl like a baby.

The child readily takes the therapist's responses and adds to them, a sure sign of the therapist's attunement to the meaning of her play.

T: You're going to crawl like a baby.

H: (*As suddenly as she got up, she lays again with her back on the floor, feet in the air.*)

T: I wonder who I should be. Where's baby's mom? Or where's another baby friend?

H: (*She throws a stuffed animal directly at me—narrowly missing me.*)

T: Was that meant for baby's mom or baby's friend? Was that baby's mom or baby's friend?

H: (*She turns on her stomach and takes a piece of chalk that was lying beside her. She begins writing on the rug.*)

T: Oh wow, look at that, baby's learning how to write, and with her left hand! I think she's trying to tell me something. What is that? Wow, baby is really trying to tell me something. Mommy. Mommy. Daddy. There you are. Baby's back to talking goo-goo talk. Wow! I wonder, does baby know how to (*the patient kicks toys away from her, thrashing from side to side*). ... I wonder what she's trying to tell me? Hmm, do you need a bottle? Maybe it's feeding time? Pampers? Do you need your Pampers changed? Oh no, I think this baby is taking a tantrum. You're wanting the toy? Sometimes it's really hard to understand baby. Play-Doh? You want the Play-Doh? All right. (*I place the Play-Doh in her hand. She looks at it and then gets up.*) Let's see. So, I wonder what will make the baby happy?

H: (*She starts ferociously, madly wiping the shelves clean, throwing everything in the cubbyholes to the floor.*)

T: Oh, what have we got here? Are you going to take everything out? How did you get so excited?

H: (*She gets to a cubbyhole that contains a large box of wooden blocks, which she is about to throw on my lap.*)

T: This is heavy, so we have to be careful. H, see how heavy this is? I know a baby wouldn't know, but I know H knows.

H: (*She backs away, grabs a rubber baseball, and begins to throw it full force at the wall. The third time, it comes very close to hitting my face.*)

T: Careful. When did baby learn how to play baseball? Wow, I think baby is gonna be an All Star pitcher by the time she's 3. I can just imagine her on the field, she's gonna be a good pitcher. Let's see. I wonder if baby's learned how to talk. ...

H: (*She is rifling through a box of Legos and assorted tiny plastic shapes. Over and over again, she picks up a shape, looks at it with disgust and throws it down.*)

T: Oh, nothing seems right. Mmmh, it doesn't.

This is a most intense interchange between patient and therapist. The patient's behavior shifts so rapidly that the therapist is almost frantically trying to catch up.

One of the hardest things to do as a beginning play therapist is to do less, to sit with the anxiety of not knowing the meaning of a play sequence. Here, the therapist is hypothesizing on the fly and out loud, and it may very well be that her words stimulate affective shifts in the child, catching child and therapist in a cycle of misattunement and generating further anxiety in both. In this particular case, the focus on the child's "baby needs" probably made her feel more anxious, shifting her from regressed messiness and "tantrums" to ferocious cleaning efforts, then to furious aggression, and finally to nothing feeling right. I might have tried to stay simple: "There are lots of strong feelings here, strong like the way a baby can feel, before there are words. I wonder what it would feel like before there are words."

H: I want to clean up. I'll get in trouble with my mom if she knew that I did all this mess. (*She begins to put things away, somewhat angrily. She finds a piece of cotton in one of the boxes of toys she is putting back in its place.*) Algodon. [Cotton.] (*She takes the cotton ball and rubs my forehead with it.*)

The child steps out of her regressed play via a "channeling" of her mother's prohibitions against her messiness. She then slips into Spanish while repairing with the therapist through a gesture of connection. I would be inclined to link these affects: "So messing feelings need to get replaced with cleaning feelings, even cleaning me feelings. Messing feelings don't seem to be very safe."

T: Oh, you're cleaning me—do I have a stain on my face? Is it all gone? (*She looks down at a hand puppet. I pick it up and put it over my right hand.*) Oh wow.
H: Stupid puppet. It's not pretty. Ugly, ugly, ugly!
T: Oh, I'm so ugly. ...
H: And that's good.
T: Oh, what, why is it good?
H: I'm gonna kick your—I'm not going to say the word.

The child has another of her mercurial shifts in which her ugly, messy self gets displaced onto the puppet.

T: I wonder why this little girl thinks I'm so ugly and stupid.
H: 'Cause you're stupid. You're freaking me out.
T: I'm freaking you out?
H: Yeah, with your stupid talking.
T: Oh god.
H: And I'm saying it for real! (*She throws a stuffed animal at the puppet.*)

The intensity of the messy feelings again breaks the plane between play and reality. This child cannot sustain the transitional space necessary for play to continue without causing real disruption. Her comment "You're freaking me out" is important to address: "Those freaking-out feelings tell us that sometimes it's scary to play and not to be sure what's play and what's real."

T: Ow, that hurt. (*The child throws another stuffed animal.*) Ow, that hurt. (*The child throws a hard doll next.*) Oh, that hurt. That actually, that actually hurt, no more throwing. ...

H: I thought you were faking.

T: I know, no, but the last time, because it's a hard thing, right? You know the difference between throwing something soft and something hard.

I would have redoubled my efforts to comment on her confusion about what is real and what is pretend: "Sometimes it's so hard to know when we're playing and when we're real."

H: I'm bored.

T: Bored, that's the worst.

H: I want to use the computer.

T: That's the worst. I hate boring feelings.

Boredom reflects the child's need to shut down and gain distance from the crashing feelings inside her, including not being sure what's play and what's real in her regressed experience. The therapist usefully tries to imbue the boredom with affect and might have added: "After all these superstrong feelings in our play, I can see why boring feelings would come to make them all go away for a while."

H: Can I use the computer?

T: Oh, you mean? Which computer? Where did you see the computer? Do you mean the invisible computer right over there?

H: Hell no—sorry. (*She begins to pick up the pieces of Play-Doh strewn around her on the floor.*)

T: How's it feel to be bored?

H: Are you playing with the Play-Doh when I'm cleaning it up?

T: Are you cleaning it up? I don't know what you're doing. You've done a lot of stuff today. So, you're going to Z on the 25th. So that means that we have today. ...

H: Eleven more days together.

T: Eleven more days, and then next week, we meet one more time before you go. How do you feel about that?

H: Angry.

T: I could tell you're angry. I wondered if that was why you were throwing stuff around. Angry feelings.

The therapist links H's departure to affect, and the child easily follows her. The therapist then validates the feeling and links it to her throwing stuff around. Well done.

H: Can we go and get some paper—if we have time?

T: Now this is very interesting, H. Very interesting that you asked me that, and there's paper where you can see it. And I don't know what, and I don't know what. ...

H: I want white paper.

T: White paper. But when you ask me that, it's like you know that I don't have it. But I think there's something else going on. Because you know there's white paper right here.

H: Nooo, there's no white paper.

The child's admission of anger at their impending separation prompts the regressive wish to have the therapist give her something, even if it is right there. The therapist is rightfully struggling with what this means for H. She could try commenting: "These hard-to-leave, angry feelings make it very hard to feel like you can get what you want. Even getting paper seems hard."

T: Let's look. How about there? (*The child reaches inside the cubbyhole where the construction paper and printing paper are. They are jammed inside, and now she is really tugging on the bulk of paper trying to get it out.*) But it's how you say it. It's like I'm not going to have any, right? It's stuck in there. There we go. Angry feelings. Hmm.

She labels the child's pulling at the paper as a reflection of angry feelings, a useful link.

H: Can we do a Father's Day card?

T: Wanna do one?

H: I want to decorate it. I'm gonna take it home. I want to do a party for him.

T: A party for your dad?

H: Because it's a special day for fathers.

T: It is.

H: Can you help me clean up, please? So. ...

T: You want some help cleaning up?

H: So we could have time to do the card.

The child has, in effect, reassembled her latency-aged self, now wanting both to make things clean again and to focus on a gift-making task outside the two of them.

T: Well I want to let you know, H, that we've got eight more minutes. Okay? So maybe we can start today and finish it the next time? All right?

H: And who's gonna clean up this mess?

T: Oh, who's gonna clean up this mess? That's a very interesting question.

H: Let's leave it like this, and you lock the door!

T: Oh really?

H: Next day when we come.

T: We can come back and clean it? Well I, you know, usually, remember how I
always say that we have to leave the room how we found it?

While the setting of limits around cleaning up the room is vital to maintaining
the structure of treatment, it seems useful to comment on H's wish to leave the
mess and lock the door: "So even though we both know about our cleaning up
rules, the feeling to just leave it all and go is very strong."

H: I'm too tired.
T: Really, you're really tired? If you're really tired, we're gonna have to start. ...

Perhaps acknowledging her tiredness would make the shift to cleaning up more
palatable: "I can see how you'd be so tired after all the strong good-bye feelings
you've been having today."

H: You have a father?
T: Yes, I have a father.
H: He died.
T: He died? (*The child's face contorts.*) What do you mean?
H: I'm asking you.
T: You're asking me if my dad died? No, he's alive.
H: Great. I'm going to make a Father's Day card for your father.

The need for reparation, to keep the therapist close despite their impending
separation, is so strong that it is the therapist's father who must be taken care of.

T: I wonder what—that's really interesting, I don't think you've ever asked me
anything about my family. Something really important, I'm usually
the one asking you stuff.

I can understand why the therapist might go in this direction, but it seems too
abstract for this patient. To my mind, the child's need to give something to the
therapist as a projection of her own wish to be given to is more relevant here, so
I would comment: "Giving something special to fathers is a very strong feeling,
and now you want to give those feelings to my father."

H: I'm going to make a shirt, and there's gonna be a scarf here.
T: Oh, think I know, you're going to make one of your special hearts. (*The child
shakes her head no.*) No, something different. So I think it's really
important that you asked me that. I wonder why. Well, if we don't talk
about it now, we can talk about it later.

By giving the impression of being able to talk about it later, the therapist is also
indirectly letting the child know that they have a future together, even after her trip.

H: It's a scarf.

T: A scarf? It seems like going to Z is gonna be happy. (*She shows me what she's made.*) Look at that! That's a shirt, and there's the collar! Going to Z is gonna be really happy, you're gonna be able to go around by yourself, but sounds like you're also gonna miss some people.

H: A lot of people.

T: A lot.

H: Not just my dad. All of my family.

T: Who are you going to miss? Let's write them down.

The therapist is trying to help H deal with her missing feelings by creating a structure for them ("Let's write them down"). Given how labile H is, this defensive superstructure is quite understandable. But, it appears from our vantage point that the child is experiencing these "missing feelings" at the more adaptive end of her affective tolerance, suggesting that it could me more useful in this moment to encourage a further expression of her affect rather than a binding of it: "Missing-all-of-my-family feelings are very strong feelings. I can see why you'd be happy and sad at the same time about going to Z."

H: There's a lot of people. (*The child is trying to fold the collar evenly.*) Do you like it like that? Is it pretty there?

T: Yeah. It looks like a shirt collar. A big white shirt collar.

H: I can't staple it from here. Shorter. I'm going to make it shorter.

T: Oh, yeah, that's a solution. There you go. And that's like a little bow tie, a little staple bow tie. It's a big white shirt, so I wonder, whose shirt is this? Whose collared shirt is this?

For the first time all session, both therapist and patient together move away from affect, suggesting that the pain of loss is too strong for either of them to mention right now.

H: Your dad's.

T: My dad's shirt.

H: Does your dad speak English?

T: I wonder why you're asking me all these questions?

H: Does he?

T: What do you think?

H: No.

T: No.

H: Yes.

T: Yes.

H: No. Yes. No. Yes.

T: What do you think?

H: I'm gonna call him. (*Goes toward the fake phone.*) What's his number?

T: We've got 3 minutes. Do you want to help me pick up, or do you want to call and figure out some stuff? Oh look, hey I found some jeans to go with the shirt. Doesn't it go?

Here is yet another common, indeed generic, problem in child therapy: how to manage the ending of a session when there are both so many important affective issues on the table *and* a room that needs to be cleaned up. My personal style is to begin cleaning up while staying with the child's play as there is usually more to gain from this approach than from placing cleanliness above all else.

H: Can I staple it?
T: Mmmh, I think the next, I don't think we should because that would be, we could have them be like that. Oh that's really good, that's really funny.
H: It doesn't matter.
T: All right H, you usually help me put the room back. I wonder what's going on that you're not helping me today.

A useful question, but one more for the therapist at this point in the treatment, as the child is clearly not yet capable of this level of linking behavior to affect. I would simply say: "Your good-bye feelings are much stronger than your cleaning-up feelings today."

H: I need to make this Father's Day card before. ...
T: I know, its sounds like you're really busy. But remember, we're going to be meeting next week and we can finish then, too. But it seems like you're really busy, that it's really important that you do that.

The therapist validates the importance the child attaches to finishing her project.

H: I'm going to try to see if the glue could come down.
T: Okay, you tried it before, but you can give it another try. Where's the, what you were drawing so that I can keep it in a safe place?
H: Can I take it home?
T: Remember what I said, well, when you finish it. ...
H: Before I leave.
T: How about we talk about it next time, okay? Because it's time to go. Alright?
H: Is it time to go?
T: It's time to go. I know it's sometimes hard to finish, H, but we gotta go.
H: I wonder who's gonna clean up all this mess. Maybe you should lock the door. Can I carry it (*referring to my keys*)? I wanna lock it.
T: You can't lock it.

I might have stayed away from the locking issue and focused instead on the mess and who will clean it: "There were so many good-bye feelings today, and they were so strong that we couldn't find the time to clean up. I will clean it up this time because it is important that we get the room back to the way it was when we first came in today."

H: Lock it!
T: I'll keep the key.
H: Can I carry your other keys? Do you have a job?
T: This is my job.
H: Do you make a lot of money?
T: All these questions!

Much as with our adult patients, there are many times when powerful issues are raised "going out the door," leaving us without the space and time to give them their proper due. The child is attempting to identify with the therapist and expressing a desire to grow up to be like her as a way to deal with their impending separation. This is far too powerful an issue to address at the very end of a session, so the best approach may be to acknowledge the feeling as something to be explored in the future: "Sounds like you're having some wanting-to-be-like-me-when-you-grow-up feelings. That's something we can surely keep on talking about when we see each other again, even after you get back from Z."

H: You know why, because I wanna be a doctor when I grow up.
T: A doctor?
H: So I can earn a lot of money!

Although this child is far less belligerent than some of the other cases explored in this section on challenges to the frame, she is perhaps even more difficult because most of her impulsivity is directed toward her own fears and concerns. The shifts between self-critical sabotage and aggressive play, with a huge dose of guilt thrown in along the way, presented a formidable challenge to this particularly well-attuned therapist. This session is especially notable for the need to rely on the concept of scaffolding, that is, to attempt to link an affect the child expresses to a future point in time when both she and the therapist will be better able to address its meaning. While this statement often carries little weight for the child at the moment, it allows the therapist to return to that moment in future sessions in the frame of "this behavior [now] reminds me of that time when you were playing with X and that same feeling of Y came up. I wonder if those two feelings are related to each other?" This not only strengthens the continuity of the child's emotional life across sessions, by linking present with past, but also further strengthens a modeling of psychological mindedness as something that exists over time.

Also noteworthy in this section is the child's boredom. I always remind my students of how common bored feelings are in a child treatment and how this boredom is almost always a signal that the child is feeling aimless and ungrounded. Much like in everyday life when a child comes to a parent stating that they are bored, the boredom is most quickly ended if the parent engages in a play activity with the child, as it is the lack of connection that is leading to the child's boredom (i.e., not feeling like they can replenish themselves). Boredom in the treatment hour is thus a signal to the therapist to try to become still more empathically attuned to the child's feelings of aloneness.

Section III

Broadening the Frame

In this last section, each of the four children presented have a nascent capacity to reflect on the links between their inner worlds and their actual behavior. The gist of the work thus changes subtly to a focus on how to broaden this frame of self-reflection, sometimes to include more affects and sometimes to deepen the links that can be made between different affects. In Chapter 10, a 5-year-old boy is aided by his therapist to use the game Mousetrap as a means of integrating anticipatory anxiety with feelings of aggression. In Chapter 11, a 7-year-old girl constructs an elaborate, transferentially charged dialogue between herself and the therapist in the roles of teacher and pupil, with several avenues available for broadening the frame of her experience. In Chapter 12, an 11-year-old girl quickly creates a play milieu in which her characters have a variety of longings and rejections to work through, giving ample room for the therapist to speak to issues of ambivalence and nuance. In our final case, presented in Chapter 13, a 7-year-old boy rapidly shifts both in and out of a play space and between play spaces with a mixture of self-awareness and "blindness" that also provides the therapist with an arena for broadening the child's capacity for self-reflection.

10 A 5-Year-Old Boy

The mother of this 5-year-old boy reported that he had difficulty dealing with anger, often taking a punitive attitude toward other children. He chronically wanted attention and had trouble following directions at school and to a lesser degree at home.

In this session, we were using a new therapy room. J begins by noticing items in this room that are like some of the things in the other room (e.g., some of the games).

T: The pad? That's right. There are some things that I keep and I bring from room to room.
J: And this!
T: Some things are the same.
J: And this!
T: Yes.
J: And this! (*This goes on for several more iterations.*)

This process of discovering what is the same, and therefore comforting to a 5-year-old who changes rooms, is affectively meaningful enough to make a comment: "I wonder what it feels like to find some of our old friends here in this new place?"

T: I also found this.
J: What? Little crayons?
T: Chalk.
J: Chalk! Let's play on the board.
T: Okay.
J: Come on!
T: Okay, let me just open it.
J: I'm trying to open it.
T: It's tough, isn't it?
J: I'm almost, I'm almost, chalk! There. Let's put the chalk right there. All of it.
T: Okay. (*J dumps all of the chalk onto a table near the blackboard.*)
J: Ay-ay!
T: Whoops! (*The chalk spills everywhere, and I put it all back on the table.*)
J: Hey, these are laying on the floor. Come on, let's go. (*Tries to draw on the board, which is hard to write on.*) I cannot write.
T: You can't write? Let's see. Let me try. (*I draw some lines on the board. J begins to draw on the board, too.*)
J: I'm going to draw a snowflake.
T: A snowflake? (*Erasure sound.*)

J: First a line.

T: Okay.

J: And then the other line.

T: Uh-huh.

J: And then the other line, and then the other line.

T: That looks like a snowflake.

J: Look outside. (*We move to the window and look out.*)

T: It's still snowing outside.

J: Yeah. That's my favorite, favorite thing.

We are so often on the lookout for instances when painful or difficult feelings can be spoken of affectively, yet here is a sweet moment that is equally worthy of exploration: "Favorite, favorite things make for favorite feelings inside. What does the snow feel like inside to you?" This question may give the child a chance to expand on the range of his positive affective experiences as well.

T: You like the snow?

J: Yeah. And why was there a table in the other one?

T: What's that?

J: Why was there a table in there?

T: The other one? Why was there a table in there? (*Not sure what he's talking about.*)

J: Like four tables.

T: In the other room?

J: Um-hum.

T: Well, every table has a room in it. I mean, sorry, every room has a table in it.

J: Okay, let's … what?!?

T: What are you looking at? (*J begins to pull Mousetrap from the window shelf.*)

J: How you … how you call this game?

T: It's called Mousetrap.

J: Mousetrap?

T: I've never played it before.

J: Me either. (*Opens box.*) Oh, that's the traps. (*Hm.*) Hey, there is … there is people. And here are the mouse. Let's see. … (*Dumps all the pieces out.*)

T: Wow, there are a lot of pieces. (*We begin to look at the pieces and try figure out what to do.*)

J: This is a hand there. Whoa! Look. This is a hand.

T: There's a big green hand on it. (*We continue to look through the pieces. I'm wondering what to do with this game, for which many of the parts are missing. I have no idea how this is going to be useful and am beginning to rue Mousetrap.*)

A most useful admission by the therapist. Especially at the beginning of one's training, there tends to be a worry that only certain kinds of play are useful, as if there is one royal road to the child's inner life and the more open-ended the game or toy, the more likely you and your patient may stay on this path. While this worry is sometimes merited (e.g., I never have Monopoly in my office as it takes too long to set up), in working with a 5-year-old, it is likely that the child will place his or her emotional signature all over *any* activity.

J: What! (*He thinks I'm looking at him.*)
T: What? I'm looking at the game. What do you think we should do?
J: We have to throw the ball to trap the mouses. The red mouse, the green mouse, the yellow mouse, and the blue mouse. There's all the mouses.
T: All these mouses.
J: (*Inaudible.*) What do we have to do with this? What do we need to do?
T: I don't know. There are lots of pieces.
J: O-ho! (*Starts trying to figure out how to fit the pieces together. He's pretty good at it.*)
J: Here *this* is. ... Here *they* are. (*Long pause.*) How you put this?
T: I don't know. I'm trying to figure it out, but it's kind of complicated, isn't it?
J: O-ho. You did it! How you did it?
T: I found that piece. See, it goes high enough. ...
J: Oh, yeah! (*Inaudible.*) ... that you found that piece. Number 10 trap! What does that? What does ... that's a trap? Those, those ...

The child's enthusiasm is infectious. I might have wanted to comment on the feelings generated by the complexity of the task: "Wow, not-knowing feelings are very strong sometimes. It's hard not to know what to do."

T: Right.
J: And then you trap the mouse.
T: Right, the mouse is down there and then you trap it.
J: Let's do it. Come on, do it!
T: Here we go.
J: Let's trap it now.
T: Trap it now? Doot doo-doot doo-dooo, ... It's Mr. Mouse walking around. Oooh, I smell cheese! Look, there's cheese! Ooh, yum, yum, yum, ... Ahhhhhh! I'm trapped. I'm trapped. I just wanted some cheese and now I'm trapped. I can't get out now.

The therapist gracefully goes into character, playing the unsuspecting mouse. His use of an open monologue and strong affect are most useful primers to engage the child's affective life. The diagnostic question then becomes which affects related to entrapment are tolerable for the child, which are at the cusp of intolerance but can be broadened, and which are so conflictual that they cannot yet be heard by the patient.

J: Dee-dee, dee dee dee, ... He's trapped. (*J traps another mouse.*)

T: Hey, friend. How are we going to get you out of there? I don't know if I can
     move this.
J: Hey! Let's put *this* right there. Now the mouse is.
T: Doot-doo-doo-doo, ...
J: Let me do it, let me do it!
T: Should I be the mouse? Okay.

    The therapist gets his first clue about the roles he and the child will play in this
game: The child is most comfortable playing the aggressor, the trapper of mice,
and wants the therapist to play the victim.

J: Doo-doo-doo-doo-doo!
T: I smell cheese. Sniff, sniff, ... (The mouse gasps.) Cheese! Mmmm. ...
     Ahhhh!

    The therapist broadens and develops the affect in the play by focusing on
the oral needs and gratifications of the mouse. This emotional gasping and
"ahhhing" heightens the pleasure the patient gains from "sadistically" depriving the mouse.

J: A-ha-ha!
T: He got hit by the ball.
J: Dee-dee-dee-dee, ... Oh yeah! The ball has to go right there.
T: Wow.
J: What the ... ? There's a shoe.
T: A shoe.
J: A big green shoe.
T: A big green shoe.
J: There's a shoe right there.
T: Oh, yeah.
J: Oh, yeah, the shoe has to kick it!
T: We might not have all the parts to it. Let's see what those are. The blue one ...
     (trying to build a new trap).

    This brief pause while they are building the next trap may be a perfect time
to comment on the affects just displayed: "So, first the mouse is full of delicious
feelings; he's going to get the cheese of his dreams—and then *bam*, the shocking
feelings of being trapped with no escape! I wonder what that big change felt like
inside for the mouse?"

J: That has to go right there.
T: That has to go where? Right here?
J: Yeah. The cheese has to ...
T: On it? Oh, that's the trap.
J: He smells cheese.

This is the child's way of prompting the therapist that oral needs should be played out again.

T: (*As mouse*) I smell cheese somewhere. Where is it. Cheese. He's feeling nervous. He's afraid it's going to be a trap. But that cheese smells so good. He says, I'm going to get some cheese anyway. Even though it might be a trap, but mmmmmmmmm. Ahhhhhh!

Now, the therapist begins to broaden the frame. He introduces anxiety to the mix and frames it in the form of a dilemma between the "cheese wishes" and the "trap worries." I might have used this type of action language to make the feelings that much more immediate and present.

J: A-ha. Now it has to go like this. Da-da-da-da. Oh, cheese!
T: Oh, cheese! Yum-yum-yum …
J: Yum yum yum yum. You eat it!
T: Yum yum yum yum yum, … . Ahhhhhh!

It is important to note how attuned child and therapist are, and how the patient wants the therapist to repeat the phraseology just so. This repetition heightens the child's pleasure because its very familiarity provides some control over his excitement.

J: Ohhh. Hm. Hm. Hmm. (*Inaudible.*) Oh, the red one! The red one. This is to go like this. Like this, and then. … This is to hold this. But how? It does not hold. There. There! (*Trying to put more pieces together, including the tub.*)

The child needs some respite from the excitement of the chase, so he shifts to figuring out the next trap. The therapist is likely on solid ground simply following the child's lead but might add: "Whew, after all those exciting cheesing and trapping feelings, our feelings need some rest to build another trap."

T: Oh!
J: The bath toilet.
T: The bath toilet? Oh, you mean the tub.
J: Tub. Yeah. (*I help him put a part together.*) Oh, yeah! Where's the thingy?
T: What thingy?
J: This one! (*He shows me the picture on the cover, pointing to the part he wants.*)
T: I don't know. I'm not sure we have that. I'm not sure we have that piece.
J: Hey, you have that game. (*We talk a bit about the games that are also in the other room that we use.*)
T: That one?
J: The man … the man is going to the yellow thingy, and then it goes …

T: What's he doing in there?

J: How you put this?

> (*As mouse*) I am still trapped. Someone …

T: Help, help!

J: No more trap (*lets the mouse free*).

T: (*As mouse*) Yay! Now I can get out, and run away. It was really terrible being caught in that trap. I felt so scared. I was just eating cheese, and all of a sudden this trap came down.

> (*As second mouse*) Really, that must have been terrible. It's so hard when you're hungry all the time for cheese, and then these traps catch you.
>
> (*As first mouse*) *Yeah, I know.*

The therapist broadens the work in a new way, having the trapped mouse confide in a buddy about his experience, thus modeling the therapeutic relationship. He also broadens the range of affects in play, adding true fear to the shock and anxiety already introduced.

J: (*Singing: two other mice come along.*)

T: Hey look, there are two other mice. What are your names? You guys like to eat cheese, too?

J: (*Answering for the other two mice*) Yes. Yes.

T: Have you ever gotten caught in a trap before?

J: No, we do not.

T: You've never been caught in a trap? Wow.

J: We do it like this. Dee, dee, dee, … . When we smell cheese, we eat it too fast for the trap should not get us.

T: Ahh. How come you guys are so fast? How did you learn to be so fast and learn to get away from the trap but still eat the cheese?

The fact that the therapist's expression of fear does not derail the play at all suggests that the child's range of affective tolerance is broad. Part of the way the child handles the fear is through the presentation of his mice as fast and invulnerable. Instead of focusing on how the mice got so fast, the therapist might have remained close to affect: "So by being so fast you guys don't have to get scared trapped feelings? Wow!"

J: Where's the seesaw?

It may be that the child switches gears here because his affect was not addressed.

T: Seesaw. … I think we've used all the pieces.

J: There is those right there. Look at … (*eating sounds*).

Again, the child is able to return to the play after a brief disruption and signals this shift to the therapist with his eating sounds.

T: He's eating cheese. Um, that smells pretty good. Can you share your cheese?
J: Sure, anybody can come and eat my cheese.
T: Yum, yum, yum. Hey, thanks for sharing your cheese. It's so good to be eating cheese and sharing cheese with your friends. (*J started to set up the trap to get the mice.*) Hey, what's that sound?
J: Not! They're still eating.

He rejects the therapist's attempt to introduce apprehension into the play, wanting the mice to be taken unaware. In this moment, he is fully identifying with the aggressor.

T: Yum, yum, yum. ... Eating cheese, eating cheese. All sharing cheese, eating cheese. (*J is preparing trap.*) Ahhhhhh!
J: (*Sinister laugh; speaking as the man piece in the game.*) Bravo! Bravo!

The therapist's dramatization of the victim's affect ("Ahhhhh!") allows the child to act out the full range of his sadism as he even mimics a sinister laugh.

T: Why is he saying bravo?
J: Because he gots all the mouse.
T: All in one trap. (*Long pause.*)
J: Now they're still safe (*lifting trap*).
   (*As mouse*) What was that?

This is a fascinating moment. The child is able to switch identifications and become the newly freed mice. This shifting of roles is reminiscent of the peek-a-boo game in which the child can make the mother disappear and then return. The child is mastering his aggression through play by the magic of doing and undoing. I might add: "What a great feeling, to know you can trap the mice, but then the mice can still get free. What a relief!"

T: I don't know what hit me. What happened?
J: They smell cheese, again! For everybody! (*J sets up several pieces of cheese.*)
T: Cheese everywhere.
J: One, two, three, four (*counting pieces of cheese*).
T: There's enough cheese for all four of us, you guys! Come on over. We're so lucky to have found all this cheese. Very exciting.

The doing and undoing now allow the child to broaden the play, including more mice, and the therapist smoothly goes along with this shift.

J: (*Making eating noises.*)

T: Eating cheese, munch, munch, munch!

J: Ahhhhhhh! (*Traps one mouse.*)

T: Let's see if we can help him and get him out of the trap. Hurry, run. Run. Let's get away. (*J uses two silver balls to chase down the mice.*)

J: Ahh (*another mouse gets hit*). Help him!

Now, the child is simultaneously identifying with the victim and the aggressor, asking the therapist to help the mice even as he continues to pursue them. I would comment on these dual identifications: "So a part of you has mice-saving feelings, and another part of you has mice-trapping feelings. I get it!"

T: If we keep running in different directions, the balls won't be able to get us. Oh, no. Yellow mouse, he got hit. Ahh! Red mouse got hit. Only two left, we have to get away. Blue mouse hit. Oh, blue mouse. Green mouse is the fastest one. He's going to try to get away. Where's he going to go. Oh, no. ...

J: (*Sinister laugh.*) Now the ... the boss sends these guys to ... the master.

T: The boss is sending them where?

J: To his master.

T: To his master. ... Who's the master? Is this the master?

J: Yup!

T: So what's the master going to do with them? What's he going to say to them?

I would stick with the affect here rather than focusing on the action: "I wonder what they're feeling, having to be taken to the master who sounds so powerful?"

J: (*As master*) Put them there!
   (*Then as falling mice*) Ahhhh! (*The mice fall through a plank with a hole in it.*)

T: They all have to fall through the hole, all the way down! Fall from so high up.

J: (*Sinister voice*) Thank you. ... He says ... he needs to say, "Thank you." ... (*Gives me the master piece.*)

T: Thank you, you silver mouse-eating balls. You did a fantastic job of getting those mice and bring them up here so that I could throw them through the hole and they could fall down.

The patient does not feel fully comfortable holding onto this powerful aggression, so he passes this role to the therapist.

J: Boom! (*Falling sound.*)

T: Boom. ... He must really hate mice.

J: He does hate mice.

T: Why do you think he hates mice so much?

The patient acknowledges the therapist's statement about the master's hatred of mice, but his question regarding why the master hates the mice is too cerebral, so the child ignores the question. He might be able to respond to a more affect-oriented question: "Those hating feelings are so strong and powerful. I wonder what it feels like to be that full of hating?"

J: (*Pause.*) He's going to go into his hole.
T: Oh, he fell down himself. They all fell down. He fell into his own trap.
J: This one needs to go. ... (*Makes sounds, tries to put more pieces together.*) The
    seesaw (*pointing to the picture on the box*). ...
T: The seesaw? We don't have the seesaw part. We don't have all the parts to the
    toy. We just have these.
J: That's it. We're. ... I ... Now let's play with the other. ... Now you clean up this
    game, and I'll get the other game.

The intensity of the child's aggression is too strong for him to maintain, so he has to punish the master in the play. He then tries to regain his affective balance by going back to building more traps, but the respite does not work this time, and he resorts to giving up the play. I might add: "So getting punished for his hating feelings ends this play for now. I wonder where all those hating feelings must go?"

T: Okay. (*I begin putting pieces away.*)
J: (*Dumps blocks out of a plastic container.*)
T: Blocks.
J: Heavy blocks!
T: That's a big box of blocks.
J: That's a hu-u-u-ge, giant.
T: Huge, huge. ...
J: Giant, giant box.
T: Giant box.
J: Watch how many there is ... (*dumps blocks*). Ooohhh! Hey, maybe with the
    mousetrap, we can play with the blocks. And let's pretend we have all
    the parts.
T: Okay, so these are all the parts.
J: Let's pretend!

The patient rebounds from the lapse in play, perhaps aided by the therapist's validation of his strength in handling the huge giant blocks.

T: Okay.
J: (*Dumps things out of Mousetrap box.*)
T: So what do you think? How should we do this?
J: Where's the seesaw ... that's the seesaw.
T: Yeah, that can be the seesaw. Will that fit?

J: Yup.

T: That can be the seesaw. (*Long pause.*)

J: Hey, this is ...

T: That'll stay there. (*We build things quietly. J is intent on using blocks along with Mousetrap.*)

The play takes on a more structured, less thematic quality. The child clearly needs more time to "recover" from the aggression stirred up by the Mousetrap game, and the therapist allows the silence to blossom.

J: No that's too far.

T: You like to figure out how things go together.

J: This ball goes here, and this ball goes there, and it has to go in here. Where did you found them?

T: That was in the box, too.

J: Let's do a little more. The mouse should be trapped. And they get upstairs ... to smell ... this is the six trap, I mean the nine trap. ...

T: The nine trap?

J: The six, the nine. ... Let's not play.

T: Okay.

J: You ... you clean up all of them!

The child cannot find his way back to the thematic play and instead modifies his hateful yet playful aggression into the here-and-now with the therapist, ordering him to clean up.

T: This mousetrap or the blocks, too?

J: The both of them.

T: Wow, you're the boss, aren't you?

The therapist usefully comments on the sudden shift to bossy behavior. This might also be a moment when the shift from play to nonplay could be processed aloud: "So we went from the six and nine trap-playing to no playing at all. I wonder where the playing feelings went?"

J: What is that there?

T: I don't know.

J: Let's see.

T: Be careful. (*J pulls a box from the bookcase.*)

J: Will you open this? And then ... (*dumps stuff out*). This is more. ... (*Dumps another bag. An assortment of tools and "doctor" toys are on the floor, along with blocks.*)

T: More. ... Will you help me put the blocks away?

J: No, you have to do it.

T: I have to do it all?

J: Yes!

T: (*Putting blocks away.*) I'm getting bossed around.

J: Hah?

T: I said I'm getting bossed around.

The child ignores the therapist's comments here, perhaps because there is no process or affect attached to them.

J: Okay. What is this? What is this? What is this?

T: It's a tool.

J: What does it do?

T: It shows if something is level. See if you put it like this, it's a level line, it will be in the middle. (*I eventually realize that I am making no sense to J.*)

J: Okay, now I'm the doctor.

T: You're the doctor.

J: And you're the sir.

The child is able to recover his capacity for play, allowing himself to transfer his bossy cleanup orders onto the role of the doctor who is in charge of the patient.

T: What is it?

J: It works.

T: This is when you're sick and put it in your mouth and then it shows how you are sick. (*Drops thermometer and picks up saw.*)

T: You're cutting. You're going to cut the box. It's a sawing sound.

J: (*Drill sound.*)

T: (*Hammering.*)

J: That's hammer.

T: That's a hammer.

J: This ... should spin around (*holding a drill*). And this listens to your heart.

T: Oh.

J: Look. ... (*Gasp.*) The game! Somebody just put this in here!

T: Oh, I see. That's where they are. The missing pieces.

J: Yes, we got it. We got it! (*Gasp.*) The seesaw!

T: The seesaw.

J: We found the missing game.

T: The missing pieces!

J: We found the seesaw! We found this.

T: That.

J: And we found the toilet.

T: We found the toilet. We found all of it.

J: Yeah!

The pleasure in finding the lost items from Mousetrap should be commented on as this exchange seems to speak to some significant issues related to separation and loss: "What special finding feelings to have when we thought those pieces were lost and could never be found!"

T: Or a lot of things anyway!
J: You clean this, and ...
T: I have to clean it up again?
J: Yes. We did not found the shoe!

He notes that not all has been found, and this should also be acknowledged: "So not all the losing feelings are gone; there are still some left because we can't find the shoe."

T: Jeesh, you're always making me clean it up.
J: Let see if they put it in the other place. Hey! There's a lot. There's a lot.
      (*Dumping out pieces from Trouble. Now seems like he's dumping things out. ...*) Now you put it back. Again!
T: Again?
J: Yup! Because I'm the officer. ...
T: The opposite? What did you say?
J: I am the officer!
T: You're the officer.

The theme of enacting control over the cleanup, now through the superego figure of "the officer," is revealed.

J: Look what they did to this. (*Pointing to where someone had drawn with marker on the top of a game box.*)
T: What does it mean, you're the officer?
J: Look, look what they did to the box.
T: Someone drew on it.
J: That's bad. Put them ... in JAIL!
T: You're the officer? What does that mean? You're the officer.

This approach feels too cognitive because it does not speak to the vehemence the patient projects onto the "bad" children who mark up the games. He is clearly wrestling with how much control he can be allowed and whether his aggression must be curbed by his inner self-punitiveness. I would speak to this conflict: "Marking up the game made for some very strong policing feelings. I wonder what those officer feelings are like?"

J: That means that you are ... the office.
T: I'm the office? What does that mean?
J: That's means you ... one red there. (*Picking up Trouble pieces.*) You forgot one block.
T: I forgot one block. Where?

J: There.

T: These things. I think they go there.

The fact that the therapist is willing to do the cleanup without fanfare or resentment probably facilitates the child's ability to shift one more time into the realm of play. Rule making around cleanup is often an overly rigidified aspect of the beginning therapist's training. While it is certainly a mistake to allow the room to become chaotic and overly cluttered, and it is often a mistake to allow the therapist to become a pawn and therefore a masochistic servant, there are indeed many times when shouldering the cleanup role is the lesser of two evils as an easy cleanup can pave the way for the child to regain his affective equilibrium and move on to other, more salient themes.

J: Let's get this. We found it! (*J takes out Mousetrap again and dumps out pieces. Sings "Found It" song.*)

T: It's exciting to find things, isn't it.

The therapist usefully speaks to the pleasures of finding things that were lost. His use of the word *exciting* feels accurate and attuned.

J: Yes! (*Keeps singing.*) Okay, let's find the ball. (*Singing.*) Where's the other ball? Just the one. Oh, no! They have to go right there. (*J is setting up a trap, and I moved one of the pieces.*) Do not move it again! It goes right there. It goes right there. Yes!

T: Yay!

J: We got it!

T: We got it!

J: Just like that!

T: Just like that!

The delight of first finding the pieces and now putting them together competently is effectively conveyed by the therapist's mirroring.

J: The pool. Pool, pool, pool. ...

T: J, we are going to have to stop for today in a minute.

J: Yeah, yeah. ... I don't get it! I don't get it! (*He turns this into a song. We try to put together some of the new pieces that we found for Mousetrap.*)

T: Where is the picture? There's a picture of it somewhere. Is it on that? The bottom? The box? Turn it upside-down. Ah. (*We look at the picture to see how the part goes.*)

J: (*Inaudible; trying to fit together parts of Mousetrap. I'm watching.*) How you put it?

T: Do you want me to help you? I can give you a hint. (*He has a piece that has two prongs in it. I point to another piece with two holes in it.*) One, two.

J: So why is it only one? Where's the other one? (*He figures it out when I point to the two prongs on the piece that he is holding.*) Dooo! (*I laugh.*)

T: Now you got it. You figured it out.

J: That's it. Okay, we can stop now.

Their pleasure in mutual play allows the child both to be self-reliant (using the box to figure out how the parts go) and to request help when needed. He seems to enjoy both roles and can end the session easily. It could be useful to reflect on the child's flexibility in this moment: "Sometimes doing-things-on-your-own feelings are best, and sometimes getting-help feelings are just as fun."

It is striking to note the many but subtle ways in which this child is psychologically healthier than the ones previously depicted. This is most clearly demonstrated by the broader range of affect he can tolerate, including on occasion the ability to tolerate multiple feelings or the feelings of both protagonists simultaneously. This manifests in his play by his being able to shift from the sadistic "master" to the frightened mice and back again. If one thinks of development as proceeding through a matrix of self, other, affects, and defenses, then the patient's better affect tolerance will profoundly affect and be affected by a more differentiated experience of self and others. The greater the child's expression of a variety of feelings without disruption, therefore, the broader will be his experience of others' emotions and then the broader his experience of self and the like in a cyclical way. This implies that this particular therapy can move more quickly than the others along the path toward greater psychological mindedness.

11 A 7-Year-Old Girl

K is in a long-term foster care placement and was originally referred for help with her behavior at home and disruptions in her relationships.

Before the session began, K came into the lounge to ask the time. This has become a ritual. In the hallway, K asked T if she had anything to say. This has become the second part of the greeting ritual.

K: Thank you—very—much. Hey, they used our chalk. (*Someone had left writing on the board in blue chalk that we got from the clinic during our last session.*)

T: Oh, I guess we left it out last time.

K: Use the white chalk, and that is the chalk that I love.

T: The white chalk is your favorite?

K: Yup. (*Pounding out the blackboard eraser.*) Okay W, listen to me, mm. You're W now, okay?

The patient is comfortable immediately switching into role-play and using the therapy room as a play space from the start. Work is therefore to be aimed at letting this play elaborate and build. It will not be necessary to spend nearly as much time creating a frame or responding to challenges to the frame.

T: Okay, I'll be W now.

K: Eh-hem, W, have you been studying? For the test?

T: Yes, I have been studying.

K: I hope you've been prepared, because the test that you're s'pposed to be taking is today. Now, since last time you was talkin', didn't want to be quiet, I just wanted to review. I said to myself, I'm just going to review with you, but I have a feeling that you might still not listen. So I said I'm just going to give you the test and give you the pen, pencil, whatever, marker, whatever you're gonna write in, gonna give you it and just let you do what you want. Because the last time, I told you I was not playing games because you were not listening to what I was saying. So I said to myself, well, we have a W that doesn't like to listen, so I should just let him get what he gets. Doesn't matter because I try to teach him, and tried to make a rhyme that time, but did I make up a rhyme that time? No, I just forget about the rhyme that time. The rhyme that time, rhymes with time. So I ss-said, if he's, if sh-, if he's gonna listen we can try it, but I said I don't want to be too big for that, so we're just going to start it, review it, and see if I want it to be correct. No, actually is it cor-rect? Because I know you haven't been studying, have you?

For our purposes, perhaps the most interesting part of this monologue is the child showing us through her role-play that she is capable of self-reflection, and that indeed she is wrestling ("I said to myself") with different ideas about how to proceed with her unruly student, W. This allows the therapist the luxury of either simply staying with the play or on occasion amplifying what it means to have an inner conversation: "I wonder how these different voices inside your head make up their mind about what to do with W?" It is important that any attempts to amplify her experience of self-monitoring be expressed through the metaphor of the play rather than through direct commentary on the patient herself. While the latter approach may break the plane of the play and may feel overly intellectualized, approaching the child's inner experience through metaphor maintains the play experience, which is the optimal way for the child to work through her conflicts.

T: I have.

K: You been studying for the test?

T: I have been, but maybe it wasn't enough.

K: Have you did your homework?

T: Yup.

K: Let me see that yup, since you yuppin' it up, let me see it.

T: Okay.

K: 'Cause if it's not all done, I can already tell what you gonna get on the test. And I'm not going to go through all them pages. Mm-hm (*looking in our notebook*). Okay, you did your homework. Yup, you did your homework, but you just forgot one thing.

T: I forgot one thing.

K: And I am not going to keep on telling you to do the spelling words that you did not do for the week.

T: Huh, the spelling words.

K: And how am I going to know who did this? No name right there, there's your name, there's no name right here. Just noticing that. Here, no name, no name, and no name. How do I know where this comes from? This could'a came from California, but did it?

T: Nope. I should'a put my name on it.

K: So why didn't you?

T: I guess I forgot.

Because the child has allowed talking about one's inner processes to be fair game, the therapist may now also do so in character: "Hmm, a part of me feels so dumb about forgetting stuff, but I have other feelings, too, like, 'Why is she always reminding me of how dumb I am?'"

K: You forget everything. You even forget your homework sometime.

T: (*I'm noticing that K has a booklet that looks unfamiliar, and I think she must have picked it up before our session.*) (*Whispering*) K, is that something that the mysterious collector brought today?

The therapist breaks the plane of the play to speak to the possibility of the patient having taken something from her. I am not sure why this would make sense in the context of their play, but perhaps the therapist has such confidence in her patient's ease of play that she can risk this diversion.

K: No, I brought this, no collector brought this. My mom gave me this. She don't need it from her old job. I'm glad she quit her old job. She said I could have it 'cause she don't use it. My sister got one, too, but she left hers home. But I brought mines because she says it got some kinda tests in here. But I'll make up my own tests 'cause my mother used to be a teacher.

T: She used to be a teacher and that's why she has some tests in there.

K: Yup.

T: But you're going to make up your own 'cause here you're the teacher.

K: Yup. So that's what. But I'm going to leave it here sometimes, because we might have more tests and more tests and more tests 'cause all these tests are going to help you with the next grade. And W, I have a feeling that you might not get left back. That's all I'm saying, you might—

The child does indeed shift easily back to play.

T: I might not.

K: And you better hope you don't because when that test comes you just better be prepared for it.

T: I sure hope I am prepared for that test and won't get left back.

This again might be a time to broaden the play to include multiple affects. The therapist is adept at speaking to the role of apprehension, but perhaps she could add the possibility of other affects: "I'm sure worried about that test, but other feelings keep coming through my head, too, like feeling sad and feeling dumb."

K: And you better hope you get a 90 or a 100 on this test 'cause I am marking this. And you should get this right. After we, we been going over this, and if you don't know it by the time, it's about time you should know it (*going through our box of things*). Now before we start, I'm gonna review. Re-view (*writing on the board*). High, made, what did high made?

T: Float?

K: And individually we will say, that, high, oopsy, oopsy (*erasing and rewriting*). High made float. So you need help? Keep looking up there. Now, you're gonna write these words down because these are the words you're gonna be using. Whatever, I'm gonna, I'm just gonna give you clues.

T: Okay.

K: Because these clues should be answers, and these answers should be clues. Now if you don't get these answers right, I just don't have nothing to say. All I'm wishing you luck is you get a 100. If you don't get a 100, sorry. Write these words down. (*Reading from the booklet.*) "Quiet."

T: (*I'm writing "quiet" on a piece of paper.*)

K: Mm-kay. Now, this is on-, this is the first clue that should be the answer. Whichever, wait, I want to say it this way. Whichever came first, came second, came third, make that first, make that second, and make that third. Whichever one made, came third, make that second, and whichever one ma-, came second, make that first. Now, action. A, T, A. Okay. And the last word is "harm."

T: Harm.

K: You may begin your test.

T: Okay. (*Wondering what that means.*)

K: You may begin your test. Teacher's guidebook, directions, nobody. Excuse me, what are you supposed to be doing now?

T: My test.

K: Looking at me, because I'll give you a big fat zero right now. Line, now come over here. I'm going to help you out. "Quiet," write "quiet." (*She's pointing to places on the page where I have to write the answers.*) Oops, I'm giving you the answers. (*Gasp!*) But I, say thanks—

T: You gave me the answers.

K: Say, "Thanks Miss X, now I'm 'na know it."

T: Thanks, Miss X, now I'll know it.

Here, it would be useful to verbalize W's inner state after receiving this unexpected gift from the teacher: "It sure felt good inside to get the answers from Miss X. I wonder why she gave them to me?"

K: Okay, just go ahead. I'm not trying to give you no more answers. Okay so, if quiet made something, what should that something go under?

T: Hmm, maybe it goes under action.

K: Up-ba-pa! You're supposed to write it down.

T: Write it down, okay.

K: That's all I was scratching for. And didn't you? Now for mine, draw a line. Put spelling errors.

T: Spelling errors?

K: Yeah, errors. Now, for your next assignment, write this, put a line, no I'll put the lines.

T: Okay.

K: Because you are just so slow, and I'm upside down. I would'a put it straighter, but I'm upside down. Now, you write this down. "Self-report. Given weekly. And reflective, interview. A-attachment, interview. Given at 1 year. Diary cards."

T: (*I see that the booklet contains psychological journal articles.*) Hmm. I hope I
　　　got it right.

K: Where's your period? Why would you put a period right there?

T: Oh, was that wrong?

K: I'm just gonna mark it the way it's supposed to be mark-ed.

T: Okay.

K: And when you mark it there, 'cause that was supposed to be a comma. That
　　　cost you, that, that, that cost you a 100%, you know that?

T: (*Gasp.*) A 100% just for the comma?

K: This. Yeah, and now it cost you 99%. You do things wrong, you get things
　　　wrong. Have you ever hearrrd of something like that?

T: I guess that's the way it is on the test.

The patient creates an authority figure who shifts erratically from benign to
malevolent. I would want to comment on what this might feel like for the child:
"Sometimes I think I shouldn't have to worry because the teacher seems to be
on my side, but then I get so worried because what I think is a small mistake
becomes something that makes me feel so scared and dumb."

K: It's, sh, but you going, but y-, you, at least you got something, at least it's get-
　　　ting hanged up.

T: (*Whispering, referring to the booklet.*) K, is that from someplace around here
　　　'cause it seems like something related to the clinic.

Again, the therapist focuses on the child's "stealing." This is always a hard
choice, between allowing "acting out" to come to its own resolution through the
play or choosing to confront it directly for fear that it would otherwise become
too strong an "elephant in the room." I would have opted not to confront it as the
play was moving along well.

K: My mom br-, I mean, my mom gave me this. We went for, 'cause I told her that
　　　I'm giving you a little test. She said, "Oh, test, let me just dig in my
　　　thing." I don't know what she be digging in, she's, I forgot what she call
　　　it. But she just said thing 'cause she don't want me to know, because
　　　'cause if I would'a went in the room with her, I would have blew on my
　　　surprise for my birthday. So I couldn't go in the room. But she gave
　　　me this, she said, "Well, this should help you with the t-test that you're
　　　giving." So I said, "Thanks mom." Then I left out the house.

T: (*I'm wondering how to respond to this because I know this isn't true.*)

This honest aside by the therapist speaks to why it might be preferable not to
bring this issue to the forefront. If the child's lying or stealing is truly inappro-
priate (the child has money or a wallet that obviously is not hers, for example),
then the issue cannot be allowed to fester. But in this, more common, case, the
child's "stealing" is relatively trivial compared to the conflicts raised by her play.

It therefore seems to make more sense to put the stealing on the back burner and to stay with the play.

K: Are you done?

T: Mm-hmm.

K: Okay. Now, W.

T: Yes?

K: Go up there. Erase the board. And if you can remember what you wrote, write it down on the board. Whether you get it right, whether you get it wrong, remember what you wrote on the piece of paper.

T: On the board, okay. Let's see. Starting from the first three words?

K: Remember what you wrote. ...

T: Okay (*writing*).

K: 'Cause this is still a test.

T: It's still a test. I just gotta do my best.

Rather than commenting solely on the action of "doing my best," the therapist could add a reflection on the inner state that accompanies this action: "Because it's still a test, I'm feeling worried test feelings as I'm not sure if I will be okay."

K: Yeah, that's all you gotta do. This is, do your best, this is still your test.

T: (*Writing all that I can remember, which isn't all of it.*) Hmm.

K: You're forgetting mighty words.

T: I know it. I'm forgetting a lot of words. Hmm. I don't think I can remember anymore. I think there's another. ...

K: Okay, so you're just gonna get that wrong.

T: Interview. ...

K: You can get what you need wrong, and you're not going to sit down until you get it right.

T: Boy, I'm probably never gonna sit down.

Again, it would be useful here for the therapist to reflect on her character's inner state as she thinks about this possibility: "I'm having never-sit-down feelings, and it makes me so worried inside." Speaking of "worried-inside" feelings both gives a name to a feeling state and locates this feeling state in the mind.

K: You're not, you're sure, right, you're not going to sit down because "self-report given weekly" was supposed to go first. You have it all mixed up.

T: I have it all mixed up. (*Trying to fix things on the board.*)

The therapist is effective at putting the feelings that arise from her passive role into action, but to broaden the frame she could articulate the feeling states that accompany these actions: "Once I start having those never-sit-down feelings, my mind gets more worried, and I can't remember things, so the worried feelings just grow inside."

K: (*Opening juice with keys.*) Excuse me, erase that that's right there, on the bottom.

T: On the bottom?

K: And right there.

T: And right here?

K: Yeah. Now continue writing.

T: Okay. Hmm.

K: If I say—okay, I'm going to give you something. All I know is "and reflect, interview."

T: Oh, "and … reflect … interview." Thank goodness you gave me that clue, I wouldn't have remembered that. Maybe now it's "attachment interview" (writing) … "diary" … hmm.

Just when it looks as though the patient will be unforgiving, she becomes generous, showing a deeper, more benevolent connection to the therapist (and hence a less-archaic superego) than the patients in Chapters 6 and 9. This allows for greater ability on the therapist's part to broaden the affective frame by including more direct expressions of ambivalence: "So, my never-sit-down feelings change when I hear you give me a clue. Then, I have I'm-not-so-alone feelings to balance the seesaw."

K: Let me see if I have that on m-, the paper that you gave me. "Self-report given weekly," I have that. "Reflective interview," I have that. "Attachment interview," I have that, but you're missing one more thing.

T: I'm missing one more thing. Hmm.

K: And I'm always saying that word, you, you better hit stuff back, you better hit stuff back, you better give his stuff back, you better gi- … um.

T: Give?

K: But what, what gotta be added to it on the bottom, to the bottom?

T: To the bottom. "Give." …

K: "Given" goes before "diary."

T: Oh, "given" goes before "diary."

K: And you should have left "diary."

T: I should have left "diary."

K: Wait a minute. Erase, no, forget it.

T: "Given," something, and then "diary."

K: Add your own year!

T: Add my own year.

K: Add 1 year.

T: "One year" (writing), comma.

K: Nooo.

T: No comma.

K: You put what you had before.

T: Oh, okay. I put a period before and that was wrong, and then "diary cards."

K: Sit down 'cause don't you feel stupid. Piary cards! (*She's referring to a small stem protruding from the bottom of my* D *in* diary *that she sees as a* P.)

T: Oh, my *D* doesn't even look right! I do feel stupid.

The therapist adds a feeling state to her description of her actions, and the patient responds with a more benign grade.

K: You got two things wrong, now you got a 94%.
T: Two things wrong, and now I'm down to 94%. Oh boy! I don't know if that's going to be good enough.
K: Let me see what I want to put. Hmm. (*Goes into the corner and lies down facing away from me with the test paper.*)
T: I don't know if I'm going to pass or fail. … Am I going to pass the test or fail it? Am I going to get promoted or get left back? I'm not sure what's going to happen.

The therapist again does a fine job of describing her ideas, which is a step closer to the child's experience than simply describing actions. Going one more step and speaking of her character's feelings would be a still closer approximation of what it feels like to be this child: "Not knowing what's going to happen makes me feel so shaky inside, and so weak."

K: (*In strange voice*) Your testimony that I have given you is really bad.
T: Oh no.
K: You have one tell (*inaudible*) to represent. And that if you don't believe me, (*stranger voice*) I'll show you. (*Comes over with paper.*) (*Singing*) Zeros are not good enough for me.
T: (*Gasp.*) A 100%!
K: (*Singing*) Zeros are not good enough for me. Zeros are not that good enough for me.
T: Zeros are not that good enough for you, but you gave me a 100%!
K: 'Cause I was telling myself, "He did try. He did. He had, he-he had it going on! He, he, if he gets everything right, of course, but in class," I said to myself, "Why should I give him a 100% if in class he doesn't even do what he's supposed to do?" But then I looked at, I looked at it again. I said, "Well, sometimes he do try to do what he needs to do." (*Breathes out.*) And then I said to myself, "This is the only time I will be giving you a 100% because next round for the science test there won't be, be giving no 100%. (*Takes a breath.*) Because you know why there won't be a 100%, because, because, okay let me just finish. Oh, the announcements are about to start. (*Looks for stethoscope to use as a mic.*)

The patient demonstrates her capacity to hold competing ideas and affects about the same person in her mind and to let herself process this "debate" until she decides what to do. I would add to this: "So it seemed like you had two parts of yourself, each with different feelings and ideas: a part that feels angry that W is not good enough, and another part that feels that he tries so hard that you can feel kind feelings toward him."

T: The announcements.

K: (*As Miss P, the principal*) Hello, students. Hello, everybody. This is my first day back because I was sick. (*Coughs.*) Excuse me, I forgot to cover my mouth. As you can see, this is everybody's first day back. Visitors are coming today, and when the visitors come, let's see what class can do the best. 'Cause whatever class is the best will be getting a pizza party.

T: (*Whispers*) A party.

K: (*Whispers*) Say, "Yes, yes!"

T: (*Whispers*) Yes, yes!

K: And I'm hoping my bestest class, and my bestest student, did well on that test. And that student is a boy, and his name is W.

T: (*Gasp.*)

K: He's in Miss X's class, here every day, not absent, always on time, and most of all he's never bad because when I walk in he's working. That's what I would like to see in Miss L's class, but I always do. I have two favoritest boys and two favoritest girls, but W is my home student because he works with me. He, he, he gets along with people. 'Cause when I'm around, he, he's all good.

T: Wow.

K: But I don't know what Miss X's talking about. When he is with Miss X, he acts a fool, but now he's fit 'cause he knows if I catch him with not doing the rrright work, he knows what's gonna happen. But like I was saying, get back to the pizza party, I know your class is probably going to be here every day. Tell their mother, just write a note to their mothers and say, "If your child can be here every day and not one student absent." Because I would like the note to be here and at my desk, P.S. 1,000. But I'll, I already know who will be being first class and second class, which I already announced. I already know them two classes, don't even have to write notes because—

T: (*Gasp.*) I hope it's Miss X's class.

The patient plays out a long, involved fantasy in which she is the generous authority figure who is no longer the critical superego but the gift-giving gratifier, and the therapist is the delighted recipient of her largesse. The therapist uses her "gasp" to connote her wishes coming true, but this is another time when positive affect could also be broadened: "What a wonderful, wish-come-true feeling, to be picked by the principal to win a special prize. It makes all my worried and dumb feelings go so far away."

K: Hmm?

T: I hope it's Miss X's class.

K: (*Nods.*) And uh, as you can see, as far as those two classes have been on time, none of them, all of them, not none of them, all of them been wearing uniforms. They wear their uniform shoes, uniform colors. If they don't wear the uniform, they wear the colors. They make sure they wear the uniform shoes to let them know that they are wearing the uniform colors. So, I want to announce the two classes that have been here on time and the teachers have been not yelling them out. The class I'm giving the award to is Miss X's class!!! Yay!!!

T: Yah!! Hurray!!

K: Everybody give a round of applause (*clapping*)! Woo! The award to get has been given to Miss X's claaasss!!

T: Yay!!

K: Once again the award has been given to Miss X's claaasss!! They have been on time! None of their students have been late!! They're THERE EVERY DAY!! BUT MISS X AND HER CLASS ARE THERE EVERY DAY!! MISS S's CLASS IS THERE EVERY DAY!! The award is once again is given to Miss X and Miss S!! (*clapping*)

T: Yaaaay!! (*clapping*)

K: So the awards have been given to them, they will be having a PIZZA PARTY!!

T: Woo-hoo!

K: Halloween party!!

T: Yaaay!!

K: CHRISTMAS PARTY!!! A Thanksgiving, Happy New Year's party! They'll be having so many parties. THEY WON'T EVEN BE GETTING ONE MORE, NAA???!!!

T: Yaay!!

K: I will be going up to classes, seeing work, but I already know Miss S's class is a fourth-grade class, Miss X's class is a sixth-grade class. They will be doing sixth-grade work. 'Cause I was giving the award to MISS X'S CLAAASSS!!

T: Yaaayy!!

K: I'm sorry to not say names, but I gotta go. (*Muffled, speaking into the stethoscope.*) What time it will begin. She'll come back on, when needed if pos-si-ble.

(*As Miss X again*) So as you can see you have been given an award. And when Miss P walks in this room we're going to give her an award. But first of all, something, write the math on the board 'cause the math is gonna consider this. (Writes 2 on the board.) Who knows what that is?

T: (*Raises hand.*)

K: What?

T: Two?

K: Good for you. That's one award for W.

T: Wow.

K: And if he gets this one he has three awards besides two. (*Writes on the board.*) That is not a number, but it's a letter.

T: A letter, *Z?*
K: You're not raising your hand.
T: Oh, oh! (*Raising hand.*) The letter *Z?*
K: Good for you, W. Three awards in a row.
T: Wow! Three awards. I can't believe it.

I would elaborate on W's feeling state here, as his fortune changes in such sudden shifts: "It makes even more of my worried, angry feelings go away. It's almost like they've disappeared. Will they stay away forever or will they come back, I wonder?"

K: Now when Miss P comes up here that's how you should be acting. Now when she calls your name on the loudspeaker, and she announces, she announced it, so of course you should be good. (*Drawing a picture on the board.*) And today we will be learning about one of W's favoritest things that he always wanted to learn about. And that is volcanoes.
T: Volcanoes.
K: Now, I won't give you any math today because W's name has been rewarded, and that's one of my students, and we have been given an award and a pizza party and he's invited for the first time. But he has three awards, and the rest of y'all don't. But y'all do, y'all don't have three awards but you have ten, but don't worry, it's just cause I'm giving it to him. It's not funny M, you have three right along with him, and actually you have none.
      (*As M*) But I need some, please Miss X. You been giving me some before W.
      (*As Miss X*) What's so funny, fat J? 'Cause if you want me to make jokes we can start the jokes. So W, would y-you like to come up here and explain about volcanoes?

The patient's gift-giving role is under duress. She appears to want to punish some of the other children but becomes a bit confused regarding whether to carry out punishments or reward others. I might carry this in one of two ways: either "Those other kids are hungry for getting these same prizes as W, and they're worried that they're not going to get them" or "W is starting to get some of his worried feelings back as he hears the principal getting annoyed at some of the other kids." The goal is to have the patient begin to own both her positive fantasies and her fears of recrimination and shame simultaneously rather than alternating between them in a more split-off manner.

T: Okay.
K: And write something about them. Huh?
T: Okay.
K: Okay. Is that the way I taught you how to say manners?
T: No, I guess I should have said "Yes."

K: Okay, don't, don't, don't say, "I think I should have said 'Yes.'" Just say, "I should have said Yes."

T: I should have said "Yes."

In the same vein, I might have added here, "Oh no, now I'm really starting to have those old inside feelings like I can't do anything right. But I'll do whatever Miss P asks so I can just have her good feelings come my way, and then maybe my worried feelings will disappear again."

K: Yeah, that's gooder. Here comes Miss P. Get ready, push your chair in, hold your thing up. (*Taping my test up on the bulletin board.*) Just hold on. Hold on just a minute, Miss P. W, spell your name again.

T: W.

K: Correct!

T: Wow, you put my work up on the board.

K: So Miss P, so Miss P can be happy.

This might be a moment when one could attempt to turn Miss P into less of a one-dimensional being: "I wonder what it feels like inside to be someone as powerful as Miss P?"

T: Miss P will get to see it.

K: This (*inaudible*). (*Instructing me on how to stand.*) Turn, facing the board, back, back, back. You're losing your mind? (*Opens the door for the imaginary Miss P.*)

T, K: Good morning, Miss P.

K: (*As Miss P*) Thank you, I got that. (*K whispers to me to show Miss P my test after we say good morning.*)

T, K: Good morning, Miss P, how are you doing?

The child is able to play multiple roles, although Miss P and Miss X are nearly identical in their praise for the therapist's character. The child is immersed in this world of gratification, sending any notion of shame into hibernation. It is fascinating, although probably coincidental, that the topic of the day is volcanoes, as one wonders where all of the patient's rage goes when she is praising this all-good, all-compliant student.

K: (*As Miss P*) I'm doing very fine. I just came up here to check on your fresh, your class that I have seen.

T: Miss P, look at my test score.

K: (*Gasp.*) A 100% on a test, W. What have you been working on? Hmm (*reads the test*). You have it wrong, but you get it right because you get (*inaudible*) "diary cards." Wow, what a coincidence. Are you supposed to be doing something up here?

(*As Miss X*) Oh yeah, Miss P, he's, he's, he's telling us about volcanoes, that we want to learn about volcanoes, and he's going to tell us about volcanoes, and you may begin. ... As you can see. ...

T: As you can see, in the volcano, the inside is very hot. And it's filled up with lava. See, Miss X drew all these lines here to show how the lava flows. And this is the outside of the volcano that is cool. (*I look at K to see if I should continue.*)

K: Draw something. Tell us about the (*inaudible*).

T: And then when the volcano erupts, all the pressure from the inside of the volcano pushes the lava out. And then the lava flows down the side of the volcano in big, red, hot streams.

K: Come out.

T: They come out. And you have to be very careful because they're so hot that they burn up everything in their path.

K: So, what do we have to do in order not to get burned? We have to. ...

T: We have to make sure that we move out of the way.

K: And, be pro—

T: Proactive?

K: Protected.

T: Protected.

K: And what will happen, W? And what he means that it just burns up? The inside right here will go into pieces, so there will not be no more volcanoes. But the inside, which is the—help me out, W.

T: The lava?

K: The inside's the lava? So which is the inside is the lava, we put a circle around that, because we know that got burnt. But if this woulda came a little closer, we woulda got killed, because this is people, or uh, this is W, even though that's not how you look (drawing two people), and this is me. And that's you. We're mad 'cause we got burnt. But these th-, these things right here are people. They're going across the sea because they want to kill us. (*Draws dots for the people.*)

Almost on cue, the split-off rage comes to the foreground as the volcano becomes a real-life danger to the characters created by the patient.

T: What are we gonna do?

K: So Miss X, we tried to walk away. W, I called him, but he walked the other way.

T: (*Gasp.*) Oh, no.

K: I tried to get him, so I went this way (*draws dots for W's path*). By the time you knew it, he was dead. So he was over here by the fire.

T: Oh, no.

K: (*Draws W by the lava.*) Crying tears like this. And here's Miss X (*draws Miss X*). "Help me" (*writes the words next to Miss X*).

T: Miss X, help me!

K: So I came to the rescue, and here am I. But I'm in the lava, too?

T: Oh, no.

The volcano saga shifts the splitting from smartness/dumbness and praise/shame to life or death: "Wow, so I used to have worries about schoolwork, but now I don't know if I'll live or die, and I so need Miss X to save me!"

K: So I'm not dead, I went over here. I picked it up, and I threw it in the water, and after you know, everything was okay. But me and W, well W was hurtin' because he was crying out tears and couldn't control himself. (*Draws tears all around W.*) So he has tears all around him, even on my letters.

T: Crying everywhere.

K: Even cried on me, ew, got me wet.

T: Oh, I cried on Miss X, too.

K: So I got split up. And he even drownded himself and still said, "Miss X, help me."

T: I drowned in my own tears! Help me, Miss X.

The therapist uses the tears metaphor beautifully but perhaps could also have expanded on the feeling states expressed by these tears: "I'm so full of scared and sad feelings that my tears won't stop."

K: And once that was saved, he came back to the rescue. He, his feet was only there, and this was me. He left me into pieces. Now I'm going over here. (*Draws dots to show circular path Miss X travels.*) I went into the lava. I said, "Why are you doing this?" He said, he came. He took me back around and put me back in here. (*Draws path.*) So W came. "Excuse me, Miss X." (*Draws W's path, the same circular path as before.*) "Why are you doing this to me?" So we took W to come a short way to put him back in there. So we both came. (*Draws the path for W and Miss X, the same circular path.*)

T: Where were we going?

K: We were taking the shortcut.

T: We're taking the shortcut.

K: Because this is the water, and we threw it on them.

T: On the bad guys?

K: Yup. And we said, "That should do." So we came back over here. We still was walking (*draws path*). We came out. Woo! (*She falls on the floor face down.*)

T: Oh no! Miss X collapsed! She must have been tired from all that walking. (*I sit down next to her.*)

K: No, I hurt my knee.

T: Oh, no! She hurt her knee!

K: (*Pretending to cry*) Rub it!

T: Oh, no. Poor, poor knee! I'll put a big Band-Aid on it. This is the bandage especially for knees. We'll wrap it up (*wrapping noises*). Oh, no, I better put some medicine on it, too (*medicine noises*).

A remarkable shift in the play has occurred. The evil of the dangerous volcano is first personified into "bad guys," but this proves too difficult to bear affectively, so the child collapses in the play and reverses roles, wanting and needing to be the one taken care of. The therapist seamlessly understands this and provides important caretaking, which could be augmented by the following: "It's such dangerous and exhausting work to protect kids from bad guys, so now Miss X can get her feelings and her knee taken care of." In this case, I would intentionally avoid fully converting the hurt into affect, instead allowing the somatization and the affective experience to coexist.

K: (*Sobbing.*)

T: And then we'll put the bandage on it. That one's all bandaged up.

K: (*Sobbing.*) Ooowww!

T: It still hurts! It hurts!

K: Oowww! Aaah! Aaaaah!

T: Should I do the other one?

K: Aaaaaahwooo!

T: Oh no! It hurts, it hurts. Maybe I should put the medicine on the other one. Medicine for stopping knee pain. (*At some point, I put my hand on her back and leave it there. She is turned away from me so I can't see her face.*)

It is evident that, although the therapist is clearly feeling that the patient is "protesting too much," the child has gone from pretending to cry through the play to a "real" experience of injury that completely disrupts the play. I might speak to this: "Oh no, it seemed like you went from Miss X being hurt for pretend to really hurting yourself."

K: (*Sobbing.*) It hurts. It hurts.

T: Yeah, it hurts. I'll put a Band-Aid on it. It's gonna be okay. I know, it hurts so much.

K: (*Sobbing.*)

T: It hurts that much. You're crying and crying and crying. Ooh.

K: (*Cries harder.*)

T: Oh. It hurts. It still hurts.

K: Oowoo!

T: Oooh!

K: Aaaaah! (*Cries and sobs.*)

T: Ooooh! Poor knee. Poor knee. Oooh. All bandaged up now. Yeah. Oooh. It hurts. Poor knee. It got hurt. Maybe we need more knee medicine over here. And more over here. And a big bandage on top.

K: Oooowww.

T: Yeaaah.

K: (*Her sister Z knocks on the door.*) Who is it?

Z: It's me.

K: What happened?

Z: I have to ask you something.

K: What ha—what? (*Crawls over to the door and stands up. Opens the door a crack.*) What is it?

Z: Do you have the right time? 'Cause we don't have the right time in there.

T: Yeah, we have 2 minutes left.

Z: Oh, okay. Thank you.

K: (*Closes the door. Sniffs and collapses on the floor against the door.*) Ow. Uuuuhh!

T: Yeaaah. Ooow. Ouch.

K: Mmm. Mmmm. Uhhh. Uuuhh. (*Crying more softly now.*)

T: That really hurt. Yeaaaah. So many tears.

K: (*Cries harder.*)

T: Sounds scary. It hurt so much, it was scary. Yeaaah.

K: (*Cries harder.*) Aaaaaaah! Oooooo! Oooooo!

T: Poor knee. Poor knee.

K: (*Strangled sounds.*) Oow! My bad knee!

It is truly remarkable to witness the degree of somatization enacted by this patient. In a profoundly visceral way, this somatization reveals the degree to which false compliance, wish fulfillment, and fear of attack were all rolled into one during the school role-play. Although this child clearly has the beginnings of ambivalence, and hence work was directed at broadening her affective range, she is still only at the cusp of being able to acknowledge such multiple feeling states. She is more broadly situated in an emotional phase in which all-good versus all-bad splits continue to predominate, and the collapse of her all-good persona into a fragile, somatized place is quite evident. The therapist is terrifically able to stay with her pained state but could also have attempted to use words to create some distance from the literalness of her physical pain: "That hurt knee is so painful, it makes the whole world feel painful and like it will never stop being painful, and that's scary."

T: Your bad knee. Ooh. You know what, K?

K: Oh.

T: It's time to stop for today.

K: My knee really hurts.

T: Oh, I know. It really, really hurts.

K: Mmm. Ooh.

T: I'm going to put our stuff together.

K: Give me my crackers.

T: More crackers. Maybe that'll help.

The child asks for her crackers to ease the pain and to continue literally to get something from the therapist. The therapist not only gives the crackers but also links them to her pain ("Maybe that'll help"). I might have added: "When you get your knee-hurting feelings, maybe the only thing that helps is to know that someone will give you something so you won't feel so alone."

K: No, all of them.

T: All of them. All of the crackers.

K: And the napkin.

T: And the napkin.

K: (*Gradually gets up.*) Your homework is to draw a volcano and write what we was doing in class. And do the rest of the homework that you have not completed.

The crackers do the trick. She is able to resume her prior role as the teacher. Importantly, although the teacher is giving out assignments, she is not overly full of praise or criticism, as if the "being-fed" feelings enable her to take a less all-or-nothing stance toward the therapist.

T: Okay.

K: Even the spelling.

T: K, I need to know where this came from (*referring to the booklet she brought*). Was it out someplace on the table or in the trash someplace? 'Cause I'm not sure that we can keep this.

K: Hmm?

T: I need to know where this came from. Um, I'm not sure we can keep this 'cause if this belongs to one of the professors, then I need to make sure that they get it back. Where did you pick it up?

K: It was, it was outside.

T: Outside?

K: In the, um, thing. It was on the floor, so I picked it up, and I brung it in here.

T: Oh, outside, outside the building or in the hallways?

K: Outside in the building.

T: Outside the building? Okay. 'Cause it seems like something from around here, and I just want to make sure that it's okay for us to hang onto it.

K: I found that outside.

T: Okay. On the floor?

The therapist ends the session by bringing back the booklet and where it came from. At first, it seems the child is admitting that she took the booklet, but then she shifts to claiming it was found outside, thus making her less liable to be condemned by the therapist.

K: It was sitting right there. And the man has said, "Hey, is that yours?" I said, "No." But I said, "No." I still remember. I have to say something. She didn't give me my present. Until she doesn't give me my present, (*whispers*) I'm gonna fuck her up. I'm gonna, I'm gonna kick her so fuckin' hard I'll fuckin' bring it all fuckin' down. That bitch don't give me back my fuckin' shit I'm gonna fuck the bitch up. That bitch better, let me tell, that bitch better, I'm gonna fuck her up like my nigger. My nigger that fucked the bitch. Bye. Bye-bye. (*K wants to listen to the recording. I rewind it for her further than the part she recorded. She hears herself crying and looks surprised. She smiles when she hears our voices when we were talking later in the session.*)

In a truly incredible demonstration of how much of the session was a "false self" representation of good behavior masking deeply malevolent material, the patient launches into a long harangue of bravado-driven, obscenity-laced "ghetto" profanity in which she can be the dominant, fearless aggressor. Fascinatingly, she then wants to play back the tape, ostensibly to hear her bravado, but is surprised by her crying. It is as though she is using the tape to help her digest and integrate these split-off aspects of her self and to have these parts of herself be witnessed and held by the therapist. The patient's ability to use the tape recorder in this way, to reveal the intensely primitive hatred that she has kept hidden, speaks both to her resourcefulness and to the significance of the holding environment that has been created in the session. I would have wanted to address this: "So in our work together, we can hear the parts of you that are full of the most angry feelings, as well as parts of you that are so hurt, and even parts of you that can be happy. We can work together on figuring out how all these different feelings make up one K."

The child's sudden shift in this moment also casts her earlier metaphor of the volcano in a different light, revealing it to have been, in fact, more than a metaphor. Rather than remaining symbolic, the idea of the volcano stirred up a desire for an actual explosion, and this is exactly what happened: At the end of the session, she literally "erupted," going up to the tape recorder and spilling out "lava." This viscerally demonstrates the gradations among play, fantasy, and reality and the ways in which these modes of being constantly shift and interact.

12 An 11-Year-Old Girl

This child has anxiety symptoms related to biweekly visitations to her father, which were court-ordered after her parents were separated. Her anxiety symptoms included compulsive thoughts and obsessive behaviors during visits. In addition, her teacher reported changes in her social behavior, which include her participation in power struggles around friendships as well as withdrawal during class activities.

L: (*Looks around the room.*) Mm … Let's play with this (*points at the dollhouse*).
T: This?
L: Yes.
T: Put it on the table?
L: (*Takes it and puts it on the table.*) Okay, I was her and … hey, let's start a new game.
T: A new game?
L: Yeah. All right, so, again, I'll be her (*white female doll*) 'cause I like her hairdo.
T: You do?
L: Mm-hmm (*yes*).
T: Okay.
L: Want to be him?
T: Should I?
L: Ah. … Who do you want to be?
T: I don't know.
L: You get to choose since I chose, you get to choose.

This child presents with a sense of fairness and, as underlies any sense of fairness, some capacity to reflect on another's experience. This permits the therapist to take some degree of reflection as a given and both to assess the limits of this capacity and to broaden it if possible.

T: Oh, I do? Oh, okay. Ah. … What should I choose?
L: Well, I think it would be cool if you'll be her (*Black female doll*) and him (*White male doll*), and I'll be her (*White female doll*) and him (*Black male doll*). That will be cool. So, how about this … how about … um … how about they are boyfriends and girlfriends (*points at one couple*), and they are boyfriends and girlfriends (*points at the other couple*), but the problem is that when they double date, these two (*Black male and Black female dolls*) start liking each other, and these two (*White male and White female dolls*) get mad because they like them, but …

Unlike the child in our previous case, this patient immediately organizes her play around a multiple set of players with multiple longings, both loving and angry. It is also striking that the child makes the couples interracial (the child is of color), suggesting a wish on her part to explore this issue. Often, a child of color will use multiracial dolls as a means of testing the waters, of assessing whether a White therapist will be able to tolerate discussing race in the treatment. It is vital for the therapist to acknowledge the child's "experiment." I might say, "I wonder what role their skin color is going to play in how they wind up feeling about each other." This incorporates the role of skin color into the larger issue of developing self-awareness in the context of relationships.

T: Oh, they do like them. Okay.

L: So. All right. So, these are the beds. Okay (*takes the White female doll and the Black male doll*). "You should probably go to work now, here is the muffin." "Thank you, honey." (*Dolls kiss.*) "Have a good day." "Bye." I'll give the rest of the muffins to them (*goes to the other couple's imaginary house*).

The question for this session becomes, "At what point do you start to add affective coloring to a child's play that is already establishing itself as affectively sophisticated?" It would most likely be best to say nothing here, but as a clinical guide, one could add the following: "Having some muffins to start the day is a very warm feeling."

T: Hello.

L: Oh, I baked some muffins, but my husband doesn't like them. Would you like them?

T: (*As woman*) Sure! Thank you.

Or, the therapist might say, "Hmm, I'm wondering why her husband would not want muffins. What was going on in his mind about that if she made them for him?"

L: You're welcome.

T: (*As man*) Thank you very much.

L: You're welcome.

T: (*Makes noises of eating.*)

L: (*Laughs.*) All right, well I'm going to do some cleaning, but I'm planning a little surprise birthday party for my boyfriend Todd. Oh, names, I forgot names. What are their names (*points at the dolls I'm suppose to play*)?

T: Ok, this is Todd. Right? And his name is, ah ... Joe. Okay?

L: Okay, that's a good name. What's her name?

T: Ah ... Joe and ...

L: Joe and ... how about ... Janet?

T: Janet? Okay, Joe and Janet.

L: All right. Hers will be Lillian, so Todd and Lillian.

T: Okay.

L: So, I'm planning a little surprise party for Todd for tonight, and I think it would
be good to go to a restaurant for dinner tonight. We're actually going to
go to a great restaurant that I saved up money for. I actually have little
money; he gets all the money because he works, but anyway, I wanted
to ask you if you want to come for a double date.

There are so many possible pathways to consider here. One is the meaning of
surprise, especially of an oral surprise: "Well, first she bakes him muffins, and
now she's wanting to surprise him with dinner. Giving food is surely an important
feeling for Lillian. I wonder why?" One might also speak to her statement of having little money and yet saving up for him: "What a sacrifice, saving up so much
money and then spending it on him. I wonder what that feels like?" Or even, "He
works for all the money, what goes through her mind about that?"

T: Oh, sure, that would be great.

L: Thanks. Oh, you guys don't have to worry about gifts. You can get one if you
want, but it's okay, he is not a gift guy.

T: He doesn't like gifts?

To further explore this dynamic around gift giving, I might ask, "What would
a gift guy feel like, and what would it feel like to not need to get gifts?"

L: He loves gifts, but he doesn't mind if people don't bring them; he is just happy to
come. Ah, see you tonight. And you can wear whatever you want, he is
a very casual person, he doesn't like. ... You can dress up if you want.

T: Okay!

L: (*Lillian*) Good day.

T: (*Janet*) Good day.

(*Joe*) Good day.

L: (*Todd*) Good day (*laughs*).

(*Lillian*) Oh, I have to buy myself a dress. Mm ... I have to go get a
dress (*falls on her way down the stairs*).

T: She fell.

It is striking that after all her gift giving, she falls just after stating that she will
get something for herself. In light of this, I would try asking, "Is it dangerous to
want things, I wonder?"

L: Mm-hmm (*yes*). All right, okay, get in the car from the driveway. Janet, I was
wondering if you want to help me pick up a nice dress. I'll buy you a
dress for it, too.

T: Okay, let's go.

L: Oh, sorry Joe; it's women shopping, but here, here is some money to buy you
         a suit.
T: You are giving me money to buy a suit?

The play is increasingly about the patient's need to pay for everything, even though she does not have much: "It seems like Lillian has two feelings, how hard it is to not have much money and how necessary it feels to buy things for everyone. What is it like to have these so-generous feelings?"

L: Mm-hmm (*yes*).
T: Can I join you?
L: Oh, sure you can, even though we're going to be in women's department stores,
         so I knew you will be bored.
T: Oh, okay, so I can stay here.
L: Well, if you want, you can come.
T: Yeah, okay, I will come.
L: Okay, jump in the back seat! (*Drives the car.*) Okay, here we are!
T: (*Joe*) Well, where are we going?
L: You will stay here. The women's department is upstairs.
T: Okay. (*I'm taking Janet and going upstairs.*) Oh, where did she go?
L: Just for the dressing room; right now we'll be downstairs. Sorry.
T: (*I'm going down the stairs to join Lillian.*)
L: Wow, look at this one. This is gorgeous; Janet, this will look beautiful on you!
         It matches with your eyes. Why won't you try it on?
T: Okay!
L: I'll try the red one. I'm sorry, Joe, you can't come with us. We'll be back down-
         stairs soon. Go look at the watches or something if you want.
T: Okay, I'll be waiting.
L: Ah, Janet?
T: Yeah?
L: The dressing room is up here!
T: Oh, okay (*going upstairs*).
L: Oh, it feels too big. That's a size 6, maybe I need a 5½. I'm going to see if they
         have a 5½.
T: Okay. I need to put this dress on. Okay.
L: Oh, that looks gorgeous! It matches so much with your eyes! The blue, and the
         purple and the indigo, that's beautiful!

I wonder if this focus on the therapist's character's eyes is also a link to her actual eye and skin color. As this is the second indirect reference to race, I would add, "Yes, White people often have blue eyes. We seem to be talking about how our skin and eyes are different from one another." It is always vital to bring patient-therapist differences into the frame of the treatment experience if they are even remotely referenced by the patient, as an exploration of these differences and the feelings they evoke can serve as yet another means of broadening the frame of reflection.

T: Oh, thank you.

L: You should love it, you should probably. Oh, here, do you want that one or do you want to look at something else?

T: Yeah, if you feel that it's good, I guess I will take it, yeah.

L: All right, let's go get it!

T: What about you?

L: I still have this dress, but you have to tell me what you think of it first.

T: Okay.

L: What do you think?

T: Let's see. (*Whispering*) Does she like it?

The therapist adroitly uses the whispered aside to allow the child to direct the play. Especially in play that is this rich in content, it would be an asset to let the child direct the content where she most wants it to go.

L: Oh, she thinks it's a little too big.

T: I think it's a little too big; I'm not sure.

L: Maybe I need a 5.

T: Maybe you do. Do you want to try a 5?

L: Yeah. Oh, no!

T: What happened?

L: There is only 4½; there is no 5!

T: Oh, do you want to try the 4½?

This is one of the first times when the child expresses disappointment, so I would very much want to bring this affect into the play: "Now, she suddenly has to deal with not getting what she so wants. I wonder how that makes her feel inside?"

L: I guess I'll have to! All right, you need to decide.

T: Okay, oh, let me see. Maybe it's a little small?

L: I guess I need to find a different dress. Oh, look at this one, it's gorgeous. Look at this black one; it reminds me of my freshman year in college!

T: Wow! It's beautiful!

So the disappointment of losing the first dress is replaced quickly by the beauty of this black one. What a relief!

L: Thank you. Let me put it on.

T: Try it on! What size is it?

L: This? This is a size 5.

T: Okay. Wow, it looks so good.

L: Thank you.

T: Beautiful.

L: Thank you.

T: You want to get it?

L: Sure, I'll buy you the dress.

T: You will? Oh, thanks.

Again, this generosity is omnipresent and should be addressed: "What a delicious feeling. Every time I want something, she gets it for me. I feel so given to."

L: You're welcome! All right, we'll take this one and that one.

　　　　(*Cashier*) To wrap it or wear it on?

　　　　(*Lillian*) We'll wrap it. Okay, thank you.

　　　　(*To Joe*) Hello!

T: (*Joe*) Hi!

L: What do you think of our dresses?

T: Well, I need to look at them first. Right? (*L shows me the dresses.*) Oh, they are beautiful, I can't wait to see you in them.

L: Thanks. Okay, let's go (*drives home*). Honey, I'm home!

　　　　(*Todd*) Hi sweetie, oh gosh, I missed you so much!

　　　　(*Lillian*) Missed you, too! So, I am going to get my dress on, all right?

　　　　(*Todd*) Have you been shopping lately?

　　　　(*Lillian*) Yes, I admit, I'm guilty. But, we are going to dinner.

　　　　(*Todd*) Really? A friendly dinner or a date dinner?

　　　　(*Lillian*) A friendly dinner. Let me go change, you—sit, read sports magazines, play video games.

　　　　(*Todd*) You said not to do that, so how come you tell me that I can do it? Can I put my feet on the couch?

　　　　(*Lillian*) Yes, go ahead! But remember, after today, you're back to "no feet on the couch."

　　　　(*Todd*) Oh … (*laughs*).

T: Because it's his birthday?

L: Aha. Put on the dress. Heels.

　　　　(*Lillian*) Tada!

　　　　(*Todd*) Oh, honey, you look gorgeous! (*Kissing and hugging.*)

　　　　(*Lillian*) We are going to go to dinner.

　　　　(*Todd*) Okay.

　　　　(*Whispering to me*) Get in the car.

T: (*Whispering*) What?

L: (*Lillian*) Get in the car quickly so he won't notice.

T: All of us?

Since surprises are becoming a central theme, this would be a good opportunity to explore the feelings stirred up by surprises: "I wonder what it feels like to give such a surprise, and I also wonder what it will feel like for Todd to get such a surprise?"

L: (*Lillian*) Aha. Okay, let's go. (*Janet and Joe are in the back seat. I am holding them and moving them as if they were in the car with Lillian and Todd. Lillian drives the car. She drives it faster and faster, so it is difficult to catch up. Then she drives in circles.*) We're here.

    (*Todd*) Honey, we passed here three times already. ...

    (*Lillian*) All right, get out! Let me get you out.

T: (*Whispering*) Should we get out, too?

L: Yes.

T: Okay.

L: (*Lillian*) One, two, three, surprise!

T: (*Joe and Janet*) Surprise! Happy birthday!

L: (*Todd*) Thank you guys so much. I didn't know we were meeting with Joe and Janet.

(*Lillian*) *Well, I tried to get the perfect party for you.*

(*Todd*) *You lllook bbbbeautiful JJJanet. ...*

They like each other, and then, like ...

(*Lillian to Joe*) Do you think they are falling in love with each other?

Trouble in paradise. There is so much generosity that one cannot help but wonder about its authenticity as well as about how available the deprivation that underlies this generosity is to the patient. Is the couple's falling in love a mask for covetousness? I would wait before commenting on this aspect of the play as we need more data before we jump in.

L: (*Todd*) I think you look awesome.

T: (*Janet*) Oh, you look good, too.

L: (*Lillian*) I get a table right here. (*Brings table and four chairs.*) Okay? Everybody sit.

T: Okay. (*I put Janet and Joe in their seats.*)

L: (*Lillian*) What are you guys going to order?

T: (*Joe*) Oh, I don't know, what are our choices?

L: (*Lillian*) Mm ... well, the chicken fingers are very good here, the salad is pretty good, the roast beef—delicious.

T: (*Joe*) Really? Okay.

L: (*Lillian*) So, we'll get two orders of chicken fingers, one big pot of roast beef, and some garlic bread with butter on the side, please. Okay?

T: (*Joe*) Okay.

L: This will be the garlic bread (*puts caramel popcorn on the table in front of Lillian and Todd*). Have you ever tried caramel corn?

T: Yeah.

L: Do you like it?

T: Yes.

L: Do you want some?

T: No, thanks, I'm not so hungry. Are you hungry?

L: Well, yeah, I just got it.

(*Todd*) Let us eat.

(*Lillian*) Honey! (*Todd started to eat.*)

(*Todd*) I think I'll go to the powder room. Will you go, Janet?

T: (*Janet*) Ah, of course, I'll go.

L: (*Todd*) I'll see you in a minute, Janet.

(*Lillian*) What are you doing?

T: (*Janet*) What? What did I do?

L: (*Lillian*) Are you kidding? I can't believe it! You're fallen for him?

T: (*Janet*) For who?

L: (*Lillian*) My husband!

T: (*Janet*) Your husband? You think I've fallen in love with your husband?

L: Mm-hmm (*yes*). (*L falls off her chair. She is on the floor.*)

This is the second time that self-inflicted aggression befalls someone when they truly desire something and it is not given to them ahead of their stated wish for it. First, it was a character in the play, and now it is the patient herself enacting this "fall from grace." Yet, this fall seems so unconscious. Is it possible to address it in some way? I might try, "Wow, two dangerous falls. I wonder if they are coincidences or whether there are falling feelings going on here?" This attempt steers clear of a content interpretation but puts the process on the table in a general enough way for the patient to accept or reject at her leisure without much intrusion (we hope).

T: Are you okay? What happened?

L: I don't know, I fell.

T: Okay?

L: Yeah.

(*Lillian*) I cannot believe it, you've fallen for my husband! What can I tell you? I don't know what to say. You think he is cute, right?

T: (*Whispering*) She does?

L: Yes.

T: (*Janet*) Well, yes, I do, but, you know …

L: (*Lillian*) But how? How could you do this to me?

T: (*Janet*) What? What did I do?

L: (*Lillian*) Now, when you like him, he likes you, meaning that he doesn't like me, and I love him.

T: (*Janet*) Oh.

L: (*Lillian*) Oh, how do you think Joe feels?

T: (*Janet*) About all this?

L: (*Lillian*) Yes! (*Lillian is walking away.*)

T: (*Janet*) I don't know. Oh sorry, just a second, oh, let's talk about it.

L: (*Lillian*) We'll talk about it at home. Let's go home.

T: (*Janet*) Okay, let's go home. Joe?

L: (*Joe*) What, Janet?

T: (*Janet*) What's wrong? You look very upset.

L: (*Lillian*) You are falling in love with Todd!

T: (*Janet*) How do you know that?

L: (*Lillian*) Because—the way you smile at him, the way you talk to him! I told you Joe will be mad. Almost as mad as I am.

T: (*Janet*) I feel very sad about that.

This last comment by the therapist raises an interesting clinical pathway question. One possible route involves expanding on the anger expressed by the patient: "They both will feel that mad, and being rejected is an awful, angry feeling." The other route is to take the therapist's approach and express sadness: "I am sad to have to make you angry, but I feel what I feel inside. I don't think I can control it."

L: (*Joe to Lillian*) Hey, this is all your fault!

T: (*Lillian*) How is it my fault?

L: (*Joe*) It's your fault because your husband has good looks, and that's why my wife liked him!

(*Lillian*) Excuse me; it's not my fault he has good looks, it is not my fault that he actually is good looking, I'm just dressing him.

(*Joe*) Oh, that's it, you better get Janet to like me or I will really, really hurt you!

(*Lillian to Todd*) Good night, honey.

(*Todd*) Honey? Will you bring me some hot chocolate?

(*Lillian*) Oh, shut up!

(*Todd*) What is wrong?

(*Lillian*) What do you mean what is wrong? You like Janet, don't you?

(*Todd*) Well, yes.

(*Lillian*) What? Did you say yes? Did you say yes? Did you say yes?

(*Todd*) Janet, what's wrong?

(*Lillian*) You like her ... you like her better than me.

(*Todd*) Janet, I mean Lillian, I will always be your husband, it's not going to change.

(*Lillian*) Really?

(*Todd*) Yes! Now, how about that hot chocolate?

(*Lillian*) Oh! (*Laughs.*) Well, let's go to bed, honey.

This is a most interesting moment in the play. I am reminded of a relatively affectively immature TAT response in which an affective dilemma is raised but resolved in a Pollyanna-ish fashion, as though painful feelings just vanish without residue. Encouraging a more complex understanding of difficult emotions and their resolution should constitute one goal of treatment with this patient. The fact that the patient laughs after abruptly restoring marital harmony implies a glimmer of recognition that it is unlikely the painful feelings would blow over so quickly, and I would start by building on this recognition: "Todd goes right back to that old hot chocolate wish, as if Lillian's upset just disappeared! Not very likely, huh?! He may want those feelings to vanish, but I wonder what her feelings are like even though he says he wants to stay married?"

L: (*Todd*) You know, I still do want that hot chocolate!
　　　　(*Lillian*) Honey, you're going to pee in your bed if you're going to have another hot chocolate!
　　　　(*Todd*) That's okay.
　　　　(*Talks to therapist*) Actually, I was wondering if you want to be him [Todd] and I could be him [Joe].

The patient makes a shift in which characters they should play, suggesting a brief disruption in the play. The therapist should be on the lookout for some defensive avoidance here as the patient is rejecting being the "betraying" Todd and opting instead for a heretofore benign character, Joe. While this is a more conscious substitution than her unconscious need to fall when aggressive, it is still highly defensive in nature. I would comment on the inner experience stirred up by playing Todd's role: "Being Todd means being full of very strong and very complicated feelings about these two women!"

T: Sure.
L: (*Lillian*) Okay. He had three hot chocolates already. I'm not making any more.
T: Does he still like her?
L: Yeah.
T: Does he like her more than he likes Janet or no?
L: Yes, but he doesn't tell her that yet.

Hmm, I wonder what he's feeling inside that makes him not want to tell her yet that he loves her more than Janet?

L: Honey. … He asks her for more hot chocolate.
T: (*Todd*) Hey honey, can you get me another hot chocolate, please?
L: (*Lillian*) Hey, this will be your fourth cup; you're going to be peeing in your bed tonight.
T: (*Todd*) Oh, no, I won't; I just want another hot chocolate, please!
L: (*Lillian*) Okay; here's another one, that's your fourth one.
T: (*Todd*) Thanks.

The child's shift from Todd's desires for Janet to still more oral desires is most striking: "That Todd has so many drinking feelings, I wonder why he so needs to fill himself up that way?"

L: (*Lillian*) Now, let's go to bed, come on.
T: (*Todd*) All right. (*Goes upstairs to bed.*)
L: (*Lillian*) Good night, honey.

T: (*L takes Joe and puts him on the roof of the house. I think she is doing it on purpose*). Oh, what is he doing?

L: Oh, he is not really there.

(*Joe to Janet*) Come on, please, you are still telling me you are mad at me?

T: (*Janet*) Well, I am mad at you.

L: (*Joe*) Why are you mad at me? I should be the one who is mad at you!

Being angry is so upsetting inside, it gets confusing to know who is mad at who.

T: (*Janet*) Well, because of the way you behaved. You didn't explain anything; you just didn't talk to me at the party yesterday, remember?

L: (*Joe*) Oh! You know what? Never mind! Okay, if you want to go with Todd, fine, go ahead, whatever. This is my house, I own it, so if you don't want to be with me—this is not your house!

(*To therapist*) And then she goes to bed, it's the only thing she can do right now.

Janet is feeling so overwhelmed that all she can do is go to bed. This shutting off of her affect is important to address as it is emblematic of how often the patient has an inkling of an affect and then must shut it down: "So Janet seems to have so many feelings all at once that she uses her shutting-down-and-going-to-sleep feelings to give her some space. I can understand that."

T: (*Janet*) I'm going to sleep, okay? Good night.

L: (*Joe*) Good night.

(*Todd to Lillian*) Honey? Good morning, honey!

(*Lillian*) Good morning. You want me to get you another hot chocolate, right?

T: Does he?

L: Yeah.

T: (*Todd*) Yes, sure! That will be great.

So even after sleeping, the first thing Todd wants is to feel that good hot chocolate and to feel that Lillian still wants to get it for him.

L: (*Lillian*) I don't understand how you didn't pee in bed. You got four cups already!

T: (*Todd*) Oh, well, I was thirsty.

And, perhaps in a whisper to avoid disrupting the flow of the play, I would add, "He still has so many feelings from last night, too."

L: (*Lillian*) All right, let me get you some.

T: (*Todd*) Thank you.

L: (*Lillian*) You're welcome. Honey, do you love Janet more than me?

Importantly, the patient can shift from this "false self" politeness to an authentic questioning of her partner's love.

T: (*Whispers*) He doesn't?

The therapist again deftly lets the patient direct the flow of the content.

L: No.
T: (*Todd*) No, I don't; I like you much better than I like her.
L: (*Lillian*) Really?
T: (*Todd*) Yes, I told you that.
L: (*Lillian*) I know; I just wanted to make sure.

Again, there is an attempt to make the bad feelings disappear, and it is the therapist's role not to let this happen so easily: "I wonder if she's feeling fully safe inside after he tells her this, or whether there is another part of her that still feels worried, or even mad, or doesn't trust him?"

L: (*Lillian*) Then again, you married me, right?
T: (*Todd*) Exactly, that's why I married you.

I would also want the therapist to see if she can create a thoughtfulness around what the male character would feel here: "I wonder if he also has more than one feeling about Lillian, too, like if he has a part that's not so sure he can love only her?"

L: Let's go there.
T: Okay.
L: He could sit here and she could sit on his lap.
       (*Lillian to Todd*) Hey, honey.
       (*Todd*) Hey. Honey, I can't see the TV.
       (*Lillian*) Oh, come on!
       (*Todd*) Really, I can't see it.
       (*Lillian*) Oh, you got to be kidding me. All right, since I am sort of in the way.
       (*Todd*) Oh!
       (*Lillian*) Breakfast.
       (*Todd*) Did you say breakfast?
       (*Lillian*) Do you like breakfast, dear? (*She passes Todd to me.*)
T: (*Todd*) I'm very hungry.
L: (*Lillian*) I'm making your favorite dish.
T: (*Todd*) Really? What is it?
L: (*Lillian*) Corned beef!
T: (*Todd*) Oh, thank you. So great.

L: (*Lillian*) You were really thirsty last night, and now you are really hungry.

This is a most opportune moment to link these oral needs to feeling states as the patient herself has made the link at a behavioral level: "Yeah, he has such strong hungry and thirsty feelings. He seems to need so much from her. I wonder what that feels like inside? I also wonder what it feels like for her that he's always so needy?"

T: (*Todd*) I am thirsty and hungry.
L: (*Lillian*) Didn't it happen after we went to that restaurant? Mm, I'll be right back, I'm going to talk to Janet.
T: Telephone?
L: Let's pretend.
T: Okay.
L: (*Lillian*) Hello, hello, Janet?
T: (*Janet*) Yeah?
L: (*Lillian*) I was wondering, has Joe been eating a lot lately and drinking a lot?
T: (*Janet*) Joe? Well, actually, a lot! I don't know what is going on. Why?
L: (*Lillian*) It's the same with Todd.
T: (*Janet*) It is?
L: (*Lillian*) And the thing is, he hasn't gone to the bathroom and he hasn't even got cramps or anything, but he has been eating and drinking all day! It's all happened since this restaurant, right? What did they have that we didn't have? Roast beef?
T: (*Janet*) Yeah, we didn't get the roast beef.
L: (*Lillian*) I think we should probably check with that restaurant, just to make sure that there is nothing wrong with that food.
T: (*Janet*) What do you think can be in that food that could cause such a thing?

The patient is in the midst of developing an elaborate, defensively induced scenario in which the desires of both men get somatized into physical maladies. I would try to articulate this process: "So, the women are trying to be food detectives to track down why the men are so hungry. I wonder if we could figure out their feelings as well?"

L: (*Lillian*) I don't know, we are going to find out. We're going to take a sample of it. We are going to eat there tonight, put it in a doggie bag, and we are going to test it at the science fair tomorrow. There is a kid I know who invented this food tester; I don't know why he made it, but come on.
T: (*Janet*) Okay.
L: (*Lillian*) Okay (*at the restaurant*). We would like roast beef. We would like a doggie bag, please.
   (*Waiter*) You didn't eat a bite of it.

> (*Lillian*) Well, we did. Thank you. Oh, look at it, it's rather yellow, don't you think?

T: (*Janet*) Yeah, it is. What do you think it means?

L: (*Lillian*) I don't know, maybe it's a virus or something. Come on, let's go to the science project.

T: (*Janet*) Okay.

L: (*Lillian*) The food tester guy says it's an energy booster. It gives the person more energy by making the person eat more food and drink more water without having any problems with the digestive system, meaning shortly ranged bathroom trips and no cramps. That is weird.

T: (*Janet*) So it is the roast beef.

L: (*Lillian*) Mm-hmm (*yes*). I have an idea.

T: (*Janet*) What's your idea?

L: (*Lillian*) I think that if we can prove that this restaurant is guilty, they will help us with our marital problems.

What a remarkably clever, if likely unconscious, link between their "marital problems" and the tainted food. Instead of linking the men's feelings to their "hunger," she thinks that if she can solve their physical problems, their gratitude will help their relationships. This appears to be just another facet of her basic dilemma: her need to give continually to others for fear that she will be rejected or abandoned if she does not. I might speak to that dilemma in the following way: "So, if the women take care of the men's health problems, the guys would be so grateful that the women would be less worried about losing them. I can see why they so want to solve this food issue!"

T: (*Janet*) You think?

L: (*Lillian*) Mm-hmm (*yes*).

T: (*Janet*) How come?

L: (*Lillian*) Well, they … they better, or we will report them.

T: (*Janet*) So, you want to tell them that we will report them, or … they better help us.

L: (*Lillian*) Mm-hmm (*yes*). All right, come on.

> (*To waiter*) Excuse me, we proved that this is contaminated with energy boosters.
>
> (*Waiter*) How did you find out?
>
> (*Lillian*) Through the kid's project.
>
> (*Waiter*) All right, please don't report us.
>
> (*Lillian*) We won't if you will help us with our marital problems. You see, she likes my boyfriend, and my boyfriend likes her, but I still love my boyfriend, and her boyfriend still loves her. That's the problem.
>
> (*Waiter*) Bring them in!

T: Okay.

I would want to speak to the hopefulness these characters are clinging to right now, even if it is a defense against their anger: "They have such hopeful feelings that the restaurant people can help save them from feeling so badly inside."

L: (*Waiter*) I knew it!

T: (*Janet*) What did you know?

L: (*Waiter*) I knew it, these men are compositive, meaning that your boyfriend is a
   100% more like Janet than you, and Janet's boyfriend is a 100% more
   like you.

T: (*Janet*) What do you mean?

L: (*Waiter*) Take a look. See the resemblances?

T: (*Janet*) What resemblances?

L: (*Waiter*) It doesn't matter that their hair matches and their skin matches, not
   only that. They have the same dress codes. Notice how Janet's sheets
   are clean, and your husband's sheets are clean?
   (*Lillian*) That's because I clean them!
   (*Waiter*) They'll be clean anyway, if you won't do anything with
   them. Notice how his shirt is dirty and yours, too?
   (*Lillian*) Mine is clean!
   (*Waiter*) Nonetheless, you guys should try to spend some time with
   each other. Janet's boyfriend is more like you, and yours is more like
   Janet. You have to let your boyfriend go.
   (*Lillian*) No, I won't, I won't do that!
   (*Waiter*) Then you'll have marital problems.
   (*Lillian*) The government would love to hear about this roast beef.
   If you do not help me any more, I certainly will tell.
   (*Waiter*) I'm sorry, but that's what I have to say.

Interestingly enough, through the play the child moves away from the use of the restaurant, away from somatizing as a defense, and back to the relationship difficulties. Her solution, however, is simply to have the women trade boyfriends. Again, this solution reveals a level of affect development mired at the relatively immature state in which feelings do not linger and are not linked to other feelings, but simply have to be dispensed with (see Thompson, 1986). I might add, "The restaurant guy is pushing them to deal with their feelings of loss by just letting go, but it's very hard to let go of loving feelings."

L: You, come! He is like, "Hey, hey!"

T: (*Todd*) Hey, hey, what are you doing?

L: (*Lillian*) We should talk.

T: (*Todd*) Okay, let's talk. What? What do you want to tell me?

L: (*Lillian*) You don't like me, that's why you are not talking. You don't want me.

T: (*Todd*) I do, why do you act like that?

L: (*Lillian*) What more do I have to do? What more do I have to do? To be continued.

The child literally cannot bear to continue with this line of play and needs to retreat from the affects it arouses. It is so poignant that she has the character repeat, "What more do I have to do?" as this line is exactly at the core of her conflict: her desperate feeling that she can never do enough to ensure her attachments. The unfolding of this theme in the play suggests that this child holds a preoccupied attachment status, and that she may often feel the need to dismiss attachments as a defense against her longings.

L: Is there time to play a little with the Play-Doh?
T: Sure. You want to do that?
L: Yes. To be continued.
T: To be continued? So we don't know what happened?

The therapist aptly tries to keep the play themes from disappearing by wondering what happened next, thus creating room for these themes to be explored through the metaphor of the play's narrative.

L: Uh-uh (no), because remember what the restaurant said.
T: Janet, she probably feels bad.

I would have tried to be more broad sweeping here: "Yes, the restaurant said the women should just let go, but feelings like getting rejected are so painful that it's too hard to just let them go. They stay in our minds in all kinds of ways."

L: Say that your best friend loved your boyfriend. (*I am taking the yellow Play-Doh.*) Didn't you say that the yellow is bad?
T: Oh, yes.
L: Okay, you get to choose again. All right, this time I'm going to close my eyes and choose a color. All right.
T: Close my eyes? Oh, close your eyes, okay.
L: I chose pink; now your turn, but first close your eyes.
T: (*I close my eyes.*) Are you moving them?
L: Yes (*laughs*).
T: Okay, brown.
L: Okay, and now you do it (*asks me to move the colors while her eyes are closed*). Green. Oh, it's the same colors we started out with, and it's the same set of colors you started out with!
T: Right!
L: Yeah, that's cool!
T: So, what do we do?
L: Anything, it's free time Play-Doh!
T: Whoa, free time?
L: So, what do you want to do?
T: Ah, what should I do?
L: A plate.

T: A plate?
L: And you can make designs on it.
T: Okay. A plate. With designs.
L: I know what I'm going to make. It's a surprise for you.

It should be no surprise to us that, even when she wants to retreat from the painful relationship paradigms she displayed in her symbolic play, the patient's wishes and conflicts are so overdetermined that she comes right back both to her need to be generous ("It's a surprise for you") and to her need to focus on oral themes and gratification. All roads do lead to Rome, for this patient at least.

T: You know what it is?
L: And we can make some forks and spoons and knives.
T: Okay, and then we can eat.
L: That's right. I'll make us a cup, and then I'll make something to eat.
T: That's a plate. What are you making?
L: A cup.
T: A cup?
L: Mm-hmm (*yes*).
T: We're going to drink from this cup?
L: Mm-hmm (*yes*).
T: What do you want to drink?
L: Well, I'm not going to make anything to put in it, but I'm going to pretend to drink water.
T: Water? You like water?
L: I love water.
T: You like to drink something other than water?
L: Aha.
T: Like what?
L: I like to drink, um, lemonade. (*Eats caramel popcorn.*) Something to eat.
T: You are making something to eat? Looks like a pie.
L: The plate?
T: No, your food.
L: Mm-mm (*no*). Something to eat.
T: Whoa, that is something to eat? What is that?
L: You'll see, ha-ha, see when I'm done. What do you think?
T: Oh, I don't know, what do you think?
L: I think you made a beautiful plate. You have five guesses to guess what it is. It is hard.
T: Okay. What will happen if I won't guess?
L: Then you win.
T: Then I win? If I won't guess?
L: Yeah. If you won't guess, then you either win or you lose. You might as well win, because if you won't guess, I guess I'll have to tell you anyway.

The child's need to be so uniformly generous precludes her from allowing the therapist to lose, even if she does not guess. I might add, "This guessing game makes me feel so safe inside because it seems like I will have winning feelings and get to know the answer no matter what I do!"

L: Okay, so, guess.
T: What could this be? Mm. I don't know, I need a clue.
L: It's something from Switzerland.
T: Chocolate?
L: No.
T: Ice cream?
L: No.
T: Is it a dessert?
L: Yes.
T: A cake?
L: No.
T: I have one more guess. It's not chocolate, it's not ice cream, and it's not a cake. What could it be?
L: People like to eat it even though it makes them fat.
T: Okay. Chocolate mousse?
L: No, it's called a Switzerland twist. It's a sort of pie, when they put warmed cooking dough and they twist it and put it right in the middle.
T: Have you ever eaten it?
L: No, I never have, but I have heard about it.
T: Who told you about it?
L: Hey, why don't we trade colors? How about, I want to trade one color with you; I have a pink, and what would you like, my green, or ... ?

The guessing game appears to have fallen flat, so the child trades with the therapist, again offering her a choice of "gifts." I would wonder about the child's experience of this generosity: "You always seem to be having a lot of taking-care-of-me feelings. I wonder what that feels like?"

T: Sure, I'll take the green.
L: Thank you.
T: We have a few more minutes. (*We play for a while with the Play-Doh.*)
L: That's pretty, what is it?
T: What do you think it is?
L: A flower?
T: A flower, yes.
L: Oh my god, it's blooming!
T: Yes.
L: Do you need the brown?
T: No. What is it?
L: It's sort of a surprise, but not really.

T: What is a "sort of a surprise"?

L: Ah ... what do you mean? Surprise? It means that you don't ...

T: No, a "sort of a surprise"?

L: Oh, hey (*laughs*)! It's a surprise. The same thing as a surprise!

T: Okay, we have to stop in a few minutes. I'll start to put these back.

L: All right, check it out.

T: Okay. Oh, this is a spoon, and an ice cream!

Food yet again. It is uncanny how locked in she is to her oral needs.

L: Yeah! Good job (*clapping*)! Well, people say I have a loud clap. Do I?

The patient is, in a powerfully overdetermined way, so affected by her oral "gift" to the therapist that she expresses her delight viscerally through her loud clapping and then draws attention to her prowess. It appears that providing oral gratification is her core method of feeling competent and viable, placing her at risk for a "false self" compliance via "feeding" others in order not to provoke their loss.

T: A loud clap?

L: A loud clap.

T: Do you think you do?

L: Maybe. We have to get in as fast as we can! We have to get it all in, fast. Stress, stress, stress.

The child shifts suddenly to the rapid, stressful cleaning up, I think as a type of manic defense against the upcoming end of the session and the loss of her therapist.

T: Or?

L: We'll die.

On some profound level, the child is literally speaking about the depths of her conflict. The loss of others leaves her feeling empty and hollow, making her need to fill everyone up with oral supplies more understandable. I might add, "Good-bye feelings, even if just for today, can be so strong and so hurting that we need to rush, rush, rush to make those bad feelings disappear. But we will see each other again next time."

T: Who will die—the colors?

The therapist responds too literally here, perhaps because the child's shift is so sudden and with so little time left in the session. It is always difficult for a beginning therapist to know how best to gain closure. Try sticking with something simple but affectively rich: "It *is* never easy to have good-bye feelings."

L: Mm-hmm. Triangle. Can we make a triangle? Yeah! (*Makes a triangle.*)

T, L: (*We put the Play-Doh back and take the keys. L turns off the lights.*)
T: It's dark; I can't see anything. L? Where are you? (*I open the door.*)
L: (*Laughs.*) I wanted to hide; I was hoping you wouldn't see me. (*Goes to hide behind the door.*)

It is fascinating, but not developmentally unexpected at all, to think that the child's impending loss of the therapist would summon up a wish to play hide-and-seek to cope with her separation concerns: "Yeah, hide-and-seek feelings always make sense when it's hard to say good-bye."

T: Do you want to stay here and hide behind the door?
L: Yes.
T: (*Whispering*) Time to go.

The therapist's whisper is a most kind and affectively attuned way of acknowledging the difficulty of the loss while staying firm in saying it is time to stop.

L: I want to stay.
T: I know it's hard, but we have to go.

Again, the therapist acknowledges the great difficulty in leaving.

L: Do we have to?
T: Yeah, we have to go. Do you want to say good-bye?

The therapist ingeniously comes up with a most simple, yet effective, way for the child to regain some autonomy over the leave-taking by having her literally say good-bye one by one to the objects in the room.

L: Yeah, good-bye room!
T: Good-bye room, see you on Thursday.
L: Good-bye chair; thank you so much for providing a sit, and made me fall! Thank you table, dollhouse, thank you other chair, thank you blackboard, thank you closet (*hugs it*). Thank you, thank you, thank you, thank you.

This good-bye ceremony is reminiscent of the classic children's book *Goodnight Moon*, in which the child deals with the loss of the parent to sleep in the same concrete manner with which this patient deals with the loss of her therapist until the next session.

T: Okay? (*I hand her the keys. She takes the keys from me, as she always does, to close the door. I am standing outside, looking into the room.*)
L: (*Laughs and whispers*) I have the power. I have the power. I want to stay inside! (*Laughs.*)

This is a beautiful moment therapeutically. The child is given the keys as part of their goodbye ritual, and she feels safe enough with the therapist to articulate her wish to defy her and keep the treatment and the room forever.

T: So, this is how you use your power.

The therapist affirms the child's power just at the moment that the child most needs the affirmation as an antidote to her feelings of loss and separation.

L: Mm-hmm (*yes*).
T: Okay? Do you want to close the door?
L: (*Closes the door.*)

Because the therapist is so able to contain the child's aggression without retaliation, the child is capable of affirming this "defiance" and, in so doing, of gathering the inner strength to tolerate being alone. This is a direct demonstration of Winnicott's brilliant theorizing (1958/1965; Tuber, 2008) on the capacity to be alone. If the parent (or therapist) can contain and not retaliate against the child's aggression, the child develops the luxury of taking the parent (or therapist) for granted and can then move on to play by herself, at least for a time. Winnicott stressed in this regard that it is the parent's misattunements, her being "good enough" but not perfect, that allow the child to experience being different from the parent and to develop an independent sense of self. In turn, the parent's attunements build a solid foundation of relatedness and connection on which this awareness of separateness can grow without causing undue disruption in their relationship. This paradigm holds equally beautifully for the therapist with her child patient. When the therapist is not perfectly attuned to the child, the child experiences herself as separate. If the therapist is then able to reattune to the child in a good enough fashion, the child has an opportunity both to reconnect and to notice what it felt like during their brief period of disruption. This sows the seeds for an increasing awareness of self and other and breeds the psychological mindedness that has been heralded throughout this book.

13 A 7-Year-Old Boy

On starting kindergarten, M began destroying school property, physically attacking his teacher, and running out of the classroom—behavior that soon became common at home.

M: I have a good idea.

T: You have a good idea?

M: Can you take that down, take that little thingy (*basketball hoop*)?

T: What little thing?

M: This (*basketball hoop*).

T: Oh.

M: Take down the orange thingy, the orange.

T: The orange thing?

M: Ah-ha, I got a new idea how to do it.

T: You have a new idea?

M: And you gonna have, you gonna have fun with it. (*Makes a funny face.*)

T: I am?

M: Mm-hmm.

T: Okay.

M: You're going to show me your new idea?

T: Okay.

M: You hold this (*orange basketball hoop*).

T: Okay.

M: And then you go like this (*moves me around*).

T: Oh, this …

M: You stay right here, stand, then I'm gonna put, you have to, and if you miss, watch. (*Throws football through hoop that I am holding up.*) If you get inside the hoop, and then, and then the person, and I have to run and get it, and I have to go around something like this (*runs around toy on the floor*), but then you go and I'll hold and you go.

T: Okay, so I have to try and get it in there?

M: Mm-hmm.

T: Okay. Why don't you move it more this way so … (*he had the hoop in front of his face*). …Yeah, okay. (*I throw ball.*) Oh, I missed, now what do I do … what happens if you miss it?

The child is intently trying to invent a game, and in true latency-aged fashion, the game is as much or more about rule creation as it is about the game itself. In light of this, the therapist is wise in simply asking him how the rules should be determined, thus giving him complete autonomy.

M: Oh, then, let me think. Oh, then you can go ... you can get ... you can just catch it.

He uses a telling phrase, "let me think," implying both that he is aware of his own state of mind and that a capacity for delay is subsumed within this mindfulness. This allows the therapist the opportunity to direct the session toward exploring which affects he is mindful of and then broadening this frame if possible: "So, you're thinking inside your head about what rules we should have. I wonder what that rule making feels like inside?"

T: Mm-hmm.
M: (*Commanding voice*) Catch it.
T: (*I pick the ball up off the ground.*)
M: And then, run around that.

The therapist handles his commands easily and without retaliation, allowing the play to proceed smoothly.

T: Okay. (*I run around the toy on the floor.*)
M: And then give it to the next person, me. (*Hands me the hoop.*)
T: And then I hold this (*basketball hoop*).
M: Ah-ha.
T: Okay. I got it. (*M looks at me to make sure I get the rules.*) I got it.
M: (*Throws ball into the basket.*)
T: Oh, you got it in.
M: (*Runs around the toy on the floor.*) Okay, now it's your turn.
T: Okay.
M: That what, that's what I did at school, at gym time.
T: At gym time.
M: Uh-huh.
T: Ohhh. (*I throw the ball.*)
M: Ohhh! You made it in. Go (*sings*) and go like that. (*Motions for me to run around the toy on the floor.*) Go!!
T: (*I take the hoop.*) Okay, I'm holding it.
M: Oh well, maybe we should do a game. (*Walks around the room picking up different toys, contemplating what to play with.*)

Another self-reflective moment by the child, and another opportunity to comment on his capacity for reflection: "There go those wondering-what-I-should-do feelings again. What are those feelings saying to you?"

M: Maybe we should play basketball. ... Um, uhh, you wanna, maybe we should play ...
T: With this hoop?
M: Um, we'll play one other game ... another game.

T: Okay.

M:(*Picks up a block and starts driving around.*) Vrrm.

T: Oh, that's a car.

*M:*Yup. Vrrrm. (*Picks up an airplane and holds it out to me.*)

T: An airplane.

*M:*I got lots of models.

T: You have lots of models?

*M:*Mm-hmm. I got lots of models of Legos, and I have a collection.

T: Oh yeah? What do you build?

*M:*Airplanes, Star Wars …

T: Star wars …

*M:*Mm-hmm.

T: What's in Star Wars?

*M:*I just build the swords, and they go jing and jing and jing (*makes sword movements*).

T: Ohhh.

*M:*With the big pieces.

T: With the big pieces of Legos.

*M:*Mm-hmm. … (*Picks up water bottle.*) Oh, potion! This is potion.

T: Potion.

M:(*Shakes bottle.*) It moves by itself. (*Shakes bottle more.*) I can see it.

T: It moves all by itself?

*M:*Yeah. (*Picks up eight ball*). Can I have some, I mean can I have some candy? (*Shakes it and holds it out to me.*) What does it say?

T: It says, "Without a doubt."

*M:*That means yes?

T: (*I nod my head.*)

*M:*Can I look at [name of TV show]? (*Shakes eight ball and holds it out to me to read.*)

T: "Concentrate and ask again."

*M:*Can I look at [name of TV show], PLEASE? (*Shakes eight ball and holds it out to me to read.*)

T: What is it you're asking?

The vehemence with which the child asks this question suggests an increase in frustration. This would be a useful moment to comment on this state of mind to see if the child can maintain a reflective stance even when frustrated: "Those are strong PLEASE feelings. I wonder what they feel like?"

*M:*It's a TV show.

T: Oh, okay.

M:"Yes, definitely." Yep, I do every day, I look at [name of TV show] every day … the TV show.

T: You do? What do the characters do?

M: They just go in and make things ... and the computer, like ... it's like a show, and they have to go inside a computer, they can have like a, they have to score and like they go like something like bigger like than, and hmm, like a rectangle, and they stand and they go pushhhhh, bump bump, and yeah you can't come on, but you got to go like this (*makes a stern face, but is struggling not to smile*). ... And then you go inside the computer.

T: You have to have a serious face.

M: Uh-huh, and guess what, and you can play, and you can lock the doors and stuff. Take out the fans and stuff and stuff, they got (*inaudible*) stuff, and they got lasers. (*Makes weapon motions.*)

T: They have all different kinds of weapons?

M: Uh-huh. I wanna use the chalk.

The child shifts the play, as if talking about the weapons might have been too intense to tolerate. This would allow the therapist to comment on the shift: "So we went from so-many-weapons feelings to talking about chalk. I wonder where all the weapons feelings went?"

T: Oh, yeah?

M: I wanna show you something.

T: Okay.

M: You're going to be amazed!

A striking comment, as if the child feels he must take on a more elaborate role as someone special and surprising to keep the therapist's interest. I wonder about his feeling deflated by the weapons play, with a subsequent need to inflate himself in her eyes. Is this a "false self" configuration?

T: (*I laugh.*)

M: (*Moves chair around so that he can stand on it to reach the board.*)

T: (*I slide closer to him to make sure he doesn't fall.*)

M: Go and get the chalk.

T: Go and get the chalk?

M: No, I already got the chalk.

T: Oh, okay.

M: Who the chalk, ohhh, the chalk. (*Singing to himself as he traces the edges of the blackboard with chalk.*) ... Chalk chalk chalk chalk chalk. Can you reach up there and go push like a square?

T: Like a square right up here? Like this?

M: No. Let me show you. ... (*Instructs me to continue to trace in the higher part of board.*)

T: Oh, finish this one. Like that?

M: Mm-hmm.

T: And up there, too?

M: Mm-hmm.

T: And what about here?

M: Ah-huh.

T: All the way?

M: Ah-ha.

T: You tell me when to stop, okay?

M: Ah huh. ... Now.

T: Okay.

They beautifully and seamlessly negotiate control.

M: (*Mumbles, drawing on blackboard.*) I'm just drawing Disney World.

T: Ohhh, that's Disney World.

M: I can remember Disney World. I remember the shooting the things and stuff and different stuff.

T: At Disney World?

M: Uh-huh. I remember. ... You went to Disney World before?

T: I've never been to Disney World. ... (*At same time as I am saying this, he is nodding yes.*)

M: It's fun. And guess what? At McDonalds ... if you secret, if you lift a pin you have to see if you won or not and if you won ... and guess what?

T: What?

M: You get to go to free Disney World! They got Mickey and stuff.

T: Oh, yeah? What did you do when you were at Disney World?

Better than a focus on action would be to say, "What feelings come to your mind when you remember Disney World?"

M: I played games, like games, and I went on the roller coasters, and I went like, "Ohhh, I can't scream, I can't scream, I can't scream," and then I (*holding himself with arms around self pretending not to be scared*).

T: And then what'd you do, scream?

The therapist gets at the feeling, but to broaden the patient's capacity to reflect on this moment, I would have framed it as a conflict: "So, you had screaming feelings and not-screaming feelings at the same time? What was that battle like?"

M: Nope (*smiling*).

T: Never?

M: Nah-ah. I just like (*holds himself and does motions of going on roller coaster*).

T: And you went all the way up and all the way down?

M: Yeah, and I don't like that. I said, "Hold on," and did like that (*wraps arms around self*).

T: And you held on tight?

M: I can draw (*inaudible*), I can draw like a cup. (*Draws on blackboard.*)

The child lets the therapist know that this screaming experience was too difficult to sit with by shifting his play, making it worthy of her attention. She could say, "Wow, so those screaming/not-screaming feelings were so strong that somehow your play changed to much safer cup-drawing feelings. I wonder what happened inside?"

T: Okay.
M: See.
T: Oh, you're showing me how you draw a cup ... with liquid in it.
M: Huh?
T: With liquid in it?
M: What's liquid?
T: With juice or water. ...
M: Let's do water.
T: Let's pretend it's water.
M: I don't want a chalk zone.

Another shift in play, this time to a phrase that is hard to interpret. The therapist should be alerted to the shift, but since the child's phrasing is unclear, it is better to wait a bit before trying to make sense of the process and nature of the shift.

T: A what?
M: A chalk zone.
T: Okay.
M: Look.
T: Was that Disney World?
M: I'm drawing chalk zone.
T: Oh.
M: (*Mumbles. Pushes over chair, and it falls. Here, I wasn't sure if he was trying to move it or whether he pushed it deliberately.*)
T: We have to be careful with the chairs ... we don't want to break them.
M: Why?
T: Because we don't do breaking in the therapy room. ... We can push it, you can push it, though (*referring to pushing the chair to move it around the room*).

The therapist is clearly a bit thrown for the first time in the session and is not sure what to make of the chair falling. She resorts to limit setting, which is certainly understandable for a second session, but ideally I might have gone for the following: "Whoa, even the chair has falling feelings. Where do they come from?"

M: Push it, I can't even push it. (*Pretends he can't move the chair, like it is stuck.*)

This is an interesting response by the child, implying that he may have indeed pushed the chair. I might have wondered, "So, the chair has stuck feelings even stronger than the pushing feelings?"

T: What's this?

*M:*That's chalk (*in front of chair*). (*Mumbles and draws on board with chalk.*) That's (*inaudible*).

T: It's what?

*M:*Nike zone.

T: Nike zone, I see.

*M:*Nike zone. I'm going to morning zone.

T: Okay, go over there to morning zone, sounds like a plan.

M:(*Mumbles*) Twenty. (*Writes it on the board on "morning side."*)

T: Twenty?

*M:*Twenty minutes.

T: In morning zone?

*M:*Uh-huh. … Then I come right back.

T: Okay.

*M:*A clock.

T: Oh. What about Nike zone?

*M:*Nooo, Nike zone's for, for after.

T: For after morning zone.

M:(*Making noises.*)

T: Beeping?

*M:*Those are the (*inaudible*) when you get up there. Beeep. Better get up. Morning, get up and (*inaudible*). … Oh, I can write another porthole.

T: Okay.

M:(*Mumbles. Draws.*)

T: Oh, it's a porthole.

*M:*Porthole.

T: Ohhh. Where do the portholes bring you?

*M:*Anywhere.

T: Anywhere you want?

This is a fascinating, if idiosyncratic and confusing, stretch of play. The child uses terms that are nonsequitors, as if the therapist should know them, giving the play a sense of being part of the child's as-yet-not-shared personal play world. The therapist is admirably able to follow the patient's lead, without impediment. The play seems to be about a process of time and space, where there are zones to go in and out of via "portholes," and where there is a certain fixed amount of time to do so. Unlike any of the cases so far in the book, here is a stretch of play full of unknowns that, despite their idiosyncrasies (or perhaps because of them), feel as though they convey some important personal meaning. As difficult as it might be, then, the best course of action here would be to wait until some meaning-laden process or content comes to the fore, even if swimming in this sea of ambiguity is anxiety provoking. There is just too great a likelihood that premature comments will direct the play away from the child's meaning making and toward a false compliance or a disrupted play.

M: Uh-huh.
T: Where do you think you'd go in the porthole?
M: (*Draws portholes and points to one.*)
T: Over here?
M: Maybe … uh, this is how you do it (*demonstrates how to draw a porthole*).
T: Okay. (*I watch and learn and try one.*) Like this?
M: (*Mumbles*) Watch me.
T: Okay.
M: I don't want to do this, I don't want to do it. (*But he is still drawing.*)
T: That's part of the porthole?
M: No, I don't want to … (*mumbles*).

The child's play becomes both more confusing and more affect laden, as if he is now dominated by an inner conflict over his drawings. I might add, "Drawing and not wanting to draw at the same time, there are strong feelings going on right now." Although purposefully vague so a shift in play is not forced, a comment like this still gets at an affective process.

M: I got an idea.
T: You got an idea?
M: Uh-huh.
T: Okay.

Again, the child shifts the play, but his labeling this shift as an idea gives the therapist another opportunity to comment on the process of his mind: "So, an idea in your mind pushes you away from the drawing/not drawing feelings. I wonder where your mind is going to now?"

M: (*Walks around room, moving all the chairs into the center of the room in a line.*)
T: Moving all the chairs?
M: I'll show you. …
T: That one, too?
M: Uh-huh … uh-oh … (*mumbles*) … shhh, just like that.
T: Just like that, in a row?
M: Ah-huh, you can sit one. You can sit in one.
T: I can sit in one?
M: I'm going to brush your hair.
T: You're going to play brush my hair?
M: Uh-huh (*points to seat*).
T: Okay, I sit here?
M: Yup. … Wait.

T: Okay.

M: (*M is holding comb in his hand. He walks over to blackboard and draws a clock with 12 written as 21.*)

T: Is that another clock?

Yet another shift in the play: "Ohhh, from hair-brushing feelings and now to clock ideas, I wonder how your mind jumps from place to place?"

M: That's 12. (*Draws another clock and corrects it to 12 on his own.*) What time it is?

T: Right now?

M: (*Nods.*)

T: It is 4:15.

M: (*Draws hands on clock but draws them at 3:00.*) Like that?

T: Let's draw 4:15. (*I go over and help him.*) ... Yup. 4:15. Okay.

The therapist decides to show him how to draw the time. Perhaps it would have been an opportune moment to ask, "Lots of clock and time feelings are coming up. Are you wondering about our time today?"

M: I'll make it clean, okay (*talking about comb in his hand*)?

T: Okay.

M: I'll do it in the sink. (*Reaches over to get paper towels out of the dispenser, but there are none.*) Hey, there's no paper!

T: I think it's empty.

M: Ah, nobody knows my secret headquarters.

T: Your secret headquarters?

M: Shhhh.

T: Okay. I won't look. (*I turn away.*)

Again, the therapist gamely follows wherever the child leads, even if she has no idea what direction the child is taking.

M: (Mumbles) I think we should color.

T: Okay.

M: Okay, let's paint then. (*Goes in box and gets out paint.*) Let's just paint, paint.

T: Okay.

M: And I got this, and then I got the water.

T: Good idea, I'll get a paintbrush.

A minor point, but using the word *good* is always tricky in child work as it implies a judgment or suggests a superego stance. Because of these implications, it should be avoided as much as possible, especially at the beginning of treatment. The inherently one-sided power differential between an adult and a child drives the early phases of treatment, such that the child is keyed into what is "good" or appropriate behavior in this new world called "therapy." Given such a frame, there should be a strong attempt to clear the way for the child's play to follow its own path freely, much as Axline (Axline, 1964) suggested many years ago. Even such an innocuous statement as the suggestion that getting a paintbrush is a "good idea" implies that other actions by the child must be similarly "blessed" by the therapist, thus prompting the child to become too focused on compliance or oppositional behavior instead of immersing him- or herself in play and seeing where his or her imagination leads.

M:(*Mumbles.*) I get the big one. I make no mess.
T: No?

The child's focus on making "no mess" suggests that he has some trepidation as to whether this new medium of expression will be a "safe" one. Using "mess" as a metaphor, I would try to help him reflect on his anxieties: "Mess feelings can be very hard to understand. I wonder what a mess feels like to you?"

M: And you get the smallest one. No, well, we'll trade the smallest one. (*He pushes the pack of brushes and paint closer to me.*)
T: Oh, you're sharing with me. You want to share yours with me?

Since his desire to share with the therapist still seems ambivalent, I would articulate his mixed feelings: "Part of you wants to have share-the-brushes feelings and part is not so sure. That can be confusing."

*M:*Maybe I should (*mumbles*) something special (*mumbles*). I think we should. (*Mumbles while painting, but paint is dry so it is not coming out well.*)
T: Maybe we should use a little more water; it might be a little dry.
*M:*I don't want to paint! I can't even put ... (*brush was not cooperating with him*).
T: Wanna try this one?

The child suddenly shows a low tolerance for frustration and a too-ready willingness to self-condemn. The following could be said: "One moment you were painting and the next moment some very strong don't-want-to-paint feelings came over you. What's that like inside?"

M:(*Takes brush and uses it.*)
T: Oh, it still has blue in it.
*M:*I'm ripping this out (*his picture*). I'm not good at this.
T: You want to take this one out? (*I start to take mine out, too.*)
*M:*No, no, don't rip it.
T: Oh, just leave it.
*M:*No more painting.

This is a striking moment in the play. The therapist empathically wants to rip out her painting so the child will not feel worse about his work, but the child makes a dramatic point of not wanting her to do that. It seems important to the child that his work be negated but that hers remain viable. I would comment on this contrast: "Ohhh, so your painting brings strong ripping-out feelings, but mine you want to keep safe. Those are two very opposite kinds of feelings."

T: (*I am about to close the paper book.*)
M: Don't, you could just ... (*moves it*). Stop painting, and I'm going to show you something.
T: Do you want me to keep on painting?
M: Hmm, what's this? (*Picks up pickup sticks from box. Struggles to open box and hands directions sheet to me.*)
T: Those are. ... I'll show you.
M: Jacks and balls! I like this game! Jacks and balls! I like this game. Jacks and balls, jacks and balls...I like jacks and balls, how do you know I like jacks and balls? Jacks and balls, jacks and balls, I love jacks and balls (*jumping up and down and spinning around*).
T: You like jacks and balls...Can you show me how?

The child is so thrilled by finding this familiar toy that he is literally jumping for joy, giving an opportunity to expand his capacity to articulate the euphoric end of his affect-tolerance continuum: "These are such strong jumping, spinning, happy feelings, I wonder what they are like inside?"

M: I took off my sneakers, okay?
T: Okay.
M: (*Mumbles*) I don't know how, I don't know how to take them off ... and I don't know how to ...
T: The jacks?
M: I can do them (*throws them up and watches them land*).
T: Oh, there's one over there.
M: Jacks, jacks, jacks, jaaaaacks. (*Inaudible*) has this game.
T: Who does?
M: My cousin
T: Your cousin.
M: She goes, she goes like this.
T: Okay, show me.
M: (*Throws ball that comes with jacks.*)
T: Oh. And then what happens?
M: It's a ball, ball, ball, ball. Got it!

The child is actually too excited to play productively, so I would have tried to use words in an attempt to increase his affect modulation: "Those ball-ball-ball and jacks-jacks-jacks feelings are so strong, it's hard to even find the place in your mind to play with them."

T: Oh, it goes really high.
M: (*Bouncing ball.*)
T: Ohhhh. Whoops.
M: You can catch it.
T: Oh, where did it go?
M: I'll get it! (*Ball had disappeared under the sink in the pipes.*)
T: Okay. Where'd it go? Did it go here?
M: Ehh, another ball (*looking under sink*).
T: Yeah, I don't see it. We'll have to wait for someone to get it for us next time.
M: Next time?
T: Maybe next time. Because I don't think it would be easy to find back there.
M: Hmm, um, well, I got a good idea.

Importantly, the child is able to show resilience here and not be unduly frustrated by the ball's disappearance. He may have even been relieved that such an exciting spasm of play could be avoided.

T: What?
M: Can you reach that, that the hot one, hot (*referring to faucet*).
T: (*I turn on hot water faucet.*)
M: (*Screams*) Hey, ewwwww!!!! (*Mumbles about the water being dirty.*) You want to turn it?
T: Okay.
M: You turning it?
T: Turning it!
M: Yup! Keep on turning it! Yup! (*Yelling and running away from sink.*) Run, run, run, just run!! (*He means for me to run away from the sink because the water is dirty, and I'm supposed to be afraid of it.*)
T: (*I run away and pretend to be scared.*)

A fascinating use of displacement in which the child's own feelings of being overwhelmed by his affect are displaced onto the "dirty" rushing water from the tap, and both patient and therapist can join together in this avoidance: "These dirty-water feelings are so 'ewwww' that it's exciting to run away from them!"

M: (*Yelling excitedly*) M's in the house!
T: I think the sink is getting clogged, so we can't keep it on too long.

The therapist appropriately sets a limit, but perhaps a bit prematurely, as it shuts down this charged play just as the child is identifying with the power of the surging, dirty water. Before setting this limit, the therapist could try commenting, "That ewwwy water is also so powerful, even though it's scary at the same time!"

M:(*Turns sink back on and yells.*) M's in the house! (*Picks up hoop.*)

T: Where does this go (*referring to basketball hoop*)?

*M:*The basketball and the catching game. ... Put it back up.

T: Put it back up? Here? (*I put hoop back on its stand.*)

*M:*Mm-hmm.

T: Okay.

*M:*We have a new basketball.

T: Yeah.

M:(*Screams.*) Oh no!! ... You goin' the basketballlllll.

T: Basketball.

*M:*I'm gonna put on my shoes, okay?

T: Okay ... oops. There. ...

*M:*I told you I don't know how to do it. Could you do it for me?

This is now the second time the child has quickly lapsed into a feeling of incompetence, in striking contrast with his wish to identify with the surging and powerful, if dirty, water. I might have added, "Not-knowing-how-to-do feelings, they are very hard to have in your mind. I wonder what they feel like?"

T: Can I help you?

*M:*I got school shoes ... (*pushes shoes in front of me*).

T: Would you like me to help you?

*M:*Uh-huh. ... What is this? ... I know what this is (*referring to papers and game pad from jacks box*).

T: What is it?

*M:*It goes with that thing right here. ... Let's see what it is. Get the paper.

T: This paper?

*M:*Ah-huh.

T: This paper?

*M:*Mm-hmm. Read it.

T: (*I open paper.*) Okay.

*M:*Guess what, my friend, guess what my friend. ... Oh, I want to play cards then. Guess what my friend did.

T: What?

*M:*He did sex in the bathroom with a girl.

Without question, one of the most remarkable and challenging aspects of play therapy with young children is how quickly they can get to "primary process" material. At some unconscious level, the child associates his fascination with dirty, surging water from the tap with bathroom curiosities, urges, and prohibitions and then simply blurts it out, making sure the therapist knows that he is clearly not the perpetrator of such "bad" actions.

T: He did? What you think about that?

The therapist responds to this shift directly and with striking equilibrium. My only suggestion would be to frame the question in terms of feeling rather than thinking: "I wonder what your feelings were when you heard about that?"

M: Uh-huh. A girl came in the boys' bathroom, and guess what. ... And at school, there was a girl sitting next to me, and there's a boy who likes her, guess what. ... They took off their, uh, she, the girl took off her belt, and let them look at their underwear, her under, underwear, and they touched it and touched it, I did NOT do that.

T: What did you think about that?

M: Nasty. And I did my work, all by myself, and I did it.

T: And you did your work.

The child clearly shows his fascination with and repulsion from this sex play. As we do not know to what extent he was actually a participant, I would be conservatively asking about the process: "So, I wonder what your mind was doing while you were having trying-hard-to-work-all-by-yourself feelings?"

M: Mm-huh. Yeah, wanna (*inaudible*), put one ... take that, and guess what, and that, to the car.

T: There.

M: Hmm, they go out to this one? No, that's not your car, vrrrrrrrrrr. I'm spinning out of controoool!!! Na na na!!! Spinning! Spinning out of controooool, spinning out of controool, man. I'm spinning, spinning out of control, spinning out of controoool (*repeats*)!

The child is telling us in as literal a way as possible how viscerally charged it is to feel these sexual feelings. Given his choice of words, he provides the therapist with a most useful segue: "Yes, thinking about that nasty sex stuff in the bathroom at school makes your mind have superstrong spinning-out-of-controoool feelings. I get how it could make you feel that way inside."

M: (*He plays with the cars we were playing with when he brought up the sex at school. As he is spinning, he is holding the car in his hand and extending his hand out toward me with the car.*)

T: Your car is going really fast.

M: I'm dizzy.

T: Now you're dizzy?

M: Oh, I'm going to the door. (He takes three steps and then pretends to fall down and pass out motionless on the floor.)

T: You're dizzy, and you fell down ... can you be revived? (*I am using the toy I used to revive him last time.*) M. ... (*He is smiling and enjoying my attempt to revive him.*) M. ...

The child's "passing out" is apparently a time-honored way for him to shut down his affective experience. I would make the link explicit: "So, the spinning-out-of-controooool feelings are so strong, maybe your mind thinks that only passing out can make those too-exciting feelings disappear."

M: Ohhh (*he twitches*).

T: Oh, I wonder what is going on? Did M bump his head and fall down?

M: (*Whispers*) Passed out.

T: (*Soft voice*) Passed out?

M: (*Whispers*) Yeah.

T: What can revive you?

M: (*Giggles, moves around, and points to the toy.*)

T: Oh, it was a shake! He must be alive! ... I wonder what will revive M? (*I use other toys to try to revive him.*)

M: (*Points to a different toy.*)

T: (*I pick up that toy.*) Maybe this will revive you ... (*whispering*) M.

M: (*Laughs.*)

T: He's moving! I can see he's alive.

M: (*Smiles more and covers his mouth to keep from giggling.*)

In a strikingly gentle, imaginative way, therapist and patient play a variation of a hide-and-seek game, providing a means for the patient to feel nurtured on a preoedipal level after the overexcitement of feeling and thinking about the sexual play at school.

T: What's the special trick?

M: Argh. (*He moves and points to the jacks.*)

T: It's the jacks.

M: Um, wait (*moves pieces*).

T: Oh.

M: I won, you lost! ... Now it's your turn.

T: Okay. (*I throw jacks.*)

M: Put it there. You have to be in, like in, people like, shhhhh, and you get it there and there and there (*referring to the game pad that looks like a target*).

T: So, I have to try and get it there?

M: Mm-hmm.

T: (*I toss the jacks on the game pad.*)

M: You got two in there.

T: I got two.

M: My turn. ... I did it! Now I go again now, 'cause I, 'cause I, watch ... bing, bing, bing.

T: Oh. How many?

M: Three.

T: Three.

M: I can beat your record.

The child has weathered the storm of the overexcitement caused by his sexual/superego struggle. He used the hide-and-seek game to shore up his earlier self-structure and can now, importantly, engage the therapist in a more "phallic-level" game in which he can "beat her record." A comment like, "Sometimes beating feelings can feel so strong and big inside" might be used to help validate and elaborate on that positive affective experience.

T: You can beat my record? (*I go again.*)

M: You got one in there. ... Beat that! (*Mumbles.*) Can I have one more? What's that in your hand?

T: What? (*I extend my hand.*)

M: Let's see it, what is that? (*Points to ring on my finger.*)

T: That's a ring.

M: You're married?

T: Am I married? Do I have a husband?

M: Mm-hmm.

T: I'm not married.

M: But you got that ring.

T: Did you think I was married?

M: Yup.

T: You did?

M: Yup.

T: And what'd you think about that?

Better, perhaps would be to say, "What would my being married feel like inside your mind?"

M: (*Shrugs shoulders.*)

The oedipal nature of the child's curiosity about his new therapist is fascinating to watch. Keeping with his phallic play, he notices her ring and creates the possibility of a triadic experience, with the therapist being married to "another man." This is a challenging moment for a beginning therapist for two reasons. First, it is always tricky to know how to handle personal questions from a child patient as there is a bias toward deflecting those questions back to the patient much as you would with an adult early in a treatment so the transference is not "sullied." I am more in favor of answering a child's question, with the addition of an affective process query: "So, I wonder what feelings come into your mind now that I said that I am X?" This situation is also challenging for a beginning therapist because it is difficult to immediately "get" the underlying developmental phenomenon expressed through a question like this—and even if the therapist does "get" it, it remains difficult to know on what level to respond as presumably the child is unaware of the unconscious derivatives of this question. I might say, "So, rings on ladies make you think about marriage and husbands. I wonder what that feels like?"

M: What are these?

His shift in play tells us that too much affect is being internally generated for him to tolerate. I would comment on this shift: "Well, we're moving again in our feelings, this time from married-question feelings to pick-up-stick feelings."

T: Those are pickup sticks.
M: Pickup sticks.
T: Yeah.
M: Can you take them apart now? I got them.
T: You want me to help you?
M: No, I got them. (*Screams and throws sticks up in the air and lets them fall down.*) Pickup sticks, pickup sticks, let's go pick the pickup sticks (*singing song and jumping around*). ... Pick, pick, pick, pickup sticks (*he starts picking them up*).
T: So we're picking them up?
M: (*Starts to pick them up quickly.*)
T: We're picking them up? As fast as we can?
M: That's how you play pickup sticks. Oh, oh, oh. There's one next to you.
T: Oh, I see one more.
M: There's one more behind you.
T: There's one more behind you.
M: And one more behind you!
M: Let's do it. Give 'em back to me. (*Throws them up again.*) PICKUP STICKS, PICKUP, PICKUP, PICKUP STICKS. (*Runs around picking them up.*) Got one left. Zrrrmmm. You got that. AHHHHH. (*Throws them again.*) PICKUP STICKS, YOU PICK THEM UP, PICKUP STICKS, THEY'RE FAR, FAR AWAY!!!
T: They went far away this time.
M: They're over here. ... That's how you play pickup sticks, right?
T: Right, you have to pick 'em up. I see one more.
M: I'll pick 'em up.
T: Okay. Should I hand that to you?
M: Ohhh, I LOVE TO PLAY, I LOVE TO PLAY!

Again, the patient's affective range is striking as he takes the raw affect of his oedipal play and curiosities and applies it with equal displaced vigor to the pickup sticks game. It is probably not at all a coincidence that, for him, the game involves throwing things far away and then finding them. He is creating a form of hide-and-seek to return to preoedipally as a relief from the intensity of his feelings about his new therapist.

T: Pick up!
M: (*Mumbles.*) Wait, I'll draw you something, okay?

Yet another shift in the play.

M: (*Draws on black board.*) ... Okay.
T: M (*reading from blackboard*).
M: What's your name?
T: Ms. T.
M: Huh?
T: T (*slower*).
M: Uh. ... I put M. Put your name? It's sorta like (*writes with chalk*) D, with a D?
T: It's with a T.
M: T. (*Writes my name on blackboard. Points to the letters M and T.*)
T: I'm going to write it, too. (*I write my name on the board.*)
M: That's you, that's me.
T: Okay.
M: And guess what?
T: Can you see?
M: Fire, fire, fire (*draws fire on blackboard with chalk*).
T: Fire?
M: I don't have to take care. ... I'm not afraid of fire.

The fascinating way this child flits from one overdetermined activity to the next speaks to the richness and complexity of a child's inner life. The child uses his nascent latency-aged skills in an attempt to neutralize the intense affective excitement he feels with the therapist by pairing them together in a sublimated way through the spelling and writing of their names. But, no sooner does he assuage his separation worries by having placed their initials side by side than an affective storm begins anew, this time in the barely disguised form of fire on the chalkboard and his counterphobic denial of its danger. I might add: "So, first you had writing-us-together-on-the-board feelings, and then fiery feelings came up right after that, but your mind doesn't seem afraid of these fire feelings?"

T: You're not afraid of fire?
M: I'm not afraid of nothing. (*Mumbles—sounds like "not afraid of the gulf or nothing."*)
T: Of the what?
M: I'm not afraid of dark, AND I'm afraid of spiders.
T: You're afraid of spiders.
M: Mm-hmmm. I HATE, HATE, HATE, HATE SPIDERS!!!
T: What will happen if a spider comes?

Although this is an interesting form of question as it asks what will happen as opposed to what will he do, the focus could more usefully be on the affect as he is admitting to a chink in his counterphobic armor: "So, sitting right next to each other in your mind are not-afraid-of-anything feelings and hate-hate-hate-hate feelings about spiders!"

M: I HATE, HATE BUGS!!
T: All bugs?
M: I HATE, HATE, HATE THEM. I HATE THEM, I HATE THEM, I HATE THEM, I STEPPED ON THEM.
T: You step on them.
M: (*Stomps on floor, stepping on bugs.*)

I would frame this action as an expression of an inner conflict: "So, one way you deal with your superstrong bug-hating feelings is to have strong step-on-bug feelings instead. What is that battle of feelings like?"

M: (*Begins to clean the eraser to wash the blackboard.*) I'll wash the wall.
T: Okay, that's good (*referring to the amount he was wetting the eraser*).

Yet again, a shift in play follows an overly intense affective expression, this time one of aggression and fear. I would try to help him reflect on this shift: "You zoomed away from those hateful bug feelings superfast. What was that like inside?"

T: Oh, to erase the board.
M: Uh-huh. You can help.
T: Okay.
M: You can do it, too, look. You can do it. (*Sits down in the chair and yells.*) KEEP UP DOING SOME WORK!
T: You'd like me to help you do some work?
M: (*Deep, mean voice*) DO IT!
T: Oh I see, you would like for ME to do the work.
M: (*Deep, mean voice*) Get it! You missed a spot, go up there, missed a spot.
T: I wonder what happens if I miss a spot?

The therapist again attempts to help the child think about what will happen next as a result of his strong shift in affect, but I would have stayed with his feelings rather than speculating about action: "Those deep mean voice orders sound like you have a different kind of strong feelings inside right now. Do they feel different to you?"

M: Go up there, you missed a spot, go up there … get that green stuff.
T: Oh, it sounds like you would like to tell me what to do.
M: And get that cup.
T: This one.
M: Ah-huh.
T: Okay.

M: And ah, get off, because I want to, AND you missed a spot.

T: I missed? What happens if I miss a spot?

M: Look at me, look at me. (*Gets up and starts to point. Nicer, normal voice.*) Do you think you could get in the "up" part?

T: (*I clean the "up" part.*)

M: (*Gets up, takes the eraser, and starts cleaning.*) And I get this spot.

T: You're getting every single spot?

M: Uh-huh … give me a, pick me up.

T: You would like some help?

M: Ah-huh.

T: Okay. (*I go over and pretend to pick him up a little, so that my hands are under his arms but not really lifting him, so that he can reach a spot.*)

After a brief depiction of his inner bossy self, he quickly shifts to his regular voice, offers to help himself, and then wants her help. Perhaps those shifts could be tracked by the following: "First there were mean bossy feelings, then there were equal cleaning feelings, and now there are asking-for-help-to-clean feelings—feelings sure can change a lot in a short time!"

M: Oww, eekk, ahhhh, you're hurting me, owww, owww! (*But he is also laughing at this.*)

T: Maybe we should use this (*a chair*).

While with young children there will almost always be times of physical contact, it is important to be cautious with them, especially in this session, with his having such easy access to extremely intense affective ties to the therapist. The therapist is thus adroit in switching seamlessly to using a chair.

M: (*He moves chair over.*)

T: All the way in the corner (*of blackboard*).

M: I think we should make the square part like what you did.

T: Over there?

M: Ah-huh. I'll do the (*inaudible*), okay?

T: Okay, you're going to help me?

M: Ah-ha … you wanna (*inaudible*) with this, you can do all, and then all the kids can write over again. 'Cause they, 'cause the kids need a turn, right? And I got a turn, right?

T: Kids are having a turn?

M: Ah-huh, they need a turn, right? Because I don't want to do their playtime, right? And they want a, and I don't want to lose my playtime, right?

T: You want everybody to have playtime?

For the first time in the session, the patient becomes conscious of other children using the room. Rather than expressing possible jealousy or competitive feelings with them at first, however, he generously wants to be fair and to give everyone a place for their names.

M: Ah-ha, and they come and they just can draw (*inaudible*), right? And the kids will say, "AHH, it's sparkly!" And they want to say, "How did somebody did that?"

T: How did somebody clean it?

M: Ah-ha, I'm gonna say we clean the chalkboard.

T: Oh, we're going to tell them we cleaned the chalkboard.

The child reestablishes a sense of mastery and distinction over these unknown peers by imagining them marveling at his cleanliness. I would remark on this: "So, your sparkly cleaning feelings will make the other children feel what inside, I wonder?"

M: Right, your, you can write like your name on a piece of paper, and then we say ah, and then they say call this number, and they call the number, the room number, right?

T: The room number.

M: And they can call you. And then on Wednesday, on Wednesday we can come here, on Wednesdays, right?

T: On Wednesdays we come here (*I nod*). ... And the chalkboard will be clean?

M: Uh-huh. And they can watch us. Mm-hmm.

T: Oh, and they can watch us.

Now, the fantasy develops into a wish that the other children could watch as they clean the room together: "I wonder what feelings you'd have if the other kids could watch you clean so sparkly?"

M: You can do this.

T: You want me to do up there, that part? (*Cleaning blackboard*) ... Ohhh, really high.

M: (*Sings in a whisper voice*) Got your name, got your name.

T: Oh, it's so. ...

M: It's coming out. ...

T: It's coming out?

M: Mm-hmmm, and it's already drying you know.

T: And it's already drying.

M: (*Mumbles about drying.*)

T: Okay, you're doing that part?

M: Uh-huh.

T: Okay.

M: Clean every spot up there, you see ... get every spot.

T: You would like me to help you clean up there?

M: Clean up there first. (*Sits down on chair with arms folded and yells in a mean, deep voice.*) I WANNA SEE SOME WORK!

T: You want me to work hard, huh?

The therapist captures the shift immediately but could add an affective label: "Wow, those mean bossy feelings are coming out again. I wonder where they were hiding and what it was like to have them pop out again?"

M: Get up there.

T: You want to tell me how to clean it.

M: Ah-huh.

T: Up here?

M: Ah-huh, because you had to draw, right, and the kids come in the room with water, and they can do it, right?

T: And then they can come with the water, and then they can write on the chalkboard?

M: Ah-huh, and that's what we can do. ... Missed a spot.

T: Up here? Did we already wash this spot?

M: Nope, I don't think so. ... I REALLY WANT TO SEE MY FACE ON IT! All done!

T: Where?

M: Upstairs.

T: Up here?

M: Ah-huh ... can you give me that?

T: That's how you do it?

M: That's how you do it ministyle.

T: Ministyle?

M: It's a ministyle. Do that, mini-me, mini-me, mini-me.

T: Mini-me style. ...

Without really knowing what the child means, the therapist ably mirrors his words, and they are clearly on the same page.

T: (*We both step back and take a look at the board.*) Oh, that is very shiny.

M: (*Whispers something*) Mini-me, mini-me ... style. Do the mini-me style. (*Whispers*) That's how you do the mini-me style.

T: Now do we wait for it to dry?

M: (*Pushes chalk off shelf.*)

T: 'Cause you wanna clean that part?

M: (*Loud voice*) We don't need those stinkin' chalk. (*Pushes chalk off shelf.*)

T: We don't need those stinkin' chalk? Because we're cleaning?

Another shift, this time a differentiation between the "clean" blackboard they cocreated and the "stinkin'" chalk: "Clean feelings and stinkin' feelings can sure be opposites!"

M: Uh-huh, you can pick up the chalk … and so then we can put some new chalk up there, okay? Like our chalk, right?

T: We could put our chalk up there and have it be new. …

M: And those kids, those kids can play with it, right?

T: Should we put these up here?

M: Is that the old one? That's the one that's been up there?

T: Ah-huh.

M: So throw them away, we don't need them, throw them away.

T: We should save them for the other kids though, huh?

M: No, throw them away, just give 'em to me.

T: I'm a little worried because we don't want to throw away the chalk. …

M: Because, we got more chalk over there.

T: So we can put those chalk up, but I want to keep these on the side.

M: Okay.

T: Okay. You can put them on the side.

M: (*Goes over to trash can, holds the chalk in his hands above the trash, and looks over at me. I shake my head, and he smiles and stops.*

Here is the first time in the session when he tests the therapist, and it comes right after she tells him what she wants to do (with the chalk) for the first time. How they come to handle limit setting versus "false compliance" is likely to be an important part of their work together, so I would comment on this dynamic: "So, I showed you my wanting-to-keep-chalk feelings, and you're showing me your I-want-to-get-rid-of-these-stinking-things feelings. I wonder what it's like when we are on opposite sides of feelings?"

T: You could put them in there (*points to a cup*).

M: New ones. Do we have them (*mumbles*)?

T: Oh.

M: Do you see them? (*Mumbles. Finds chalk, takes pieces out, and lines them up in a row on the blackboard shelf.*)

T: What about that one, right there?

The child again has access to his "obsessional" latency-aged defenses of orderliness in the face of disorder, and the therapist goes right along with those defenses by asking about a piece that is not in line.

M: That's one of the old parts.

T: It is?

M: Ah-huh. (*Sings a little to himself.*) And I have two more MINI-STYLE.

T: You're going to do the mini-style … ?

M: Ah-huh, and then we could put the new chalk (*mumbles*).

T: Oh, the new chalk.

M: (*Mumbles.*) New chalk. (*Lines up chalk again.*)

T: We should line them up?

M: So kids can look at them ... look at the right stuff.

T: This color?

M: Mm-hmm.

T: Blue.

M: Don't worry about this color ... (*mumbles*) ... just give 'em one, okay?

T: Okay.

M: For the others?

T: So we're going to share with the other kids?

M: That's how you share. ... I'm good with sharing, and I'm trying to be nice. Do you know where the chalk is? Oh, there it is.

T: Sharing with the other kids and cleaned all the blackboard.

The therapist deftly links his two "good boy" behaviors but perhaps not explicitly enough. I might have added: "It takes a lot of work with your feelings to try to be nice. We often have other parts of us that don't always have those trying-to-be nice feelings."

M: You need to clean this.

T: That part's still dirty?

M: (*Cleaning the blackboard with eraser, making a straining face.*)

T: Oh, you're working so hard.

M: Beep, beep.

T: You know what? It's almost time for us to go.

M: (*Ignores me, walks over to sink, fills up a bowl of water, and begins to pour the water on the blackboard shelf so it spills all over.*)

T: Oh, you know what. (*I get up and walk over to him.*) It's okay to do the cleaning game, but it's not okay, it's not a therapy game to spill water, okay?

This is a strikingly common occurrence in any early treatment and a most difficult moment for the beginning therapist. The therapist brings up leave-taking, and the child immediately enacts what this impending separation means to him: He must ignore her to ward off the pain of her impending loss, and then he goes to a behavior that is likely to be both an extension of his trying to be good (here he wants to further clean the already-clean blackboard) and an unconscious aggression at being "rejected" by her. In this session, the therapist physically sets a limit and distinguishes between okay and not okay behavior. This is a vital part of her therapeutic work. What is much harder to include, however, is to speak reflectively to the patient's feeling state while still setting a limit. To do this, I might add, "Time-to-go feelings are very strong and very hard and maybe your spilling feelings and your good-bye feelings are sitting right side-by-side with each other."

M: Okay, but can I do something? (*Starts to pour water again.*)

T: I want you to hear that we are not allowed to spill the water in therapy games, okay? You can hold the thing (*empty bowl*), but you cannot spill the water.

M: It's done cleaning it.
T: It's all done? Should we put this back up?
M: (*Screaming and pointing to a streak on the blackboard.*)
T: Oh, there's a big, big mark. How did that happen?

The child focuses on a streak that mars his attempts to be clean, and this affectively overwhelms him. The therapist could say, "Oh no, all your good-cleaning feelings are getting so upset because of that one streak. We need to protect your cleaning feelings from your messy ones."

M: (*"Passes out" on floor.*)
T: Oh, and now you're down for the count. … Can we revive you?
M: (*Screaming a lot.*)

It is impossible to know, of course, whether a different, more affectively toned intervention could have avoided this screaming, or indeed if the screaming is what he most needed to do at that moment. I might have addressed his need to "faint" as the only way he knew of at the moment to shut down his affective life: "Oh, I see [in a very quiet voice], with all these superstrong screaming feelings needing to just pass out sounds like the only way to not feel so jumbled up inside."

T: You are making a very big noise. …
M: (*Mumbles.*) It's messy!

Importantly, the therapist does not retaliate for his screaming. I believe this is what allows him to articulate his upset about the "mess."

T: Okay, M, it's time for us to start cleaning up.
M: Can we write a note (*on blackboard*)?

Her reiteration of his need to clean up comes at just the time when he wants to get rid of a mess, allowing him to recover affectively and regain his latency-aged defenses.

T: We can.
M: Like … (starts to write).
T: Right there?
M: M (*writes his name on board*). Write your name.
T: Okay (*I write my last name on board*) … T.
M: T (*sounds it out*). … What's your name for real? I call you (*by first name*).
T: Okay, you can call me X.
M: When I tell them, can I say Ms. T?
T: You can. … (*We write both X and T on the board*).

Both therapist and patient regain their connection to each other through the use of the blackboard.

M: Tomorrow, we should bring in a snack.

The patient wants to add to their connection through a snack, showing a striking degree of faith in the therapist that she would not be repulsed by his needs.

T: Bring a snack?
M: I could have a cookie ... MAGIC POTION!! (*M has picked up the bottle of water, which is colored from the watercolors, and starts shaking it.*)
T: A magic potion.
M: (*Pretends to drink it.*)
T: What happens if you drink the magic potion?
M: I'll die, right?
T: You think that something bad will happen?

The contrast between the wish for oral supplies and the fear of drinking a dangerous potion is striking. I do not think it would be useful to speak to that linkage with so little time left in the session, however.

M: Nope, I'll think (*mumbles as he is helping put things away*).
T: Oh, I forgot about those. We have to put those in the box, too.
M: Oh, let's put them back.
T: Okay. Let's put them back, that's a good idea. ... Yup, and what about this?

The child is being especially compliant, perhaps as a way to earn future snacks. The therapist needs to watch out for stating how "good" he is being by being "clean" as his messy self needs to be authentically modulated rather than obscured by compliance.

M: (*Closes the box.*)
T: It's closed! Should it go in there?
M: Uh-huh.
T: Okay ... the box is closed, so now we have our sign (*on blackboard*).
M: And what about cleaning the chalkboard? Clean the chalk board, let's get this from the chalk board. ... WE DON'T NEED YOUR STINKING CHALK! WE GOT, there's no more chalk, right?
T: It's in there. What happened to the chalk that was in there?

The therapist is a bit too concrete here. Instead, I might have focused on the shift from clean to stinking: "So, those stinking chalk feelings are still very strong."

M: Ohhh, there's none anymore.
T: Where'd it go?
M: I don't know ... they can bring in the old chalk.

T: We don't know where it went?

M: Nope, see I put them in the *(inaudible).*

T: Oh, they're in the back?

M: *(Mumbles something about next time.)*

T: We can do it next time?

M: They can bring, they can bring their own chalk … and we did a nasty job, look.

T: We cleaned the whole board?

M: Nooo, it's a mess, right? Look.

T: It's a mess still?

M: Look, look … and this is still dry, look and look, and it's dirty, right? No more, we not cleaning it, we're not cleaning no more because it keeps … ahhh, AHHHHHHH. *(Points to a dirty place on board.)*

The child feels frightened and angry about having to leave with some messiness still obvious. I might have said: "So, you're feeling so strongly that we have to be all clean to feel okay about leaving, and that little mess makes leaving feel so much harder. But we will have more times to play, and more times to clean, and even more times to mess."

T: Because that's what happens?

M: AHHHHHH. *(M then sits on the floor and asks me to help him tie his shoes. I tied one and he did the other, and he talked his way through it and left easily.)*

The child is adroitly able to get some last-second "mothering" from the therapist, allowing him to leave with apparent ease.

Of all the cases presented in this book, this case shows the greatest range of developmental issues. Indeed, it is a walking compendium of Freudian psychosexual stages. Shifting from powerful phallic play to oedipal curiosities about the therapist to sexual stimulation by his peers, to the need for oral supplies, to the "anal" preoccupation with stinky smells, to the hide-and-seek of separation paradigms, this child reveals both how much he has attained developmentally and, at the same time, how vulnerable these states of mind are to disruption. He regresses and progresses so dramatically and so often that his therapy is likely to be one in which both child and therapist learn volumes about the vicissitudes of psychological development.

This child is well on his way to internalizing the reflective stance we have been advocating. He is driven by his unconscious needs and conflicts yet at the same time is able to depict the dynamic shifts he goes through with striking clarity. He does not yet know why these shifts are happening, and as with most children, he experiences them more viscerally than intellectually. Despite this, however, he feels safe enough to articulate what it feels like to go through these changes because of the open, reflective space that has been created with the therapist. The prognosis for this child will likely be good because he has such access to his affective life, which will allow him to use the therapist's interventions as catalysts to increasingly link his visceral states to different states of mind and therefore to begin to understand why he feels as he does. When a child is so aware of the "what" of feeling, it becomes much easier to help him figure out the "why" of feeling and to give him the tools to continue these explorations in his life outside the context of therapy.

14 Conclusion

This book has tried to give as up close a view as possible of what early sessions with beginning therapists are actually like. These invaluable data are not sufficiently available to beginning therapists, and even keeping the supervisory comments aside, I hope that simply reading the sessions themselves will be invigorating. They may indeed be the closest viewing many beginning therapists will ever get of another beginning therapist's work; I believe that in and of itself is useful. The supervisory comments provided throughout the sessions may also be viewed in this light as giving new therapists an open look into the experience of supervision, a process they might not otherwise get to observe outside their own supervisory sessions.

Beyond simply providing a window into early sessions and into the supervisory process, however, I have also sought to integrate the three major conceptual developmental models I described in the Introduction as "in my bones" throughout each and every clinical vignette. Each of my comments was designed to heighten both the patient's and the therapist's capacity to mentalize and hence to foster a sense of psychological mindedness, even if the children, as in the middle section of the book, were antagonistic to that way of being. Each of the comments was also an attempt to embody Winnicottian notions of the importance of play, the quest for authenticity, and the creation of a transitional space to enhance play and creativity best. Last, the comments were also an attempt to integrate vital aspects of ego psychology into this discussion of Winnicott and Fonagy through a depiction of how these children's intrapsychic conflicts involving affect, drive, and defense interact with the matrices of both the capacities to play and the capacity to recognize the mental states of self and other. These three models have been the lifeblood of my clinical work over the years, and I truly hope they may also be of help to you as you begin your journey as a therapist. My hope is that each transcript provided you ample opportunity to see how these three conceptual pillars interact in the mental life of each child. I would argue that mentalization or psychological mindedness is the goal of each of these initial forays into psychotherapy. Play in the Winnicottian sense is therefore to be seen as the primary means through which mentalization is enhanced. To make the linkages among the three models even more explicit, it is the conflicts created by the interplay of drives, affects, and cognition as depicted in ego psychology that provide many of the conscious and unconscious obstacles both to play and to mentalization. Thus, rather than attempting to tease apart the three models within each session, my premise instead has been that following their intertwining threads is a vital means of helping the patient.

I would like to conclude this book by touching on another area of vital importance to the therapeutic process that I have not yet addressed. I have spent almost the entire book detailing the private world of patient-therapist interaction with little to no regard for the therapist's feelings about his or her patient. Because these sessions are drawn from so early in the treatment, there are relatively few signs that I saw of systematic and entrenched transference or countertransference paradigms. A detailed depiction of such experiences is thus more appropriate to a work detailing later phases in psychotherapy. Certainly, all of the children had strong feelings at times toward their therapist. In the four cases in the section on responding to challenges to the frame in particular, each of the cases depicted a generalized antipathy to the therapeutic process that could be described as a type of generically negative transference. It is equally true that some of the therapists' reactions to the children, also within that section, showed how trying work with such patients can be, although it is again beyond the scope of this work to differentiate between what was generic to a beginning therapist with a difficult patient and what might be particular areas of concern within the therapist's psyche that a specific patient happened to evoke.

If we cannot in the present context speak to a true transference or countertransference experience, I want instead to end the book by speaking of how difficult it is personally to be a beginning therapist, and thus how much courage it takes to enter the process. Your tolerance for ambiguity has to be enormous, as there is so much to learn about any child's personality, and you start knowing next to nothing about this person with whom you will be engaging so closely. Yet, despite knowing so little, you are expected, by both parent and child, to know so much. Even further, you are also supposed to be vulnerable and open about your fragile beginning therapist self to both supervisors and professors, often in front of your peers. To be simultaneously openly vulnerable and aware of all your shortcomings and ignorance while still presenting a notion of calm assurance and professionalism to your patients demands enormous authenticity. At the same time, this authenticity is challenged by the all-too-understandable and commonplace wish to be seen by one and all as talented, knowledgeable, and on top of things. In Winnicottian terms, as a beginning therapist, the pull toward a "false self" presentation is ever present and must be fought against at every turn.

Putting up a good fight against this false assurance while trying to stay available and helpful to your patients is a most arduous endeavor. It may thus be useful to reflect briefly on the aptitudes that I believe will help you in this challenging task. First is receptivity to play. This is far from easy, as this receptivity implies a degree of freedom from the internal and external anxieties generated by the child's play material as well as from the inherent difficulties in being a therapist. Second is a willingness to be comfortable with silence and to give the child the space to create play scenarios. This is also deceptively difficult, as the beginning therapist is so stressed and strained by what he or she does not understand that silence can be seen as indicative of ignorance or confusion, and thus can be avoided when it should be nurtured. Third is the capacity to generate warmth and acceptance as the prevailing winds of your relationship with your patient. This is probably much more a function of your body language and tone of voice than it is of anything you actually say to the child. Fourth is the avoidance of superego-based constructs (the "shoulds" or "good work" statements) in response to a child's behavior, as opposed to ego-based constructs that emphasize a sense of curiosity and wonder about the meaning of the child's play. Fifth is both having access to and feeling comfortable with your sense of humor. Despite the often tragic and painful quality of much of a child's play content, your humor may provide a source of perspective and solace to both you and your patient that will enhance the humanity of both of you. These five aptitudes and qualities can be enormously challenging to sustain over the course of a given therapeutic hour, much less over long-term psychotherapy. This challenge has always struck me as one reason why I feel our calling as child therapists is a most noble one, as there are far easier, but few more rewarding, ways to earn one's keep. It is thus my sincere hope that this book has been of some service to you in your development within this remarkable, yet not quite impossible, profession of ours. Good luck to you in the process.

References

Axline, V. (1964). The basic principles of child psychotherapy. In M. Haworth (Ed.), *Child psychotherapy* (pp. 93–94). New York: Basic Books

Bion, W. (1962). *Learning from experience*. London: Heinemann.

Bucci, W. (1997). *Psychoanalysis and cognitive science: A multiple code theory*. New York: Guilford Press.

Fonagy, P. (1991). Thinking about thinking: Some clinical and theoretical considerations in the treatment of a borderline patient. *International Journal of Psycho-analysis, 72*, 217–233.

Fonagy, P., Gergely, G., Jurist, E., & Target, M. (2002). *Affect regulation, mentalization and the development of the self*. New York: Other Press.

Mayman, M. (1967). Object relations and object representations in Rorschach responses. *Journal of Personality Assessment, 31*, 17–25.

Mulley, H. (1938). *Explorations into personality*. New York: Oxford University Press.

Slade, A. (2005). Parental reflective functioning: An introduction. *Attachment and Human Development*, 7, 269–282.

Thompson, A. (1986). An object-relational theory of affect maturity: Applications to the Thematic Apperception Test. In M. Kissen (Ed.), *Assessing object relations phenomena* (pp. 207–224). New York: International Universities Press.

Tuber, S. (2008). *Attachment, play and authenticity: A Winnicott primer*. Lanham, MD: Aronson.

Winnicott, D. W. (1965). The capacity to be alone. In *Maturational processes and the facilitating environment*. New York: International Universities Press. (Original work published 1958), 29–36.

Winnicott, D. W. (1965). The aims of psychoanalytic treatment. In *Maturational processes and the facilitating environment*. New York: International Universities Press. (Original work published 1962), 166–170.

Winnicott, D. W. (1965). Communicating and not communicating leading to a study of certain opposites. In *Maturational processes and the facilitating environment*. New York: International Universities Press. (Original work published 1963), 179–192.

Winnicott, D. W. (1971). *Playing and reality*. London: Tavistock.

Index

Made in the USA
Middletown, DE
21 September 2016